Women in Israel

About the Author

Nahla Abdo (Ph.D.) is an Arab feminist activist and Professor of Sociology at Carleton University, Ottawa, Canada. She has published extensively on women, racism, nationalism and the state in the Middle East, with special focus on Palestinian women. Among her recent publications are *Gender, Citizenship and the State: The Israeli Case* (in Arabic, 2009); *Women and Poverty in the OPT: Some Conceptual and Methodological Notes* (2007); *Women and the Politics of Military Confrontation: Palestinian and Israeli Gendered Narratives of Dislocation* (co-edited, 2002); and *Violence in the Name of Honour: Theoretical and Political Challenges* (co-edited, 2004). In addition, Professor Abdo has published numerous articles in academic journals. She has recently returned from a six-month research trip to Palestine/Israel where she worked with various civil society organizations and conducted research on Palestinian women political detainees.

Women in Israel

Race, Gender and Citizenship

NAHLA ABDO

Zed Books

LONDON & NEW YORK

Women in Israel: Race, Gender and Citizenship was first published in 2011 by
Zed Books Ltd, 7 Cynthia Street, London N1 9JF, UK and
Room 400, 175 Fifth Avenue, New York, NY 10010, USA

www.zedbooks.co.uk

Copyright © Nahla Abdo 2011

The right of Nahla Abdo to be identified as the author of
this work has been asserted by her in accordance with
the Copyright, Designs and Patents Act, 1988

Designed and typeset in Monotype Joanna
by illuminati, Grosmont
Index by John Barker
Cover designed by www.alice-marwick.co.uk
Printed and bound in Great Britain by
CPI Antony Rowe, Chippenham and Eastbourne

Distributed in the USA exclusively by Palgrave Macmillan, a division of
St Martin's Press, LLC, 175 Fifth Avenue, New York, NY 10010, USA

A catalogue record for this book is available from the British Library
Library of Congress Cataloging in Publication Data available

ISBN 978 1 84813 955 8 hb
ISBN 978 1 84813 954 1 pb

Contents

Preface

THIS BOOK is the culmination of many years of academic work and feminist political involvement. The impetus for writing it, while timely in terms of its contribution to existing debates on citizenship, is also important personally. In the book I carve a space in which I situate my personal experiences theoretically and locate myself politically. The book represents the embodiment of my gendered, racialized and marginalized citizenship in the State of Israel.

Before choosing the diaspora as my living and working place over my birthplace and country, historically known as Palestine, I spent my childhood and the better part of my adult life in an exclusively Arab/Palestinian town. Sheltered in my culture and language, attending Arabic schools, leading my everyday life in my town, little did I know that my Arab or Palestinian presence was anything but normal. At that time, the only struggle for me was to ensure that no one in my society or family took advantage of me, as a female. As a child, in the summer of 1967 and for six days, I remember watching the men in my family gathered around the radio listening to the news, with great anxiety showing in their grim faces. This was the time referred to in Arabic as the Naksa (the Six Day War) and the defeat of Arab armies by the Israeli army. But my wider political consciousness was to develop only in my late teens as a high-school student, listening daily to teachers preaching to us about the risks of being 'political' or critical of Israel, and silencing any student who dared to criticize the state publicly. It was only then that I began to find some answers to my growing questions about the larger world around me.

This world began to show itself to me in equally significant terms as a university student who had to use her second language (Hebrew) as the primary language of instruction and communication. It was at Haifa University that I began to comprehend fully what, as Palestinian citizens, we meant to the state which insisted – and continues to insist – on calling itself the Jewish state. Working in the academy and belonging to several feminist and political anti-racist groups in the diaspora have reaffirmed the importance of my identity and the need to retain that part of the world as mine too. For the last thirty years or so I have turned Palestine/Israel, and its social, economic, gender and racial complexity, into the core of my academic research and political activism. My knowledge of and concern for marginalized Palestinian women have been the driving force for this book.

I have learned a great deal from being directly involved in various groups, especially women's groups and civil society activism in Palestine/Israel. Of these, I would like specifically to mention three: Women Against Violence in Nazareth, al-Tufula and Mada al-Carmel. In many ways this book would not have been possible had it not been for them. My thanks go to them all. Many thanks are due to the staff of the Centre for Women Against Violence in Nazareth, and especially to Aida Touma and Naela Awwad, who gave me the opportunity to facilitate several workshops around the issues of gender, citizenship and the state. The amazing enthusiasm of the participants, who came from all walks of life (academics, social workers, teachers, activists), broke down traditional taboos. With open minds and hearts these women have shared with me their personal, work and life experiences.

At Mada al-Carmel (the Arab Center for Applied Social Research – Haifa), I gave several public talks and facilitated a number of workshops on Palestinian women and the political economy in Israel. While the participants were largely academics, they were all keen to translate theories into their experiential lives. For this, I would also like to thank the staff, especially Nadera Shalhoub-Kevorkian, Himmat Zubi and Areej Sabbagh. At al-Tufula Centre (Pedagogical and Multipurpose Women Centre – Nazareth) I also had the chance to present my research publically and gain important feedback from participants. My thanks here go to Nabila Espanioly and the staff at the Centre, who, like the other two organizations, shared with me their data and publications. MADAR (the Palestinian Centre for Israeli Studies) has published an earlier version of this book in Arabic. Many thanks go to Mufeed Qassoum and Hunaida Ghanem for their enthusiasm and dedication to publish and distribute this edition of the book.

Finally, I would like to thank my children, Beisan and Hadaf Zubi, who, while still trying to figure out the meaning of their Israeli citizenship, enthusiastically volunteered to read the first draft and shared with me their concerns as well as their unending support and love. It goes without saying that writing this book meant spending a good deal of time away from family duties. I am deeply grateful to my partner Sami Zubi, who gave me all the time and space I needed, with love and admiration. While all these people helped shape this book, sole responsibility for it is mine.

Introduction

FEMINIST LITERATURE on citizenship has grown significantly in the past decade or so, most importantly in terms of its gender critique of male-stream Western theories of citizenship. Feminist critique of Marshall's theorization of citizenship, which ignored the role of gender in civil society, the polity and the state, has significantly improved our understanding of the relationship between citizenship and the state. Carole Pateman's contribution in this area is particularly significant. In *The Disorder of Women: Democracy, Feminism and Political Theory* (1989), Pateman argues against male-stream citizenship theories that divide civil society into a public and a private sphere, relegating men to the public sphere while containing women within the private sphere and viewing them as politically irrelevant (Pateman 1989; Pateman and Mills 2007).

Challenging the divided and seemingly disconnected spheres of the public and the private has been forcefully taken up by Sylvia Walby's classic *Theorizing Patriarchy* (1990), wherein she demonstrates the fallacy of gender-neutral citizenship theories, arguing that patriarchal control over all spheres of civil society, including the social, political and economic, is the primary reason for excluding women and marginalizing them. Most pertinent in this key text is Walby's question, posed subsequently in an article, 'Is Citizenship Gendered?'

I

(Walby 1994), a question that drew the attention of feminists. One response came from Ruth Lister, who began her article 'Citizenship and Gender' with 'a resounding yes'. According to Lister,

> Citizenship has always been gendered in the sense that women and men have stood in a different relationship to it, to the disadvantage of women. Yet, for much of its history, a veil of gender-neutrality has obscured the nature of this differential relationship. Today, as feminist theorists have stripped away this veil, the challenge is to reconceptualise citizenship in gendered terms in the image of women as well as men. We are thus talking about citizenship and gender from two angles: as a historical relationship and as a political and theoretical project. (2004: 1)

This said, engendering citizenship is but one step in fully comprehending the importance of women's participation in civil society and nation-state building, including, or perhaps especially, in Western liberal democracies. Thus, as important as gender is in theorizing citizenship, the issue of race/ethnicity, it is argued here, is of equal importance. In other words, citizenship is not only gendered but also ethnicized and racialized, as Nira Yuval-Davis has aptly demonstrated in her work on Britain and Israel (1991, 1997). The nation-state creates the Other as a racialized subject and places persons so categorized at a disadvantage in relationship to citizenship rights. Hence the racialization of Southeast Asians and other people of colour in Britain, and of Palestinians in Israel.

The process of othering and racialization, as this book will show, is not only externally induced (e.g. by the state or the 'superior nation'). Thus, unlike for example the case of Britain or the United States, where the state has established a system of hierarchies based on, among other things, a distinction between white and non-white (or non-European origins), in the case of Israel racism/ethnicization is practised within the preferred group (Jews) as well. This book, which theorizes citizenship in Israel, will demonstrate that racialization occurs not only between the Jews as a majority and Arabs/Palestinians as a minority, but also among Jews – between European (white) Jews and Mizrahi Jews (the overwhelming majority of whom came from Arab countries).

In order to comprehend the processes of citizenship hierarchies in both their external and internal manifestations, the discussion in this book will proceed from the general (e.g. general theories of citizenship with their gendered and racialized components) to the more specific, highlighting the historical and regional specificity of the Israeli case. Theorizing citizenship in the latter case, it is argued here, necessitates a serious consideration and critique of feminist literature on the Middle East, which tends to overemphasize the roles of cultural institutions, such as the 'family', 'nationalism' and 'religion', in determining female citizenship status while de-emphasizing the role of the state and colonialism. Moreover, as Chapter 1 argues, the majority of the literature on citizenship in Israel has largely been produced by males and remains gender-neutral or gender-blind, even when marginalized groups such as Palestinians and Mizrahi Jews are included. The current book is intended to fill the gap in existing literature on citizenship by focusing on women's citizenship in Israel. Three categories of women will be considered: Palestinians, Mizrahi Jews and Ashkenazi Jews. However, our emphasis will be largely placed on the two most marginalized categories, namely Palestinians and Mizrahi Jews.

Understanding these major groupings of women in Israel, it will be shown, necessitates a comparative and historical analysis of their status, position and role in state-building in Israel. The challenges such a task presents are considerable, if not daunting. Part of the reason for the difficulty lies in the relative scarcity of a substantive literature and separate data on Palestinian Arabs and Mizrahi Jewish women, the two marginalized groups.[1] For example, the literature produced on Palestinian women in Israel by both academics and civil society (especially NGO) feminist activists has undoubtedly grown in the past decade or so. Still, as Chapter 1 demonstrates, the overwhelming majority of this literature is ethnographic in nature, is centred on a micro-level analysis and revolves, in large part, around issues of identity, family, violence against women and political representation. While such factors are important, the lack of structural situatedness or a theoretical framework makes the analysis substantially deficient.

For example, there are no studies by Palestinian feminists that outline the role played by the Israeli state in shaping and reshaping the status of women; nor there is a study which contextualizes women's status and positions within a framework that is capable of outlining the socio-economic and political forces at work. The major lacunae in feminist writings about Palestinian women in Israel are the lack of structural analyses and the basically ahistorical nature of the studies. Existing studies fail to capture the role of history in shaping women's status, particularly around the Nakba (Catastrophe, referring to the events of 1948) and the Palestinian confinement to Israeli military rule between 1948 and 1966.

Compared to the works published by Jewish Ashkenazi feminists, which cover their history, early experiences as members of the Zionist settler movement and their citizenship status in Israel, feminist scholarship on Mizrahi women remains scarce.

As will be argued throughout this book, knowledge about the social, economic and political upper hand gained by the Ashkenazi Jewish women as members of the settler-colonial group − or what Oren Yiftachel calls 'the Charter Group' (1999) − is well established. Jewish Ashkenazi feminists not only write about their history and contemporaneousness, they also control the epistemological sphere through their investigations, research and even representations of the 'Other' − Palestinian and Mizrahi women. This state of epistemological control on the part of Ashkenazi women has not escaped the attention of a growing number of Mizrahi feminists in their writings, who resent their 're-'presentation by Ashkenazi women. Scholarship by Mizrahi feminists about their experiences and those of their community, while it is growing, is still in large part focused on issues of identity, representation and individual narratives, as will be seen in this book. The one advantage Mizrahi feminist literature might have over that written by Palestinian feminists is the emphasis placed by most on their historical experiences. Most writings by Mizrahi feminists, it will be seen, are largely written from a post-colonialist perspective and are concerned with the question of 'beginning'. This concern gives Mizrahi feminist literature an added value over that of Palestinian feminist literature, as it frames Mizrahi female citizenship as being produced structurally and historically, emphasizing simultaneously the role of Israeli colonialism vis-à-vis its differentiated Jewish ethnicities.

Feminist literature on women in Israel seems to be concerned largely with one's own 'national' group rather than with women citizens in Israel. Ashkenazi feminists' access to power and knowledge allows them to write about the Other; Mizrahi and Palestinian feminist literature remains mostly confined to the topic of the self. By providing a comparative analysis of the three different categories of female citizens in Israel, this study hopes to fill a major lacuna in existing literature on citizenship in Israel. Each category, albeit with more focus on the two marginalized groups, will be studied individually and relationally, or in relation to the other categories.

The lack of historicized and contextualized literature on marginalized groups of women in Israel constitutes an important factor and incentive for this study. In addition to the historical approach this study takes, the comparative approach it employs in understanding the three major categories of women citizens in Israel presents an original contribution to existing theorization on citizenship. In other words, this study bridges the wide gap between the male-stream, yet gender-blind, structurally and theoretically grounded literatures on citizenship, on the one hand, and the largely micro-based analysis characteristic of most feminist literature in Israel, on the other.

The book is divided into four chapters. Chapter 1 examines the literature on Israeli citizenship in general while simultaneously providing a feminist framework for analysing women's citizenship within the context of settler colonialism. It investigates the problematic of existing literature, which tends to follow the work of Sami Smooha and strives to theorize Israel as an 'ethnic democracy' (1997). It also provides a critical analysis of the literature that uses the ethnocentric approach in understanding citizenship in Israel. In an attempt to develop an alternative theorization of female citizenship in Israel, this chapter adopts a historical approach and articulates female citizenship through a critical feminist lens that emphasizes the roles of gender, class, colonialism and racialization. Palestinian women – unlike other ethnic groups, including both Ashkenazi and Mizrahi Jews – will be viewed as a national collective with indigenous rights and status. Citizenship, this chapter argues, is not only gendered and racialized, but classed as well. The Israeli state not only invented Palestinians as an 'ethnic' group, but also disadvantaged them economically by stripping them of their historical rights to their own land or territory. Landed property or territorial rights, especially for indigenous peoples under settle colonialism, constitutes a major citizenship right. Restoring the relationship between territory or land and the state to its rightful place in the debate on women's citizenship provides for a more comprehensive understanding of existing feminist literature on citizenship in the Middle East.

Considering the importance of history in comprehending women's citizenship status, Chapter 2 addresses the specific historical context and moments which have influenced, shaped and reshaped the position of women in Israel. Recognizing the differences in the historical moments that marked the lives and experiences of the three categories (Palestinian, Mizrahi and Ashkenazi women) will facilitate our understanding of the origins of marginalization, oppression and the silencing of the women 'Other', especially Palestinian and Mizrahi women, in Israel. At the outset, however, it must be noted that the three categories of women referred to throughout the book are not homogeneous entities, self-contained or mutually exclusive. Each of these categories is also differentiated on at least the level of class, marital status, age or other considerations. However, for the purpose of this book the three categories will be discussed separately and on their own terms.

This chapter provides the historical and material background for explaining the bases on which Israel's exclusionary and exclusivist or racialized policies and practices rest, and implications of these for marginalized Palestinian and Mizrahi women citizens. The impact and implications of the nature and character of the Israeli state on women's socio-economic and political position and status are examined through detailed examination of two crucial areas of life and experience: economic rights and status, and educational experience. Chapter 3 analyses women's economic status in Israel. Using a comparative approach, the status of Palestinian women is compared to that of Jewish Ashkenazi and Mizrahi women. Areas examined and analysed include women's economic conditions in general, their labour force participation, employment, unemployment, poverty and productive performance in general. Israeli official discourses on Mizrahi and Palestinian women's economic status are analysed and juxtaposed to their lived reality. Women's economic status is investigated both separately (for each group) and comparatively or in relation to each other, whenever data make this possible. Special emphasis in this chapter is placed on the gender bias of official Israeli data and on the ethnic-based approaches adopted by officials and the academy in reporting on the status of women, especially among Palestinians.

The fourth and final chapter takes up the issue of women's education. As in Chapter 3, emphasis in this chapter is placed on the two marginalized groups of women: Palestinian Arabs and Mizrahi Jews, the primary victims of Israeli racist policies. Their education is analysed both historically and contemporarily and is compared to that of Ashkenazi women. The chapter deals with education in its wider context, not only in terms of the normative definition of education as an official form of literacy, but also in terms of the extent to which it is capable of addressing the historical injustices which befell the marginalized groups of women. This expanded definition of education is also assessed for the extent to which it is capable of providing women, especially the marginalized, with human and cultural capital. Moreover, and in a manner similar to the discussion in Chapter 3, the final chapter provides a critical examination of Israeli official and academic literature on Mizrahi and Palestinian women's education, contrasting it with their actual lived experiences.

ONE

Women, State and Citizenship:
The Israeli Context

UNDERSTANDING GENDER RELATIONS and women's position in society, and in the Middle East more specifically, necessitates a conceptual framework capable of explaining the moments and movements within which such relations and women's status are produced and reproduced. The complexity of such a framework requires the articulation of different forces, among which the state and land occupy a central place. These two forces, as will be argued in this book, construct, shape and reshape the socio-economic dynamics in which various relations, including gender, race, class and ethnicity, are situated. Such forces are particularly pertinent in studying the case of citizenship in Israel.

Feminist Writings on Women in Israel

The feminist literature on women in Israel has basically followed the racial and ethnic divide that characterizes the nature of citizenship in Israel. The hierarchical state of citizenship that is expressed in the differential distribution of rights allocates more power, access and resources to Ashkenazi men and women, enabling them to control and monopolize epistemological production, whereas the marginalized Other such as Palestinians and Mizrahi Jews tend to be relegated

8

to an inferior position with much less access to power and resources, negatively affecting their production of knowledge and human capital development. In other words, the racial and ethnic hierarchy which characterizes the Israeli state and society reproduces itself at the level of academic production. This state of affairs recalls Dorothy Smith's notion that 'knowledge is power',[1] both of which largely become the property of the male (and to a lesser extent female) Ashkenazi Jews within the Israeli state and academy. Power/knowledge differentiation is not only racially distributed between different social groups, but is also gendered within the same group of Palestinians, Mizrahi or Ashkenazi citizens; males more than females acquire power positions and consequently become major contributors to knowledge. In this state of hierarchical power/knowledge distribution, the Other is often represented or written about by the powerful, whether in general studies or within feminism.[2] It is not surprising, therefore, to see that most literature on and about the silenced Other comes from the powerful, even within feminism. Such is the case of literature on Arab Palestinian and Mizrahi women in Israel, the majority of which, and especially that produced locally, is written by Jewish Ashkenazi feminist or female academics (Lavie 2002, 2005; Shohat 1999; Abdo and Lentin 2002a; Motzafi-Haller 2001).

In the past decade or so, however, one has begun to witness the growth of literature on and by Palestinian women, partly due to the growing number of local NGOs (as they produce documents, reports and other forms of study[3]) and partly on account of the growing number of female academics. Still, most of this literature, especially that on and by Palestinian women, tends to be localized and based on empirical case studies, and in the main provides descriptive accounts of selected ethnographies or individual social phenomena.

The corpus of feminist literature, especially on Palestinian women in Israel, is growing among academics and activists alike. This literature covers important phenomena, with topics such as tradition vis-à-vis modernity, especially in the case of women and education among the Bedouin (Abu-Rabia-Queder 2006); violence against women; Israeli police treatment of crimes against women; and so-called honour killings (Shalhoub-Kevorkian 1999, 2000, 2004; Mojab and Abdo 2004). It also deals with issues such as women, familial patriarchy, nationalism and reproductive technologies (Kana'aneh 2002). Having said this, the literature remains ungrounded theoretically and lacks connectivity to structuring forces such as the state, political economy, territory, and so on. This observation has also been made by Amalia Sa'ar (2007), who notes that the overwhelming bulk of this literature remains at the empirical level with little conceptual or theoretical framework capable of locating phenomena within the larger structure within which they are situated.

In fact, with the exception of Sa'ar's (2007) article, which provides an important critique of Palestinian feminist literature on women in Israel, and Barbara Swirski's essay on women and citizenship in Israel (2000) – which is insightful, albeit theoretically problematic, as will be seen later – it is safe to argue that the overwhelming majority of existing studies on Palestinian women in Israel are still located at the empirical, subjective, ethnographic and local/micro-level of analysis. There is thus a major disconnection between the latter studies and the largely 'objective' structural and theoretical studies at national/ regional level, including studies of state and citizenship produced by Palestinian Arab and Israeli Jewish male academics.[4]

The state of knowledge about Mizrahi women is not very different from that on Palestinians. In this case, while some Mizrahi feminist scholars deal with more objective and structural issues, especially the question of Zionism and Israeli racist policies, they all acknowledge the dismal state of epistemological production on Mizrahi women in Israel and call for more scholarly work on this section of the Israeli female population (Shohat 1988, 1999, 2002; Dahan-Kalev 2001, 2003; Motzafi-Haller 2001; Lavie 2002). To address this disconnect between the local and the national, between the empirical and the theoretical, and between the subjective and the structural/objective, this chapter will build on existing literature to provide a conceptual framework for articulating women's socio-economic position, especially that of marginalized Palestinian and Mizrahi women, within the context of the Israeli state and citizenship therein. As will be argued throughout this book, in a settler-colonial state such as Israel, issues of race and class are fundamental to understanding gender dynamics and women's position. Therefore a political-economy analysis of women in the context of settler colonialism is provided here as a contribution to theorizing the role and position of women in Israeli society.

Before proceeding further, it is important to note that this chapter takes for granted the fact that women – all women, in all societies, and whether taken within the context of a liberal democratic state or a settler-colonial state – are marginalized and discriminated against on a gender basis. Patriarchy – which is characteristic of all social structures, including the economy, the polity and law – marginalizes and discriminates against all women. This is also true within the Israeli settler-colonial state, and especially the context of nationalism, national security and militarism, as will be seen later in this chapter. However, this assertion should by no means be taken to suggest that all women are equally oppressed and similarly marginalized. Women do not constitute a class on their own; nor do they define and identify themselves in the same way(s). In addition to being gendered, women are also classed, racialized and ethnicized, and their position and citizenship status are constituted around multiple identities. Adopting a multilayered frame of analysis to comprehend the status of women in Israel is aimed at avoiding the trap of essentializing women, viewing them instead in their fluid and changing identities within which they perceive themselves. Having said this, and for various reasons, especially the need to preserve the voice of the marginalized and silenced, this book will place special emphasis on Mizrahi and Palestinian women. Thus, unlike Ashkenazi women, whose concerns and voices have tended to be heard on account of the large space made available to Ashkenazi feminists, Palestinian and Mizrahi women and feminists continue to be largely absent from a privileged space of representation. After all, the feminist methodology adopted in this research is not concerned with 'objectivity' (read: neutrality); it rather aims at opening up a space to give voice to the marginalized and silenced.

Existing Debates on Citizenship in Israel

In order to theorize women's citizenship status in Israel, this chapter will engage with the existing literature on citizenship and the state as it concerns Israel. A general review of the existing scholarly work on citizenship in Israel suggests that the current debate is largely situated within the 'ethnic' state or 'ethnocracy' paradigm. This ethno-centred approach to women in Israel, as will be seen later, is also representative of Barbara Swirski's work on women and citizenship in Israel (2000). The 'ethnic-centred' paradigm, it is argued, provides a step forward from the classical functionalist (Eisenstadtian) definition of Israel as a liberal democracy.[5] In critiquing the functionalist notion of 'liberal democracy', Sami Smooha adopts the term 'ethnic democracy' to characterize the Israeli state. For Smooha 'ethnic democracy' is defined as 'a system that combines the extension of civil and political rights to individuals and some collective rights to minorities, with institutionalization of majority control over the state' (Smooha 1997, 1999). Smooha specifically attempts to distinguish 'ethnic democracy', which accords inferior rights to minority groups while still remaining democratic, and *Herrenvolk* (Master Race) democracy, which denies political rights to subordinate groups and is not a democracy at all (1999: 234).

Smooha's notion of ethnic democracy was heavily critiqued by various Israeli 'revisionist' or 'new' sociologists, as well as by Palestinian scholars. One such response was *Questioning 'Ethnic Democracy'* (Ghanem et al. 1998). Here the authors challenge what they argue has become a dominant position among social scientists inside and outside of Israel regarding the character of the state. They argue:

> using ethnic democracy as a model fails to capture the political situation in Israel on several levels; structured, state sanctioned inequality are not compatible with democracy, 'Arabs' are structurally prevented from mobilizing politically due to the increasing 'Judaization' of the state and the tyranny of the majority, and also, the model overlooks the ambiguous boundaries of the Israeli polity which expands into the settlements and Jewish Diaspora. (Ghanem et al. 1998: 254–5)

Instead, Ghanem et al. suggest the term 'ethnocracy' as a replacement for 'ethnic democracy'.[6] Ghanem et al.'s notion of ethnocracy provides a more expansive, elaborate and critical approach to theorizing the structural forces of marginalization and discrimination undergone by Palestinian citizens. However, besides the fact that their work excludes gender as an important analytical tool for understanding citizenship, they end up reproducing a binary between 'superior Jews' and 'inferior Arabs', obfuscating other subjects and identities in between. The authors take the concept of 'ethnos' to mean 'members of a common origin', a definition they place at the centre of their notion of ethnocracy (Ghanem et al. 1998: 261–2). Constructing 'Jewishness' as a unified ethnicity, this book argues, is ideologically and politically problematic. This construction follows a Zionist ideology in assuming that all Jews necessarily have a common origin (Nimni 2003a; Shohat 1998, 1999, 2002). Ethnocracy in this paradigm lumps together Mizrahis, Ethiopians, Ashkenazis and other Jewish ethnicities into a whole and presents it as opposed to Palestinian Arabs as a binary.

Palestinian Arab and Israeli Jewish scholars have engaged in the ethnic-centred paradigm using different reference points. Still, as will be argued further, almost all authors in this paradigm remain, at least on one level, gender-insensitive and rather male-biased. The ethnocracy paradigm developed by Shafir and Peled for discussing Israel's 'multiplicity of citizenship' will be taken up here. In *Being Israeli: The Dynamics of Multiple Citizenship* (2002), the authors provide a rather complex and comprehensive discussion of ethnocracy in accounting for citizenship in Israel. To begin with, both Shafir and Peled (Peled and Shafir 2002)[7] use the context of settler colonialism to characterize two historical epochs in Zionist development: pre-1948 and post-1967. The authors accept the notion that the Zionist movement in pre-Israel Palestine was a settler-colonial movement in terms of its policies and practices towards Palestinians. Settler-colonial policies and practices, they also concur, represent Israel's treatment of Palestinians in the post-1967 occupied Palestinian territories (OPT). However, when it comes to 'Israel proper' (1948 and on), they drop the term 'settler colonialism' as a manifestation of state policy and replace it with the notion of ethnic-based policies. Furthermore, using a 'neo-institutionalist' approach to characterize citizenship in Israel, an advancement over that of Marshall (who theorized citizenship focusing on the relationship of the individual to the state through the medium of formal rights), the authors view citizenship not only as 'a bundle of formal rights, but as the entire mode of incorporation of individuals and groups into society ... recognizing in the process the collective "ethnic" rights of the different collectivities' (Shafir and Peled 2002: 11).

Adopting the concept of 'incorporation regime' to characterize citizenship in Israel has allowed the authors to include in their definition of citizenship factors such as 'social, political, economic and cultural institutions that may stratify a society's putatively universalist citizenship by differentially dispensing rights, privileges, and obligations to distinct groups within it' (Shafir and Peled 2002: 335). This definition has also enabled the authors to identify the hierarchical structure of the different citizens' groups (e.g. Ashkenazi, Mizrahi, Palestinian, women, immigrants, and so on) where the positioning of each, as they argue, is based on their 'conceived contribution to the Zionist cause' (22). This 'multilayered citizenship' framework, they contend, is what accorded 'second-class ethno-national citizenship for Mizrahis and women ... and third-class citizenship to Palestinian Arabs' (73).

The authors' specification of a complex citizenship regime is also characterized by the presence of two different contending (and, I may add, contradictory) citizenship discourses, namely 'liberal democracy' and 'ethno-nationalism'. These contending discourses represent the sources of the hierarchies in rights and privileges accorded to the different segments of the population. In this twofold paradigm Jews are positioned in the 'liberal democratic' frame, with Ashkenazis being more privileged than Mizrahis, while Palestinians acquired a third-class citizenship within the 'ethno-national' frame of rule.

Unlike what reality on the ground has dictated now and in the past in terms of Israel's exclusivist and exclusionary policies towards its Palestinian citizens, namely in terms of the racist and racializing character of Zionism and the Israeli state,[8] the authors come to the conclusion that further globalization, expressed in 'further economic liberalization of the state and market', is bound to open up the Israeli market to the incorporation of different ethnic groups, leading to the development of Israel as a 'liberal democratic' state/country. 'Within the tension between liberal and ethno-nationalist discourses', the authors contend, 'there lies the promise of a democratic and multi-cultural incorporation regime' (Shafir and Peled 2002: 73).

Theorizing Israeli citizenship: a critique

The problematic embedded in the above conclusion, which pertains to the authors' 'promise of a democratic regime', represents a funda-mental misunderstanding of Israel's citizenship regime, both histori-cally and contemporarily, especially as it relates to Palestinian citizens. Lived experiences of Palestinian citizens both past and present tell a very different story. On the one hand, their basic rights to work, live and move freely have been and remain largely restricted if not denied outright. The state's land policy, namely land confiscation and expropriation and the exclusion of Palestinians from ownership of land, has not abated (see Rouhana and Sultany 2003). Finally, since the recent elections which brought right-wing Prime Minister Netanyahu and Foreign Minister Lieberman into office, a long list of racist laws and proposed laws have been introduced in the Israeli Knesset (parliament), producing in the process a more closed off and exclusionary regime rather than liberalizing it or opening it up to include the Other – as Shafir and Peled would have us believe.

To reiterate, the authors exhibit an ambivalent position on their view and understanding of the true mission of Zionism: while they reject its settler-colonial project for the pre-1948 and post-1967 periods, they seem to suppress the whole question when discussing 'Israel proper'. The authors' position on Israel's settler-colonial prac-tices within its 'proper borders' will be discussed in further detail later in this chapter. At this point it is important to note that their theorization, which is premised on the 'promise of a democratic regime', has been challenged by a growing number of scholars, including Avishai Ehrlich, who argues that 'Israel will become more particularistic and oriented towards "political Judaism" (Jewish "fundamentalism") to the detriment of secular Zionism' (Ehrlich in Nimni 2003a: 79).

The authors' position, developed in 2002, does not fundamentally differ from the position Peled had articulated one decade earlier in 'Ethnic Democracy and the Legal Construction of Citizenship: Arab Citizens of the Jewish State' (1992). In this article, Peled argued that Israel is a 'successful example of a democratic yet deeply divided society' which serves as a positive example for other Western democracies struggling to reconcile 'ethnic claims and democratic values' (1992: 432). His argument, then and ten years later, is that the confluence of republicanism, liberalism and ethnicity as legitimate political principles in Israel has created two sets of citizenship rights: republican citizenship for Jews and liberal citizenship for Arabs; Arab's liberal citizenship allows them to conduct their political struggles within the boundaries of law (1992: 432–3).

The nuances developed in Shafir and Peled's book (2002), especially in their articulation of the system of multiple citizenship, which allows for partial inclusion of Mizrahis and women – albeit that the focus is on Ashkenazi Jewish women – are largely to be appreciated and welcome. However, this inclusion remains largely superficial and highly problematic, especially when the authors lump together Mizrahis and all Jewish women (Ashkenazi and Mizrahi) as one category accorded second-class citizenship.

Ethnocentric approaches, it is argued here, are problematic on all counts: at the levels of gender, race/ethnicity and class. Later in this chapter a feminist analysis of citizenship in Israel is introduced. Here the critique of ethnic-centred approaches to citizenship in Israel is developed further. Ethnic-centred approaches, whether they describe the Israeli state as 'ethnic democracy' (Smooha 1997) or 'ethnocracy' (Rouhana 1997; Farsakh 2006; Rouhana and Ghanem 1998; Shafir and Peled 2002) or even as 'singularist ethnocracy' (Butenschon et al. 2000),[9] all tend to dismiss a central feature of the Israeli state, namely its settler-colonial character. As mentioned above, most scholars whose theories are ethnic-based use the concept of settler colonialism but only in reference to contexts outside of Israel proper (Shafir and Peled 2002). In other words, settler-colonial policies on which Zionism is premissed disappear from these analyses of the State of Israel.

Yuval-Davis has noted that the concept of ethnic democracy creates complacency by constructing 'the ethnic domination of the Jewish collectivity in the Israeli state as "normal" and as compatible with the construction of Israel as a democratic state'.[10] This is true, as we have seen above, in most cases of Israeli Ashkenazi literature on citizenship and the state. 'Ignoring or marginalizing the construction of Israel as a settler society, with its own specific characteristics, prevents most Israelis, both emotionally and analytically, from understanding some epistemological and ontological aspects of the Israeli Palestinian conflict' (Yuval-Davis 2003: 193). In fact, the ethnic-centred paradigm in general, I would add, raises the question of whether this concept is used more for 'convenience' or as a political strategy than for its 'theoretical validity'. After all, ethnocentric approaches provide softer, less politically charged concepts to describe what are basically racist policies and practices embedded in the Zionist ideology on which Israel has been – and continues to be – founded.

There are further theoretical and methodological problems associated with the use of ethnic-centred approaches to characterize the Israeli regime of citizenship, especially in reference to marginalized women like the Palestinian and Mizrahi collectivities. One such problem lies in the way in which these approaches mask the lived experiences of marginalized women citizens. In this paradigm, the term 'ethnicity' is presented without a clear definition and left as an elastic concept. It is stretched to include all sorts of other definitions; sometimes it is equated with religion (Swirski 2000; Levanon and Raviv 2007). In this case, ethnicity as a framework has the potential to segment the population, especially the Palestinians, into scattered groups, as is the case with various works which treat Palestinians not as an indigenous people but as segments made up of Muslims, Christians, Druze and Bedouin, an account which removes the historical specificity of the indigenous Palestinians in Palestine/Israel. In other instances the term 'ethnicity' is used synonymously with culture, while in the case of most of the Palestinian literature the concept is employed in a manner such that it is synonymous with nationalism (as with Rouhana and Ghanem). In all of the above, the ethnic-centred approaches create a seeming equality of rights of historical, geographic and cultural belonging between Jewish Ashkenazi or 'engathered settlers' and other immigrants, on the one hand, and indigenous Palestinians, on the other.

Moreover, this paradigm tends to overemphasize *demography*, undermining in the process the role *geography* plays in shaping citizenship and the state. More specifically, the role of territory or land, which is at the centre of the history of dispossessed Palestinian citizens as well as at the heart of the history which enabled the establishment of the Israeli state, is hardly articulated in the ethnic paradigm. As will be seen in the following discussion, territory and deterritoriality, expressed in land appropriation or expropriation, have played and continue to play a vital role in the reproduction and the further expansion of the Israeli state, on the one hand, and in the further alienation and oppression of Palestinian citizens as a national indigenous collective, on the other.

The use of ethnic-centred paradigms to explain Israeli citizenship and the state, while remaining predominant within the Israeli left academy, is only one form of theorization. In fact, and contrary to this body of literature, there is a growing body of academic work that provides an alternative theoretical framework. This scholarship is largely produced by what Edward Said once referred to as 'exilic intellectuals', a concept which refers to those who 'confront orthodoxy and dogma, representing people and issues that are routinely forgotten or swept under the rug; and they do so on the basis of universal principles, such as freedom and justice' (Said 1994: 11–12).[11] These are the intellectuals who confront Israel as a racist or racialized settler-colonial state. This literature, which includes, for example, the work of Uri Davis (2003), Ephraim Nimni (2003), Ella Shohat (1988, 1999, 2002), Ronit Lentin (2002, 2008), and Farsoun and Aruri (2006), among others, contests the validity and analytical usefulness of the concept ethnicity. Instead, they emphasize the historical continuity of Zionism as a settler-colonial regime, characteristic of the State of Israel: before, throughout and after the establishment of Israel. This body of literature, which, as will be further demonstrated, has opened up a larger epistemological space for questioning, on the one hand, the notion of Jewishness as a homogeneous national or ethnic collectivity, and, on the other, Zionism as its national expression, allows Mizrahi Jews a greater voice and a wider ontological space. Conceptualizing Israel/Zionism as a racialized settler-colonial project, moreover, provides an analytical tool not only to comprehend Zionist exclusionary policies at the demographic level, but also to make sense of the Zionist state's geographic policies of systemic and systematic land theft based on racist policies, with their devastating consequences for the indigenous people.

Defining Israel as a settler-colonial and racist state more specifically restores the notion of land or territory to the citizenship debate, emphasizing in the process the import of 'economic citizenship' (Davis 2003), a factor which has often been excluded from most, if not all, post-modernist and post-colonialist paradigms. Putting it differently, settler colonialism as a frame of analysis provides a more inclusive account and appropriate conceptual tool for understanding the classed, racialized, ethnicized and gendered nature of Israeli citizenship. Restoring the economic to the political system and the material to the historical is important inasmuch as it opens up a wider space for challenging the present and envisioning a future without existing forms of oppression.

In other words, approaching the state as settler-colonial and racist allows us to see the exclusion of Palestinian citizens (and also Mizrahi women), and their racially based inclusion or marginalization, not in terms of ethnic, religious or cultural polarity, difference or differentiation, but rather as fundamental components of the political economy of the settler-colonial state. It is for all the above reasons that in this study I use the terms 'racism' and 'racialization' to characterize the Israeli settler-colonial state and object to its characterization as an 'ethnic' state. Throughout the book I try to distinguish between ethnicity and racism, or ethnicizing and racializing, as two distinct sets of state policies. I here share Yuval-Davis's observation that adopting the term 'ethnic' and prioritizing it over other more apt descriptions and characterizations of the Israeli state – that is, 'racism' and 'racialization' – is methodologically more appealing to Israeli liberal and left Zionist academics and activists (Yuval-Davis 2003). This method of enquiry removes from such academics the responsibility to dig deeper into the racist nature of their own upbringing – Zionism. Racist and racialized policies characteristic of Israel's settler-colonial project are not akin to ethnic divisions or policies adopted by the state. Racism and racialization concern the exclusivist and exclusionary nature of Zionism and its state manifestation. Ethnicity and ethnic policies, on the other hand, go very well with the notion of liberal democracy, with its catchwords 'different inclusion', 'accommodation', and 'tolerance'. They also go well with the naming of Israel as a democratic state.

While I consider the distinction between 'ethnic' and 'racial' vital in characterizing Zionism and the Israeli settler-colonial state, I also find myself in some instances falling into the trap of using the concepts interchangeably. This is particularly true when quoting directly or indirectly existing literature on citizenship and the state in Israel. One must always remember that the overwhelming body of literature on these issues has been and continues to be written by Ashkenazi male academics, who are part of the Establishment but use liberal critiques to reconcile what otherwise are vast and irreconcilable contradictions. This is also the case with Israeli feminist scholars, the overwhelming majority of whom are liberal or radical but not anti-Zionist or anti-racist.

Gendered Citizenship and the Settler-Colonial Racist Regime

Territory and deterritorialism and women's citizenship

Geography expressed in the presence or absence of territorial boundaries constitutes a major element in the feminist definition of citizenship.

The concepts of state and territory are not new to the feminist debate on citizenship. Whether citizenship is perceived to be affected by globalization or imperialism, and thus defined by the absence of territorial boundaries or 'deterritorialization', as is the case with the 'postnationalist' or 'externalist' approaches (Soysal 1994, 2001; Shaw 1997), or whether it is defined in the context of the nation-state with defined territorial boundaries, as in the case of the 'traditionalist/internalist' approaches (Jenson 2000, 2001; Joppke 2002), state and territory or land constitute basic elements in defining citizenship in general and women's citizenship more specifically. However, land/territory is not just an expression of borders and boundaries.

In the settler-colonial state, land or territory is concerned less with defining or fixing borders than with keeping these borders fluid and undetermined. In this context land/territory is about establishing space, history and national presence (Butenschon et al. 2000; Davis 2003; Rouhana and Sultany 2003). Restoring land and the state to Middle East feminist debates on women's status and citizenship is to help make good the disconnect between civil society activism (NGOs) and the 'national' at the practical/empirical level, and that between feminist and the main male-stream literature at the abstract/theoretical level.

The centrality of territory/land in defining women's citizenship and the state in the Israeli/Palestinian context is paramount. On the one hand, the place of territory and deterritorialization has been and continues to be the focus for the reproduction and expansion of the State of Israel, while, on the other, these constitute a source for the perpetual diminution of the social, economic and political position of indigenous Palestinians. In theorizing the Israeli state as settler-colonial with a racist or apartheid-like regime that impacts even on its own citizens, Davis (2003) reaffirms the role of territory/land by emphasizing the primacy of economic citizenship in defining citizenship and the state. Economic primacy in Davis's work refers to the systematic abrogation of the rights of the indigenous Palestinians to their economic resources, primarily land, as part and parcel of Israeli Zionist policies. The very history of the Zionist movement that became the basis for Israeli state ideology and practice, Davis writes, has been and continues to be predicated on the expulsion of the indigenous Palestinians and the consequent confiscation of their landed property, with restrictions (sometimes total) placed on their living, using or even working on their confiscated lands. This form of confiscation and exclusion, he argues, is tantamount to the apartheid regime which governed the lives of indigenous Blacks in apartheid South Africa (Davis 2003). It is worth noting that Palestinian citizens, although they comprise around 20 per cent of the total population, live on less than 3.5 per cent of the land and control even less, as almost half of the land they live on is outside the jurisdiction of the Arab village councils (see National Committee for the Heads of the Arab Local Authorities in Israel 2006).[12]

In the settler-colonial state, land has a multiplicity of functions. On the one hand it is used by the state as the physical and material condition for its maintenance, reproduction and expansion (building settlements, providing infrastructure and accommodating more settlers). Yet, for the indigenous people land/territory carries a rather different meaning and has a different function. For indigenous nationals, land, as noted by Davis above, serves as a source of life and survival and a material basis for cultural production. As Rosemary Sayigh has reminded us, land for Palestinians, especially refugees, has served and continues to serve as the repository of history and memory transferred through generations, as well as the space from which material and cultural subsistence and wealth is derived (Sayigh 1979).

In many respects, land is also a gendered concept. Historically land for Palestinian women has served as the primary means of survival, productive activity, public socialization and as a resource for future security. It is also a means of marginalization and exploitation. While this issue – namely, the relationship between women, landed property and their socio-economic status – has yet to be fully researched, the literature suggests that landed property can have an intimate relation to women's social and economic status (Tucker 2000, 2002).

Historically, landed property has played an important role in shaping the form and even dynamics of marriages, affecting the very structure of patriarchy and family relations or familialism. It is possible to argue that certain forms of traditional marriage such as polygamy and *badal* (exchange marriage)[13] are a function of economic situations and historically have been tied to the control over land and the drive to keeping it within the agnatic line of the family. Rosenfeld's and Al-Haj's studies of Palestinian villages established a strong correlation between the number of offspring and the size of family land holding (Rosenfeld 1968; Al-Haj 1987). In other words, historically land more than nationalism has formed the impetus for Palestinian women's reproductive activities.

Politically, land for Palestinian citizens has served as the single most important rallying point for women's and men's political activism. Harakat Al Ard (the Land Movement), which was established during the 1950s and subsequently violently repressed and forced underground, is one example. Another is the national demonstrations which started on 30 March 1976, known in Arabic as *Yom al-Ard*, 'Land Day', during which six Palestinian citizens, including one woman (Khadija Shawahneh), were shot dead by Israeli soldiers. Since then, Land Day has become an annual day of demonstrations in all centres of Arab population in Israel.[14]

Symbolically, land also functions as a social and cultural space for women, especially for the majority who spend much of their life at home, the centre of activity for most women. The absence of sufficient land for Palestinians, combined with Israel's use of a systematic house demolition policy against citizens – especially Jerusalemites, Bedouin and people living in the so-called 'unrecognized' villages – violates women's right to safety and security and obstructs their socio-cultural productivity. It is no surprise, therefore, that many women end up with no alternative but to go back to increasingly cramped familial accommodation, usually with their immediate family, or, if that is not an option, the extended family.

Finally, land and more specifically Israel's landed policy have placed an additional restriction on women citizens in terms of their movement. Restrictions on women's right to choose their living space are a case in point. Palestinian citizens are legally excluded from their historical land, which, after being expropriated, is placed in the possession of either the Keren Kayemet Li-Yisrael (Hebrew for the Jewish National Fund (JNF) or the Israeli Lands Authority – the two authorities coordinate to ensure that the confiscated Palestinian land formerly owned by citizens is kept under total Jewish control.[15] The case of Fatina Zubeidat is an example for Palestinian citizens barred from owning or renting a house in Jewish areas.

After their marriage in the summer of 2006, Fatina and husband Ahmad Zubeidat, both graduates with distinction from the College of Architecture at Bezalel Academy of Arts and Design in Jerusalem, filed an application to live in the 'community town' – recent Jewish settlement – of Rakefet in the Galilee. Following their interview with the Selection Committee, they were declared 'socially unsuitable' and their application denied. As Adalah (the Legal Centre for Arab Minority Rights in Israel) noted, all 'Selection Committees in Community Towns illegally exclude Arab citizens, Mizrahi Jews, single parents and gays' (Adalah 2007).[16]

The devastating impact of Israel's landed policies on Palestinian citizens is particularly grave with respect to the socio-economic condition of the Bedouin community. Such policies have led to their further impoverishment, and consequently to an increase in social and gender problems. Finally, Israel's tight control over Palestinian lands has the potential to annul all citizenship rights of certain communities; for example, the proposed land swaps suggested for Palestinians living in the Triangle area.[17]

The above discussion demonstrates the important role of territory/ land not only in defining the Israeli settler-colonial rule but also in comprehending women's citizenship status in Israel. Incorporating land/territory in its multiple roles and functions in defining the settler-colonial state and understanding women's citizenship therein should be viewed as a primary analytical tool for framing the debate on citizenship. This analytical perspective on the relationship between gender, land and the state, it is argued, is dearly missing in most feminist literature on citizenship in the Middle East in general and Palestine/Israel in particular.

Feminist theorizing of citizenship in the Middle East: religion, familialism and nationalism

By going beyond the Western feminist theories that locate women's citizenship directly within the state, within (or outside) its national territorial boundaries, Middle Eastern feminists have undoubtedly contributed to a new body of literature which expands the purview of citizenship to include concepts historically specific to the region. These concepts, namely 'familialism', 'religion' and 'nationalism', constitute significant players in the discourse on the rights and status of Middle Eastern women. Suad Joseph (2000), Deniz Kandiyoti (1996), and Abdo and Yuval-Davis (1995), for example, argue that women's rights point up the most serious fault line in modern concepts of citizenship in the Middle East and call for a more pluralistic approach that takes into account the multiple tensions and contestations within each specific context. Elaborating on the role of patriarchy, which is embedded in the familial, religious and national institutions, individually and relationally, and their consequent role in shaping and reshaping of women's citizenship rights has undoubtedly enriched the citizenship debate and produced a more nuanced account of the differences between the Western liberal democratic state and the Middle Eastern and Arab states.

In the context of Israel, an attempt has also been made to use the above approach, which focuses on the relationship between the three institutions of family, religion and nationalism and the mediatory role they play between women and the state, as a tool for understanding women's citizenship status (Swirski 2000). While this approach provides important insights for the analysis of women in Israel, it nevertheless fails to understand fully or account for the historical specificity of Israel as a settler-colonial state. It is to this discussion that we now turn.

In Israel, and in contrast to Western liberal democracies, there is no separation between state and religion. Quite the contrary, religion in the form of Orthodox Judaism has been embedded in the character of the Israeli state since its establishment. As Connie Jorgensen has stated, 'The 1948 Declaration of Independence stated specifically that

Israel was to be a Jewish state. The Jewish religion, particularly the Orthodox version, has become the central identifying characteristic of both the people and the state' (Jorgensen 1994: 281). Orthodox Judaism, as many feminist scholars observe, is paternalistic if not patriarchal in nature, as it considers women to be inferior to men. For example, in the Jewish *Halacha* (Jewish law), one finds many references to the subordinate position of women. These include the prohibition of marriage between Jews and non-Jews; the cleansing of the bride; the consent of the bride's father and the groom in order for the marriage to take place; the right of a brother-in-law to veto the remarriage of a widow; and the husband's veto power over divorce (Jorgensen 1994; Swirski 2000). Similar forms of restriction and the inferiorization of women are also present in Muslim judicial courts and shari'a courts, as well as in the church ordinances that form Israel's primary institutions for dealing with personal status laws or family laws concerning Palestinian Arabs/Muslims and Christians alike.

Regardless of the highly political nature of Judaism as the official state religion, proclaimed by Ben-Gurion as a means to entice world Jewry to immigrate to Palestine (Jorgensen 1994: 281), to date Israel – sixty years after its establishment and now as a powerful state with nuclear weapons – continues to use religion to cement its policies both externally and internally. Internally, the Jewishness of the state serves to reproduce and strengthen its racist, exclusivist and exclusionary politics and policies towards indigenous Palestinian citizens, keeping them under control. Externally, however, Israel uses Jewishness as a tool to cement its settler-colonial (or immigration) policies; it also functions as a tool to serve the interests of the Western imperial centre in the Arab region and beyond. A state of all its citizens would obstruct such functions and render the political-ideological construct of Jewishness unnecessary. In fact, this is why Western strategists and politicians in visits, meetings and discussions re-emphasize the Jewishness of the state. A stark example of this is US president George W. Bush's letter to Sharon on 14 April 2004; and when in a 2007 visit to Israel he made it clear that Israel would remain a Jewish state. Another example is Gordon Brown's speech to the Knesset on Israel's sixtieth anniversary.[18] The lack of separation between state and religion (between Israel and Jewishness) explains the important role religion as a political ideology plays in the lives of women citizens in Israel.

It is important to note that religion, as an institution rather than a spiritual relationship between the individual and her God, is not an essentialist or stagnant force. It is not an ahistorical notion fixed in time and space. Depending on the state in question, institutionalized religion can play different roles with varying impacts on women; it can also have a transformative character. In other words, neither Jewish nor Muslim religious codes should be seen as written in stone. For example, a survey of women's family status throughout the Middle East and North Africa suggests the presence of varied shari'a interpretations and consequently laws governing women's position in almost all of life's domains (including marriage, divorce, polygamy, alimony and custody over children).[19] With a sincere commitment to democracy, social justice and equal citizenship, the presence of political will at the state or decision-making level can influence change in this realm. In fact, recent feminist activism, both Jewish and Palestinian – albeit not without tremendous resistance – has enabled an important change in women's status law or family law. Building on the successes of other feminist organizations, including their Jewish feminist counterparts who successfully lobbied the state to enact a civil Family Law in 1995, a campaign by Palestinian women's NGOs and various other civil and human rights activists succeeded in amending the Personal Status Code for Palestinian (meaning Christian and Muslim) women. Prior to this, the code stipulated that only Jewish and Druze women could take their cases of alimony, child custody and divorce settlement (but not marriage and divorce proper) to the civil court instead of to the religious court; this excluded Christian and Muslim Palestinian women. It is important to note that Druze women were seen as non-Arabs by both the Israeli establishment and official feminism, hence their inclusion in the campaign. Palestinian women in Israel fought a long, hard campaign, which began in 1995; they proposed an amendment to the Knesset in 1998, and saw the law passed on 5 November 2001. All Palestinian women can now take their personal status cases (except for marriage and divorce, which are still controlled by religious courts) to civil courts if they so choose.

Furthermore, as a relational concept, to use Joseph's notion (2000),[20] religion, or more correctly the religious institution, is intimately related to familialism, the institution of the family. The relationship between the two is in fact mutual and reciprocal: the family can and does serve as a repository of religious codes, norms and modes of daily behaviour, and in this relation functions as a primary institution for conserving, reproducing and spreading religious doctrine. On the other hand, institutionalized religion serves, among other things, to organize family and gender relations. And in so far as women are concerned, both institutions work as a mutual reinforcement of patriarchy. But the mediatory role these institutions play in determining citizenship, especially women's citizenship, is only defined when contextualized within the nation-state, which appears as the overarching structure and ideology that oversee, control and govern religion and the family.

A study emphasizing the articulation of religion, familialism and patriarchy as important components of women's citizenship must also account for the historical specificity of the 'state' and its situatedness at a particular historical juncture. More specifically, I refer here to the contentions that 'the institutions of the family and religion have dominated Arab Palestinian culture historically and were heavily entrenched in the Ottoman and British imperial rules over Palestinians', and that 'Israel has inherited the Millet system from these two previous regimes',[21] a position taken by Swirski (2000: 35–6) to explain Palestinian women's seeming fixed state of oppression.

There is no doubt that patriarchy embedded in the religious and familial institutions is heavily entrenched in the traditional culture of Palestinian women. It also constitutes an important restrictive force on women's status, mobility and development. Existing ethnographic literature that deals with issues of so-called honour killing and violence against women is replete with examples on this front, as pointed out earlier. However, the concern here is with the wider socio-economic and political context within which such institutions are situated. For, as will be seen in the next chapter, neither the Turkish Empire nor British colonial rule had similar, let alone equal, policies and practices concerning the colonized indigenous Palestinians, especially in terms of their daily survival and reproduction as landowners, tillers or sharecroppers. Nor did these two states have landed policies similar to those that Israel has had, and continues to have, regarding indigenous Palestinians. The point here is that family and religion cannot be treated as ahistorical concepts detached from the specific historical state within which they operate. The concepts of family and religion, like any other socio-ideological or political construct, have their bases in real material conditions and within a specific time and place.

The next chapter shows further how landed property, either in the form of *waqf* (private land endowed to religious institutions) or in other forms of landed property, has played an important role in structuring the Palestinian family and women's position during the reigns of both the Turks and the British. Still, neither Turkish nor British colonial rule was able to effect the total expropriation of Palestinian lands and peasants; nor were these waqf lands threatened, let alone confiscated, by either of the two previous colonial powers. Israel, on the other hand, has physically and by force removed about 80 per cent of Palestinians from their historic land. It has also confiscated their religious waqf lands, affecting the very relationship on which various ideological forms, including familialism, have been shaped. Moreover, Israel's colonial policy of demographic control and confinement has put its imprint on the Palestinian family, even after most of the indigenous land has been confiscated by the state. One such intervention, as will be explained later, concerns the role of the Israeli state in propping up the institution of the *mukhtar* (village head), using it as a political and social tool for controlling the local population (Zeidani 1995; Nakhleh 1977).

To argue that family, patriarchy and religion are vital cultural constraints on women's citizenship, that they have always existed, and that Israel has merely inherited these structures from previous colonial rule, as Swirski (2000) has put it, is a simplification of reality and politically problematic. For the assertion, I maintain, feeds into existing Orientalist and racist perceptions of indigenous Palestinians as 'backward', 'less', other, 'inferior' and 'primarily oppressed' by their own family and religion, justifying in the process Israel's Zionist 'civilizing mission' towards not only indigenous Palestinians but Mizrahi Jews as well.

The fact is that Israel has played a major role in shaping and reshaping familial roles among its Palestinian citizens, a point that cannot be overemphasized. The lingering effects of Israel's military rule over its Palestinian citizens between 1948 and 1966 on the structure and form of the family, and more importantly on gender relations, cannot be ignored. This period of military rule has largely restricted women's mobility, their economic/productive role, as well as their access to education, thereby stunting their development, an issue that will be further examined in the next chapter. Israel's exclusionary physical, economic and cultural policies have undoubtedly strengthened women's dependence on their husbands, fathers, brothers and other male family members. And the long-term impact of similar policies of confinement on a limited geographical area allocated to Mizrahi Jewish immigrants, especially in the early years of their settlement/immigration, continue to linger on, especially in so far as Mizrahi women are concerned.

In the late 1980s, the concept of nationalism was introduced as an important structure or institution through which women in the Third World experience their agency. Introduced first by Kumari Jayawardena, the notion of nationalism as an institution gained more popularity, especially among Middle Eastern feminists.[22] Feminist critical work on nationalism as a social and political construct having a tremendous influence and role in shaping and reshaping women's status in the Middle East has largely been based on Benedict Anderson's seminal work *Imagined Communities: Reflections on the Origin and*

Spread of Nationalism (1991). For Anderson, nations as imagined political communities could only arise historically when three cultural concepts lost their grip on the minds of people: the ontological verity of sacred texts; the dynastic order of a power hierarchy with a ruler envisioned as linked to the divine; and a comprehension of time in which cosmology and history were indistinguishable. The rise of print capitalism contributed to the idea of calendrical time, in which strangers who read the same daily text could incorporate themselves into a new idea of community imagined as the same (Anderson 1991: 26). Anderson's calendrical time here refers to the Marxist notion of colonial capitalism.

Unlike the concept of 'people', characterized in the work of Marxists as based on historical material origins, nationalism is culturally rooted. The nation is often imagined as living within defined geographical borders, as a sovereign entity, and as a community. Despite the actual inequality and exploitation that may prevail in each nation, it is always conceived as a deep, horizontal comradeship. Ultimately it is this fraternity that has made it possible, over the past two centuries, for so many millions of people, not so much to kill, as willingly to die for such limited imaginings (Anderson 1991: 6–7). Herein lies the important contribution of the feminist critique of nationalism. Women in this critique are seen as the keepers, the biological and social producers and reproducers, of the nation-state, and as such their domestic, familial or mothering roles are seen to be a priority over all other (public) roles they might play. This is true for all women in Israel, particularly for Mizrahi, Ashkenazi and Palestinian women (Yuval-Davis 1991; Joseph 2000; Swirski 2000; Katz 2003; Berkovitz 1997).

Within the Israeli-Palestinian nationalist context, feminist literature – except for literature specifically dealing with the Palestinians in the West Bank and Gaza – has largely focused on the similarities of marginalization and exploitation of nationalism towards all women citizens. In so doing, literature has produced a seeming equality between Jewish nationalism and Zionism, on the one hand, and Palestinian nationalism, on the other. The work of Barbara Swirski

(2000) and that of Sheila Katz (2003) are prime examples here. Both provide detailed accounts of how nationalism past and present has constituted a primary force in subjugating women to the national interest by keeping them confined to the domestic sphere and away from the public political realm where major political decisions are being made.

In the abstract, the assertion that nationalism and all nationalisms are forces which contribute to women's oppression and marginalization runs the risk of overgeneralization. Ashkenazi, Mizrahi and Palestinian women are oppressed by their respective nationalisms, as the latter are largely constructed by males and organized around masculine, patriarchal values. Yet this construction is differentially distributed between the colonizers and the colonized, rendering the relationship between the two asymmetrical: colonial nationalism has the power to oppress the colonized on a multiplicity of levels, including gender, race and class. In other words, to argue that both Arab-Palestinian women and Jewish Israeli women are equally oppressed by their respective nationalism, as Swirski and Katz do, masks the true relationship between the colonizer and the colonized and the oppressor and the oppressed. Within the context of Jewish women, Israeli (Ashkenazi) feminists have extended their critique of nationalism to what many consider to be that most influential and perhaps sacred institution, Israel's national security or military-industrial complex. The Israeli military-industrial complex, feminists argue, is the most important force that defines who belongs to the nation and who is excluded from it (Izraeli 2001; Swirski 2000; Golan 1997). In this literature, Israeli militarism is conceived as central to the Jewish state and is perhaps the major if not the sole institution responsible for creating, maintaining and certifying Israeli citizenship. On this, Izraeli notes that service in the military is equivalent to serving the Jewish collective and is 'constructed to be the basis for entitlement to full citizenship in the Jewish state and in a sense, even for consideration as a normal human being' (Izraeli 2001: 284). But this body, she adds, is essentially gendered:

The gender regime of the Israeli military is based on a gendered division of labour and a gendered structure of power, supported by a gendered ideology that combine to sustain and reinforce the taken-for-granted role of women as 'the Other' and their proverbial role as 'helpmates' to men. (Izraeli 2004: 282)

Feminist literature on Israel's 'military–industrial complex' seems to suggest that the production/reproduction divide that is characteristic of citizenship – namely, the presence of production-oriented citizenship, often expressed in the roles played by male citizens as soldiers and producers, and the reproduction role of citizenship relegated to women's biological and social roles – is replicated in the military (Berkovitz 1997; Amir and Benjamin 1997). This divide is further entrenched in the Defence Service Law (1986) which exempts women if they are married, pregnant, have children or declare convictions that prevent their service in the military – Haredi or Orthodox Jewish men are also exempted from military service (Berkovitz 1997). These exemptions are based on the idea that the roles of mother and wife are incompatible with the role of soldier, as women in the military service will adversely affect the Jewish birth rate. Thus participation in the army would prevent women from fulfilling what Ben-Gurion called their 'unique destiny' – motherhood (Berkovitz 1997: 610).

In recognizing the intimate relationship between Israel's military establishment and the leaders of the state, the specificities of the patriarchal nature of the military becomes clear. As in the case of other Jewish (Ashkenazi) feminist literature, the literature on the militarized aspect of Israeli nationalism is also ethnic-blind and fails to account for the historical and culturally specific conditions under which Mizrahi women find themselves. The question that needs be addressed here is, which women and whose Jewishness are being discussed? One could perhaps argue that more Mizrahi women marry and have families earlier than do Ashkenazi women, and as a result their contribution to the Israeli military and national establishment is less. It is also possible to argue that because of their lesser contribution to national duties Mizrahi women are less rewarded in the public sphere than their Ashkenazi counterparts, a common argument often used to justify exclusion of Palestinians from important public positions. However, these are not the arguments advanced in such literature. Ashkenazi feminist literature on Israeli military and Zionist nationalism, while not only ignoring the offensive and destructive role of Israeli's military establishment towards Palestinian Arab women (and men), also silences the Mizrahi Jews who have been turned into the other by the state itself. The Jewish Ashkenazi literature is concerned instead with one nationalism and one Jewishness; it provides an essentialist meaning of Zionism as an expression of the national movement of all Jews. The concern here, rather, is with the ramifications of this white liberal feminist approach. This approach conceptualizes gender in isolation from its class and racialized context. It is primarily oriented towards reproducing Israeli Jewish nationalism or Zionism as given without challenging its Orientalist nature, which undermines if not excludes its Jewish other – Mizrahi or Arab Jewish women – let alone its settler-colonial policies towards indigenous Palestinians.

Israeli Jewish (Ashkenazi) feminism is often blamed for skewing Mizrahi women's identity, and consequently their positioning within the Israeli citizenship debate. This is particularly so in as far as the intimate relationship constructed between Zionism and Jewish nationalism (Yuval-Davis 1995). Zionism cannot be used as a totalizing concept for all Jews; Mizrahi Jewish feminists are almost unanimous in claiming that such a definition not only excludes them but also masks their history, reality and identity. Mizrahi feminists refuse to see Zionism as a frame of reference for defining their identity (Shohat 1997, 1999, 2002; Dahan-Kalev 2001, 2003; Lavie 2002).

In 'Intervention of the Mizrahis', Ella Shohat (1999) provides an eloquent critique of the seemingly necessary connection between Zionism and 'Jewishness' and examines the problems of ethnic discrimination and racism in the Jewish national imaginary. Mizrahi or 'Easterner' is the term she gives to Israel's population of Jewish immigrants from the Arab and Islamic world. Many of these Arab Jews, Shohat contends, are Sephardic, practising the Jewish rituals and liturgy passed down among the Jews who were exiled from Sepharad

(Spain) in 1492. The designation Mizrahi, however, draws attention to the ethnic differences that have marked Arab and Muslim Jews as the Oriental Other to Israel's founding Zionist leaders who were Ashkenazi (Eastern European). State practices, such as the spraying of early Mizrahi immigrants with pesticides, or the consideration of Mizrahi Jews as test subjects for biological weapons intended for Palestinians (assumed to be the same racial group), draw attention to the ways in which Zionism has sought to construct a nation founded on Jewish sameness while essentializing Jewish ethnic, racial or sexual difference as inherently outside the privileged space of the nation (Shohat 1999: 5–6).

For Shohat, the term 'Mizrahi' is being constructed by Mizrahi Jews as a challenge to the artificial dichotomy created through the Zionist discourse on Arabs and Jews. She argues that the Zionist state has attempted to systematically suppress Sephardi/Mizrahi identity through a variety of mechanisms. These mechanisms included the rejection of an Arab Muslim context for Jewish institutions, identity and history, leading in the process to the subordination of Arab Jews to a universal Jewish experience – a process, Shohat contends, intended to create a 'master narrative of Jewish victimization' (Shohat 1999: 6).

Shohat calls for the creation of Mizrahi studies in a new form which would be related to Palestinian studies. Such an approach to Mizrahi studies, she argues, would furnish the grounds for a critique of the treatment of Mizrahis in Zionist discourse on a wider geographical and historical level. Moreover, framing Mizrahi women's experiences in Israel, Shohat adds, has the potential of intervening at the point of convergence of multiple communities and identities, crossing the boundaries of essentialized identities (Shohat 1999: 17). In a similar vein, Motzafi-Haler takes up the concept of Zionism and critiques its racist nature towards Mizrahi women. In a discursive analysis aimed at answering the question of why Mizrahi women are absent from Israeli Ashkenazi feminist accounts, Motzafi-Haler locates the answer in the 'silencing' and 'erasure' of Mizrahi women's experiences within Zionism (Motzafi-Haller 2001: 699). Mizrahi feminist discourse, she argues, can contribute another layer of critique to the post-Zionist debates by re-examining democracy and racism from the multiple levels of Israeli society that are excluded from access to power.

The debate within post-Zionism revolves largely around scholars who take Zionism as a settler-colonial project to refer to Zionist practices in pre-Israel, Palestine or the Occupied Territories only, suggesting that Israel proper has gone global and as such is now beyond a history conceived of as settler-colonial, a position adhered to by scholars such Peled, Shafir and Yuval-Davis. A detailed analysis of this position is found in Nimni (2003a).

For Ilan Pappé, Post-Zionism labels

a cultural view from within Israel which strongly criticized Zionist policy and conduct up to 1948, accepted many of the claims made by the Palestinians with regards to 1948 itself, and envisaged a non-Jewish state in Israel as the best solution for the country's internal and external predicaments. (Pappé 2003: 44)

I extend Pappé's formulation in my definition of post-Zionism to include any critical reflection on the foundation myths of Zionism, from within or outside Israel, which assumes a homogenous Jewish nation with a birthright to the territory now designated Israel. Included in this expanded definition of post-Zionism is the rethinking of Israel's physical and spiritual violence against Palestinians both inside and outside its borders and the racist treatment of non-European Jews. Although post-Zionist literature articulates alternative views of Israel as a racist society, opening up a space to bring Zionist racism into the foreground, and highlights its exclusionary nature and character, it is important to note that this is not the only alternative vision. Anti-Zionist scholars such as Ilan Pappé (2003), Avi Shlaim (2001, 2009), Smadar Lavie (2002, 2005), Ella Shohat (1999, 2002), Uri Davis (2003) and Ronit Lentin (2002, 2005, 2008) have articulated a clearer vision of the racist ideology of Zionism and the Israeli state. Anti-Zionist literature is also clear about the settler-colonial and racist nature and character of Zionism and the Zionist movement throughout its history – that is, in the pre-state period in Palestine as well as subsequent to the creation of the State of Israel. This is particularly true in so far as its Palestinian citizens are concerned. It is this clear anti-Zionist visioning and theorization, I argue, which needs to develop more and spread widely, as it carries the true potential to create an alternative Israel in the Middle East, one that is secular, democratic and inclusive.

Framing Palestinian women's citizenship, especially in terms of its relationship to nationalism, is rather more complex. Throughout their history Palestinians as a people have never lived within a state of their own; Palestine has always been under the control of foreign colonial and settler-colonial regimes. In other words, Palestine as a sovereign territory or nation-state has never been the primary source of meaning for Palestinian nationalism. Still, Palestinians have always understood the cultural roots of their nationalism – cultural roots with a material basis. Palestinians associated themselves with others of their kind and identified their community not as an imaginary construct called a people or a nation located outside of their historical materiality, but as an expression of their material connectedness to the land or territory called Palestine. Geography for the Palestinians was not a mere demarcation of borders and boundaries, elements often imposed from the outside. Land for Palestinians was the space on and from which they produced and reproduced themselves as an agricultural people. Historically, then, as peasants who tilled, worked and established a close relation to Palestine as a geographical space, Palestinians developed a strong material culture, which made them a close community. The goal of the Zionist state since 1948 to erase Palestinian national and cultural markers of community, obliterate their collective memory and fragment them as a people through their expulsion, dispossession and dispersal, has failed. Instead, these circumstances have cemented their collective memory as a people and revived their national consciousness (real or imagined) as a nation. The development in the 1950s of Harakat al-Ard (the Land Movement) in Palestine/Israel; the emergence of the PLO among diaspora refugee Palestinians in 1964; the celebrations of the Land Day, which has become an annual event since 1976; the emergence of the first Intifada in 1987, followed by the second Intifada in 2000 – all constitute strong expressions of the connectedness of Palestinian national identity to material geography/land. Moreover, these historical moments have strengthened the individual and collective memory of Palestinians as natives of the land. They also heightened consciousness of and resistance to the state. The latter for them became the primary symbol of their oppression. Given this context, it is not surprising that the bulk of feminist literature produced by and about Palestinians has tended to focus not on 'citizenship' or the 'nation-state' per se (a condition Palestinian women historically and those living in the Occupied Territories more specifically never experienced as their own), but on issues concerning women and national liberation as a resistance movement. It is, moreover, in this context that authors Jad, Johnson and Giacaman described the notion of citizenship in the context of the 1967 Occupied Palestinian Territories as 'perplexing' and mystifying (Jad et al. 2000: 134).

This perplexity notwithstanding, women's active participation in the struggle against Israeli occupation and settler colonialism, especially during the first Intifada, has generated a large body of feminist literature. While mostly critical of the male politics of the Palestinian national leadership, of the national government and its economic and social institutions, this work in fact painted a rather positive picture of women's active role in the resistance (Abdo and Lentin 2002b; Kuttab and Abu-Awwad 2004; Labadi 2003; Dajani 1994). Reflecting on this body of feminist literature, one can ascertain that framing women within the national context, even when the latter still takes the form of a liberation movement, can be somewhat limited and limiting. While not wishing to belittle the right of the colonized to struggle against their oppression, especially when the major enemy is embedded in a racist settler-colonial regime, it must be said that the theorizing of women's status ought to be more inclusive if not comprehensive. We need theory, as Marx reminds us, not just to describe the world we live in; we need it in order to analyse our world critically and eventually change it. Theorizing feminist citizenship according to a long-term vision, one in which Palestinians can envision a state without racism, oppression and exclusion, one that is not based on nationalism or ethnicity, seems to be what is missing in existing Palestinian feminist literature on women's status and role. By examining and understanding critically the forces of oppression embedded in the structure and ideology of the Jewish state, feminist theorizing of citizenship must allow a space for envisioning an alternative state in which women, and especially the marginalized, can attain their full rights and entitlements.

This vision, it is argued here, holds true for Palestinian women at large and those who are citizens of Israel more specifically. After all, despite the fact that in theory Palestinian women who are citizens of Israel enjoy certain citizenship rights, they also, unlike their sisters elsewhere in the diaspora, endure many forms of oppression, including dispossession, economic deprivation, social inferiority and political under-representation. They also share a collective and individual memory which has been constructed around their constant cultural alienation and denial. Their historical and contemporary life experiences have largely shaped, and continue to construct, their ontological being. What actually differentiates the status of Palestinian women in Israel from their counterparts in other parts of the Middle East is the ambiguous relationship they have with the type of state imposed on them as their own. Palestinian women citizens find themselves in a unique position where the self-defined Jewish state became the only force which accorded them partial and inferior citizenship status while simultaneously removing them from the nation-state. This contradictory position in which Palestinians find themselves – citizens of the state but not members of the nation – has been given little or no attention by Palestinian feminist scholars, whereas it surely deserves special attention. Israel, it should be noted, is the only state in the world in which its citizens are not its nationals.

Women's citizenship in Israel: between exclusion and racialized inclusion

Contradictions and contestations constitute a central feature of every state, but more so in a settler-colonial state such as Israel. Women's citizenship status in Israel can best be comprehended in terms of the presence of two different processes operating simultaneously within the Israeli state: one of exclusion and racial separation, which affects the Palestinian citizens at large; and another of racialized (and ethnicized) inclusion, to which Palestinian and Mizrahis (especially women) are subjected. Both processes, while seemingly contradictory, have been implemented hand in hand since the creation of the state.[23] This dynamic, as will be argued in the following pages, provides a comprehensive framework for understanding not only the racism and classism practised against indigenous Palestinian women, but also the racialization, ethnicization and Orientalization of Mizrahi women as Other.

Exclusion or racial separation lies at the heart of the Zionist colonial-settler project. It aims at establishing an exclusionary and exclusivist Jewish state in Palestine. Control over space (geography or territory), as well as over demography, lies at the centre of this citizenship regime. The Zionist exclusionary ideology enshrined in the Israeli legal, constitutional[24] and institutional regimes is expressed in a number of important laws. These include the Law of Return (1950), which offers the rights of full citizenship and nationality to Jews all over the world while simultaneously excluding Palestinians from the right to return. The Law of Return is directly linked to the Nationality Law (1953), which establishes Israel as the state of the Jewish people. Further to this is the Absentee Property Law (1948), also known as the Law of Hader-Ghaieb (present–absentee law), which enabled the state to legalize the confiscation of the overwhelming majority of Palestinian land, homes and property. This law has targeted all movable and immovable (landed) property belonging to about 80 per cent of the Palestinian population who were expelled from Palestine between 1948 and 1951. It also targeted many of those who stayed in the country but happened to be outside their homes or villages at the time of the census. This law is of particular significance to a sizeable section of Palestinian citizens who became internally displaced (Al-Haj 1986), as well as a large section of the Bedouin whose right to their land was denied and who have since been living in some fifty 'unrecognized villages'. Finally, the Nationality and Entry to Israel Law (2002) was introduced to cement previous policies banning family unification, thus denying Palestinian women (and men) the right to citizenship in their own places of residence, officially defined as Israel proper, such as is the case for Palestinian Jerusalemites.

In addition to the legal and constitutional exclusion, Palestinians are also geographically confined, excluded and to a large extent separated from Jewish residential locations. In fact, as some studies have shown, even in the so-called 'mixed' cities, Palestinian Arabs and Israeli Jews are not quite mixed; they continue to occupy their own quarters and work and live in their respective neighbourhoods. Racialized separation of residency was also extended to less desired Jews, such as Mizrahis, as will be elaborated below. And, as will be discussed in Chapters 3 and 4, exclusionary processes exercised against indigenous Palestinians are also expressed in the so-called enclave economy (or the racialized Arab market in the so-called Arab sector), as well as in the separate and inferior educational entitlements accorded to other citizens, especially Palestinians.

As for the Mizrahi Jews in Israel, whereas they were legally and institutionally included in the state, and considered as part of the Jewish nation, historically and to a large extent contemporarily they have been subjected to various forms of geographical and cultural exclusion from the Ashkenazi community. As will be elaborated on in the next chapter, Mizrahi Jews were not considered proper Jews and were placed in highly underdeveloped residential areas, being moved from ma'abarot (Hebrew for 'transit camps') to Ayarot Pituach (Hebrew, with Ashkenazi spelling, for 'development towns'), mainly in the Naqab (Negev) area but also in border zones and military areas after 1967, as well as in places such as Dimona, Beit She' and Beit Shemesh, most of which were built on depopulated Palestinian villages. For those who were able to lift themselves out of the inferior residential locations and for the many others who continue to live there, this racialized geography has greatly shaped their lived experiences. While this will be discussed further in the next chapter, for present purposes it is sufficient to register that the history of Mizrahi in Israel provides a stark example of their racialized inclusion in what the Zionist leadership imagines as real or proper Jews.

Unlike the case of the Palestinians, who were and are considered undesired citizens, Mizrahi Jews were considered by the state as nationals and deemed essential to its national project. While the socio-economic and cultural effects of Mizrahi Jewish exclusion and racialized separation continued to linger, the Israeli state, army, economy and polity became gradually open to their inclusion. The need for and the consequent integration of Mizrahis, especially males, into the Israeli military and the more frequent intermarriage between Mizrahi and Ashkenazi Jews have lessened their geographical exclusion, allowing them more access to reside in, own and work in other parts of the country. Still, it is important to re-emphasize that the major advancement in the position of Mizrahi Jews has affected men more than women, as the former were heavily represented in the military. This position allowed them greater access to the advantages offered by the military in terms of economic and political public participation and positions.

Without intending to make light of the harsh experiences of Mizrahis – for whom spatial exclusion has affected their economic and social status and deepened gender cleavages within their community and between them and Ashkenazi women in almost all spheres – the racist exclusion of Palestinian women (and men) has touched their very material culture, in which land is the depository of the people's collective memory. The constant settler-colonial expansion and expropriation of indigenous Palestinian land has altered the ontological and epistemological identity of Palestinians. The loss of land became the loss of their economic rights, the loss of their social status and the loss of their material symbol of culture and security.

Economic exploitation, political marginalization and social oppression are capable of communalizing the plight of the poor, including Palestinian, Mizrahi and other women citizens in Israel. However, the issue of territory or land operates as a major differentiating factor within the culturally and racially marginalized. It marks the difference between the indigenous-cum-citizen and the immigrant in fundamental ways. For indigenous Palestinians, as the preceding analysis maintains, the loss of land penetrates the cultural and symbolic spheres of the national collectivity of the indigenous people. Losing this cultural and material character is tantamount to losing an integral part of their indigenous identity.

The concept of racialized inclusion or of marginalization as a state of lived experiences has also been employed by Mizrahi feminists in describing their citizenship status both historically and in contemporary Israel (Motzafi-Haller 2001; Lavie 2002; Shohat 1988, 1999, 2002; Dahan-Kalev 2003). Whereas the regime of exclusion and racial separation operates on, or is enacted at, the structural level (including that of the state and its laws) and is primarily oriented towards indigenous Palestinians, racialized and ethnicized inclusion concerns both Palestinian and Mizrahi women and lies at the core of Israel's social, economic, political and institutional realms. Racialized inclusion refers to the process of partial inclusion – albeit with an inferior status – of Palestinian women, and to some extent also Mizrahi women,[25] in terms of employment and the availability of state services and entitlements. These benefits include the rights to adequate health care and education, the right to employment and political representation, and the right to financial redistribution from national taxes towards their city and village councils. Racialized inclusion is characterized by various forms of racism, including institutional racism embedded in all state structures (Kretzmer 1989). The extent to which this marginalized inclusion is utilized and acted upon by indigenous Palestinian women citizens depends partly on the size of the opening or space available to them in the public sphere of politics, but more on the space allowed them in the labour market. This ontological state also partly depends on women's agency, and their own active struggle for public presentation and equal citizenship.

In this structure of exclusion and racialized inclusion, Palestinian women are located at the edge of the most marginalized collectivities/groups in Israel. They are marginalized on a racial basis (as Palestinian citizens in a Jewish state), on a class basis in so far as other Israeli Jewish (especially Ashkenazi) women are concerned, and also on a gender and social status basis as female members of a traditional Arab society and family. Mizrahi women, who in most of the literature are considered second-class citizens, are best understood in the context of racialized or ethnicized inclusion. This framework provides a more appropriate context for appreciating their status both today and historically, as will be demonstrated throughout the book.

Racism, which is embedded in the Zionist ideology and practice of the Israeli state, has been and continues to be the primary source of victimization for indigenous Palestinian women (as well as immigrant Mizrahi women). Both, albeit differently according to the historical moment, have experienced the attempts at Israelization aimed at forcefully denying them their historical and cultural roots, whether these originated in Palestine or not. Such attempts were and are expressed in the policies and practices of the state in efforts to remove the Arab identity of Mizrahi or Arab Jews (Shohat 2002), while denying Palestinian Arabs their national or Palestinian identity.

The preceding articulation of women's citizenship in Israel has been largely situated between two contending sets of theories: a male-based structural theory, which places the state at the centre of its analysis, and a feminist culturally oriented theory, which places cultural institutions such as the family, religion and patriarchy at its core. The main argument advanced here is that a comprehensive understanding of women's citizenship status in Israel requires the articulation of both sets of theories in a manner capable of bringing the existing feminist theorization of citizenship in the Middle East to bear on the structural framework of the male-based theorization. It also points to the need for gendering male-based citizenship theory. More specifically, current theorization of women's citizenship accepts the structural and state-based theorization of the existing critical literature, which views Israel as a settler-colonial regime, perceives Zionism as a racist exclusionary project, and calls for the end of the

'Jewish state'. It also understands the role of the cultural, expressed in institutions such as the family, religion and patriarchy, but points to its structural lacunae and the somewhat absent role of the state, the legal and the economic in such theorization. Theorizing women's citizenship in the context of settler-colonial regimes, such as in the case of Israel, it is argued here, cannot overlook the historically specific ways in which gender is intrinsically linked to the forces of class, race, ethnicity and nationalism.

Structuring the gendered and gendering the structural are necessary steps for comprehending women's citizenship status in Israel. They are also steps necessary for restoring territoriality and economic rights to the feminist debate on women, state and citizenship by going beyond the narrow definition of 'territory' as borders or boundaries. This approach has the potential to open up a wider space for envisioning an alternative state and citizenship rights based on equal and not racially differentiated citizenship status. Such an alternative, which could be possible with Israel as a non-Jewish and non-Zionist state, has the potential to build strong alliances with women across religious, national, ethnic and racial divides.

Feminist theorization of women's citizenship in the Middle East, as seen above through the works of Joseph (2000), Swirski (2000) and others, has distinguished itself from Western feminist theorization of citizenship in general in one major respect: it shifts the centre of analysis from the relationship between the individual and the state to one that emphasizes the role of cultural institutions, such as religions, patriarchy and the family. While the latter institutions play important roles in shaping women's status, they are by no means the only or most important forces at work. First, as argued earlier, such institutions are not free-floating agents or independent of the state. The state plays an important role in shaping and reshaping these institutions, as seen above. Equally important is the fact that the state and no any other institution has the absolute power to confer citizenship, employ differential citizenship rights and statuses, and even withdraw citizenship rights from its subjects, as the Israeli case demonstrates.

The need to structurally situate feminist theory of citizenship not-withstanding, the reality is that the marginalized cannot be viewed as simple or silent victims of their status: they are not mere recipients of oppression. Women, both globally and in Palestine, are also agents of change. Similar to their male counterparts, women have been able to utilize myriad openings available to them to empower themselves and their community. For example, in the late 1990s, Palestinian women's activism in the area of violence against women and so-called honour killings succeeded in establishing two women's shelters, one for abused adult women and another for female youth. In the past decade or so they have also established a number of women's and feminist organizations dealing with issues ranging from violence against women to issues of sexuality, including a forum where the voices of homosexual men and women can be heard safely. At the academic level, the establishment of a women's research centre within Mada Al-Carmel (the Arab Centre for Applied Social Research) is an important advance, encouraging young Palestinian academics to hone their critical research skills, thereby enabling them to counter and challenge the inculcation practised by the Israeli academy.

The development and further growth of Palestinian women's agency and organizational activism have lately gained more momentum. Palestinian women, as individuals and collectives, are assuming a more visible public presence. A well-organized protest against Israeli policies of house demolitions in the Naqab, the Triangle and the Galilee was initiated by thirteen women's organizations in April 2008.[26] Palestinian women citizens are actively involved in the making of their history, and for the first time since 1948 Palestinian women citizens of Israel are organizing to claim their right to decent work and economic justice, following the founding on 8 March 2008 of the Union of Arab Women's Works Committees. The establishment of this collective emerged as the culmination of a long and arduous struggle waged by women over the last decade, a struggle which peaked with the introduction of welfare-to-work (the Wisconsin Plan) in the Arab sector.[27]

Working on multiple fronts, Palestinian women citizens have also engaged in joint efforts to challenge their citizenship status.

Despite Israel's protracted history of denial, isolation, exclusion and marginalization, Palestinian national consciousness and determination to continue the struggle for the right to equal citizenship in their land have strengthened considerably. The struggle over the right to land and equal citizenship culminated in 2007 with the emergence of a new and widespread campaign for a Bill of Rights and entitlements addressed to the Israeli state and policymakers – this despite their constant attempts to suppress these rights, to deny their legitimacy, and their use of force to quell Palestinian citizens' resistance. At the heart of this organized and diligent campaign lies indigenous Palestinian affirmation of their material and cultural rights and the rejection of the State of Israel as Jewish. This assertion was publicly announced in 2008 through the publication of what became known as the *Three Documents*, which publicly criticized the state as Jewish and outlined a future vision of citizenship for all its citizens in a state that would enshrine equal rights in a new legal and constitutional system.[28]

The constant resistance undertaken by Palestinian citizens in Israel, especially women, furnishes the grounds for a wide resistance movement against the Zionist settler-colonial regime of the State of Israel. Granted, such struggle cannot stand alone either locally or nationally, but needs the support of a wider global movement – as has in fact been forming over the past five years or so. At the time of writing, some sixty campuses across the globe are involved in what has become known as 'Israeli Apartheid Week'. Students and faculty of various national, ethnic and religious backgrounds are organizing educational sessions drawing attention to what they perceive to be Israel's apartheid policies and practices against Palestinians in general and its own citizens more specifically.

Challenges to Israel's state policies and citizenship regime have also come from the other marginalized groups: Mizrahi or citizens both from within Israel and from the diaspora. The form of such challenges, however, differs from those of an activist nature practised by Palestinian citizens. The voice of marginalized Mizrahi women and men in the past decade has been expressed in the development of a new and alternative body of epistemological production challenging the very premisses of the state. Central to this literature is a critique of Zionism as the state's political ideology and practice. From a growing body of work promoting the 'one state solution' to the existing racist state (e.g. Tilley 2005; Kovel 2007) to those who fundamentally challenge Israeli politics (Nimni 2003a; Aminov 2005; Lentin 2005; Ghanem 2005), the purview of conceptualizations of Israel's regime and citizenship has undoubtedly expanded.

It is maintained here that deconstructing the concept of Zionism and reconstructing it as what it actually means in and for Zionist practice – that is, the principle that directs the settler-colonial regime – is crucial for theorizing equality of citizenship. Important contributions in this regard are also seen among a growing body of Mizrahi feminist scholars. The next, historical, chapter deals with this literature in more detail; for now, suffice it to mention the important scholarship of Mizrahi feminists whose challenge to Zionism as an exclusivist and exclusionary ideology has undoubtedly enriched our understanding of the Israeli state (Lentin 2002, 2005; Lavie 2002; Shohat 1988, 1999, 2002; Dahan-Kalev 2001, 2003; Motzafi-Haller 1997, 2001).

A theorizing of women's citizenship in a settler-colonial regime is successful when historically grounded and contextually situated, as the discussion above has indicated. It is important to understand the role of the cultural (family, religion and the national) in the formation of citizenship, but this should not be prioritized over the material conditions expressed in the relationship between the settler-colonial state and indigenous land. It is land/territory that distinguishes the settler-colonial state from the 'liberal democratic' state and differentiates indigenous citizens from the subjects of the liberal state. Land/territory, as stressed above, must be analysed not as a marker of state borders or boundaries, but in all that it entails in terms of economic, social, political and symbolic significance and power. Placing this expanded conceptualization of land/territory at the centre of feminist theorization of women's status and citizenship enables us to account for the contradictory processes of exclusion and racialized inclusion or marginalization articulated earlier. After all, the settler in the hyphened settler-colonial needs to exclude the other in order to accommodate and expand its own, while the colonial needs to include a marginalized other as economic producer.

Finally, there can hardly be a stronger indication of the turning of the Zionist state into a 'purely' Jewish state than the current 'Loyalty Oath', passed into law on 10 October 2010 by the cabinet. This oath, which requires 'non-Jewish citizens' to swear allegiance to Israel as 'Jewish and democratic', is aimed specifically at Palestinian citizens. A year earlier (25 May 2009), just a few months after the coming to power of Israel's right-wing prime minister Benjamin Netanyahu and foreign minister Avigdor Lieberman, a host of similar bills were introduced with the intention of: preventing Palestinian citizens of Israel participating in the political life of the country; turning citizenship from a right into a conditional privilege; criminalizing political expressions or acts that question the Jewish/Zionist nature of the state (e.g. the Nakba Law); and using the criterion of having done military service as a justification for discrimination (Adalah 2010). The bill awaiting approval by the Knesset, while not emphasizing the punishment of those who contravene the 'Oath', raises the question of how to interpret the term 'loyalty'. Since discussion of the 'loyalty to the Jewish state' was introduced in 2009, two Palestinian human and equal rights advocates have been imprisoned for their anti-racist work calling for citizenship equality; several Arab MKs have been impeached; and Haneen Zoabi, the first Arab elected MK, was stripped of her diplomatic immunity for speaking about Israel's treatment of the flotilla to Gaza.

The Act is not only intended to derail the so-called peace process, as is commonly argued, and to halt or annul the existing applications of hundreds of Palestinian families seeking reunion (especially involving Palestinian citizens married to members of families from the post-1967 occupied territories, or from other Arab countries); it also sends a clear message to the Palestinians and the world community regarding the state's intended rejection of the right of millions of Palestinian refugees to return to their homeland.[29] If passed by the Knesset, this bill can be used to legalize the 'transfer' or expulsion of Palestinian citizens outside of their historic lands. The process of 'ethnic cleansing', the term used by Ilan Pappé to describe the Nakba of 1948, while practised under various land policies and forms of population transfer (especially among the Arab Bedouin in the Naqab), will only expand to include all Palestinian citizens of the state.

Methodological Notes

The following notes refer to the challenges of researching women in Israel, especially when both qualitative and quantitative research methods are applied. Writing about women in Israel, especially Palestinian and Mizrahi Jewish women, is a theoretically complex but also methodologically challenging undertaking. There exists an epistemological hierarchy which characterizes academic production of knowledge on state and society (including citizenship) in Israel. It is Ashkenazi males who are generally involved in knowledge production, followed by male Palestinian and Mizrahi scholars, with the overwhelming majority of their studies being gender-blind if not actually biased. As for the production of knowledge on women in Israel, it is Ashkenazi feminists, more than any other group of women, who tend to dominate in the work on state and society. This hierarchy of epistemological production and distribution poses a major challenge to feminists within marginalized groups. Palestinian and Jewish Mizrahi women in particular are adversely affected, requiring them to double their efforts. Before attempting to produce knowledge by and about themselves, marginalized feminists find themselves responsible for deconstructing existing myths and the falsified history within which their lived experiences have been portrayed. It is only after such processes of deconstruction are accomplished that they can begin to write or present themselves as they actually are.

A clearly anti-racist and anti-colonial feminist methodology situated within the larger context of Marxist political economy has informed the writing of this book. While the book is not an ethnographic account, it nonetheless has benefited from the concept of 'militant ethnography' coined by Jeffrey Juris (2008) to refer to an approach to global justice movements in which the author/researcher is placed inside the social movement and is actively involved in it. My involvement in the Palestinian women's and civil rights movement in Israel for the last two decades is a major source of information for this book. Knowledge gained through my personal and political engagement with women's groups and human rights organizations, especially among Palestinian citizens, reflects the movement's desires and aims, to which I am tangibly committed. In other words, this is a politically engaged book which is based on the author's long-term involvement in activism among various Palestinian women's and other civil society organizations in both Israel and the occupied territories of the West Bank and Gaza Strip. Hence, the positioning of this research lies not only within the critical feminist anti-colonial school, but also in the growing Palestinian, Jewish and international movement involved in developing an alternative vision to existing forms of oppression. It is in this sense that I also see the approach to be in the spirit of Said's notion of exilic intellectualism.

Quantitatively, using a comparative approach that is both historical and contemporary for studying women in Israel poses additional challenges in terms of the use of data. This is particularly true when the required data pertain to issues such as economic participation (employment, unemployment, poverty, social assistance and so on). The challenges come partly from the problematic of discerning development trends, say in education and health services. The reason for this is that Israeli statistical data, especially census data, divide the population into two major categories: Jews and non-Jews. This official methodology, unfortunately, has also largely been adopted by most male scholars of Israeli citizenship.

One major challenge in locating specific information on women is in terms of their labour participation. For example, what is the exact rate of Palestinian women's participation in the labour force? Is it the official rate, put at 17 per cent, or the rate of 23.4 per cent reported in the 2004 *Socio-Economic Survey*, which was reaffirmed in 2008 in the report put in front of the special economic committee in the Knesset?[30] The issue, as will be explored further in the following chapter on women and the economy, is about inclusion and exclusion. As Nabil Khattab has rightly observed, there is 'a reasonable basis to believe that the Palestinian Arab female labour market participation is underestimated by official statistics due to unreported paid jobs such as housekeeping/domestic labour, unskilled workers in agriculture and in local small textile manufactures' (Khattab 2002: 93). To Khattab's list of exclusions we must add all women who work out of their homes. While the problem of underestimating and marginalizing women's labour participation in official statistics is general to women all over the world, Israel's settler-colonial regime, with its constitutionally and institutionally based exclusionary policies, complicates this problem further. For these reasons, this study will also use data from Jewish and Palestinian civil society organizations as well as other international reports, as these are more neutral than Israeli ones.

Finally, the contradictory processes of racialized (and ethnicized) inclusion and exclusion adopted by the settler-colonial state poses major problems for questions of identity and naming, especially for the two categories of marginalized women, namely Palestinian Arabs and Mizrahis. Thus, whereas on the one hand this contradictory process makes it difficult to provide an empirical account of Palestinian Arabs as a national collectivity or indigenous people, on the other hand the totalizing and generalizing concept of Jews used by Israeli officials (as well as the overwhelming majority of Ashkenazi scholars, including a large number of feminists) veils the historical specificity and difference of Mizrahi Jews. These processes also mask their contemporary marginalization and struggle.

Still, the choice over what concepts to use for naming, defining or identifying groups, collectivities or categories of people – for example, 'indigenous people' or Palestinian Arab instead of 'Israeli Arab' or 'Arab-Israeli' – is a political choice, based on the overall principle of critical feminist anti-racist and anti-colonialist analysis of marginalized women. By emphasizing the actual lived experiences of marginalized citizens in Israel, it also places Israel in its proper context: a settler-colonial and racist state with its Zionist ideology alive, rather than in the 'past' or the 'post' state. This also holds for adopting the term 'Mizrahi' instead of 'Oriental' or 'Sephardi' to name or identify Jews who migrated to Israel, whether by choice or by force. Finally, this position is politically informed and based largely on the feminist ethic of respect for marginalized voices and definitions of self. As will be seen in the next chapter, this is a strong statement against the collapsing of women into one class or category, and in favour of seeing them historically and culturally differentiated.

Finally, I would like to note that, in common with the convention for naming Arab Palestinian citizens adopted in this book, I have opted for a particular mode of transliteration from the Hebrew language. As Ashkenazi authors (male and female) have historically and contemporarily produced most of the knowledge – literature – on Mizrahi or, primarily, Arab Jews, Arab names of Mizrahi scholars were often dismissed or changed to accommodate Ashkenazi pronunciation. For example, the letter h (ح in Arabic), which is found in many Mizrahi names and concepts, has been Ashkenazified and turned into ch to suit Ashkenazi speech. In this book, Mizrahi names such as Tzfadia and Yiftachel are kept in the Ashkenazi form as found in the Hebrew literature. But when the literature is found in Arabic, the Arabic letters and terminology have been retained. Tzfadia as present in Arabic literature is written as Safadiyya. Safadiyya is an adjective that refers to the person who originated from the Arab city of Safad. However, after the depopulation of its original Palestinian inhabitants, Safad was Hebrewized and turned into Tzfad, hence the name Tzfadia. The same applies in the case of the name Yiftachel, which in Arabic literature is recognized as Yiftahel (an Arabic term). Similarly with other terms such as pituach (development), which is adapted from Arabic with ch replacing the Arabic letter h. In fact, the very term Mizrachi is Ashkenazified from Mizrahi (people originating from the East or Mizrah). This is why in all references I have kept the term Mizrahi and avoided Mizrachi.

TWO

Women in Palestine:
The Relevance of History

HISTORICIZING MARGINALIZED SUBJECTS, specifically women, constitutes a significant element in understanding their presence at both ontological and epistemological levels. The argument in contemporary discourse that in order to move forward we need to put the past behind us is nonsensical. History is not an act of the past; nor can it be ignored or considered irrelevant to analysing the structural and cultural, the material and ideological, contexts within which people in general and women in particular find themselves. A historical materialist analysis of women's experiences in contexts of colonialism and settler-colonial regimes that focuses on women's, men's and children's daily lived experiences is most appropriate here. Such analysis reveals not only the sources and roots of their subordination and marginalization by exposing the forces of oppression; it also presents the oppressed as living subjects and not reified objects of discussion. Moreover, such an analysis of Palestinians is particularly pertinent for appreciating the processes of social, economic and political change they have undergone and continue to undergo, and so informs the path to the future. The historical epochs of particular concern here are those of the British and Zionist colonization of Palestine, which occurred simultaneously. Although this epoch carries the legacy of oppression inherited from the Ottoman period, changes at the local, regional and international levels during the first half of the twentieth century rendered this epoch particularly significant. These forces served to transform Palestinians into stateless refugees and subordinate citizens, on the one hand, and led to the establishment of the State of Israel, on the other.

A feminist history of Palestinians during this period is clearly needed. There are a few ethnographic accounts drawn largely from the area of Jabal Nablus and pertaining to certain aspects of gender–family relations (e.g. Moors 1996; Tucker 1988), but a comprehensive account of Palestinian women in this era is lacking. A similar instance is the Mizrahis (especially Yemeni) and the small number of Ethiopians brought to Palestine in the early twentieth century by the Zionist movement as cheap labour power to replace indigenous Palestinian labourers in the 'Jewish sector': this marginalized community, as will be seen later in this chapter, has also received little if any serious attention.

In contrast, and unsurprisingly, there is a relatively large body of literature written by and about Ashkenazi or European Jewish women who were part of the Zionist settler movement in the early twentieth century in Palestine. This literature, it is argued here, not only fails to speak in its own voice or present the reality of life there; it appropriates the voice of Others – especially indigenous Palestinians, but also Mizrahi Jews – and 're'-presents them as a construction moulded by the writers' own imaginations rather than as they experienced their lives. Studies in this vein include those of Barbara Swirski and Marilyn Safir (1991), Barbara Swirski (2000), Tamar Mayer (1994), Alice Shalvi (2002), Sheila Katz (2003) and Deborah Bernstein (1998), to mention just a few. While all such feminists situate themselves within the radical strand of feminism holding critical stances on all forms of patriarchy, they nevertheless all share a liberal approach and ignore the destruction of Palestinian women's lives, in which Ashkenazi Jewish women have taken part, in pre-Israel Palestine. The liberal and somewhat pro-state position of these scholars is also evident in the way they identify Zionism not as it was and continues to be, namely a settler-colonial and racist

movement, but as a 'national movement for the Jews'. The problem
with this premiss, as will be seen, lies in its biased conception of
the relationship between colonizer and colonized. This bias, which
positions these authors in support of Zionism (as a national movement), while denying the inherent settler-colonial, racist nature
of the movement, confutes their self-defined feminist identity as
radical and anti-patriarchal. It also places their writings within white
Western Orientalist ideology, which disguises racist relationships in
its critique of nationalisms.[1]

In the overwhelming majority of Ashkenazi feminist studies on
pre-Israel Palestine, whether British colonial rule is used as a reference point (Swirski 2000; Mayer 1994; Swirski and Safir 1991) or
whether the whole study is devoted to this epoch (Bernstein 1992;
Katz 2003; Hertzog 2003; Bernstein 1998, 1991) the approaches
taken remain largely ahistorical. In such literature European Jewish
settlers are abstracted from the historical environment of Palestine
and studies as if they were an insular community and not part of
the Zionist settler-colonial project which built its very existence
on the ruins of the indigenous Palestinian society. No class or race
analyses are found in such literature; furthermore, the analyses are
themselves implicitly racist as they fail to question the exclusivist and
exclusionary nature of the Zionist movement. Total dismissal of the
indigenous Palestinians pre-1948 is emblematic of Ashkenazi feminist
literature. For example, in most of her work Deborah Bernstein does
not shy away from deleting Palestine from the historical memory,
referring to the pre-1948 state as Israel (1998, 1991).

In a manner reminiscent of conventional Western Orientalist
(read: racist) literature on Arab women, Ashkenazi feminist literature
largely works within the cultural − if not 'culturalist' − paradigm,
treating women's issues, especially indigenous Palestinians, in an
ahistorical and immutable way. Mahmoud Mamdani's notion of
the 'culture talk' or 'culturalist' paradigm is characteristic of this
literature (Mamdani 2007). Hence the overwhelming concern of this
literature is with issues of nationalism, religion, tradition and family,
and the ideological constructs deemed by Ashkenazi authors to be

the primary agencies of oppression of women in all spaces and at all times, regardless of historical circumstances.

Both Swirski's (2000) and Katz's (2003) studies represent prime examples of the culturalist claim that Palestinian (and, for that matter, Jewish) women's primary sources of oppression reside in their culture (i.e. religion, nationalism and familialism). This approach, as argued in the first chapter and detailed below, is methodologically evasive and logically ahistorical. It is evasive in that it equates two nationalisms: that of the colonial and that of the colonized. It is ahistorical in that it provides very little or no historical material evidence concerning the actual lived experiences of the subjects of Zionist settler colonialism. Still, even if one accepts the argument that all nationalisms express masculine projects with patriarchy at their core, and that all nationalisms constitute a source of women's subjugation, the solution is not, as most Ashkenazi feminists argue, a united women's struggle against nationalism. The reality is that, on the one hand, a struggle against nationalism alone is not a guarantee of women's emancipation. On the other hand, the argument obfuscates the primary struggle in the context of settler colonialism, namely that between the colonized and the colonizer, between the indigene and the occupier.

A close review of the only comprehensive account of this historical epoch provides a more detailed example of what has so far been argued. The case in point is Sheila Katz's *Women and Gender in Early Jewish and Palestinian Nationalism* (2003). This book discusses the period that I believe constitutes the most significant stage in the history of Palestinian women; the roots of their expropriation, displacement, oppression and disintegration speak volumes about a large number of events and phenomena. As is seen later in the chapter, this epoch forms the historical turning point in the lives of the Palestinian people, as it furnished the grounds for their expropriation and impoverishment, the destruction of their homes and villages, and their eventual expulsion in massive numbers from their country. Unfortunately, however, very little of this historical reality is discussed by culturalist authors. In her book, Katz abstracts women, both Ashkenazi (European Jewish) settlers and Palestinians, from the dynamics of then-existing socio-economic and political contexts and miraculously represents both Palestinian indigenous women and European Jewish settlers as equal victims of their respective nationalisms. For example, in a chapter on 'Sacrificing Sisters', Katz attempts to validate her constructed vision of 'Jewish–Palestinian sisterhood' by quoting Audre Lorde:

> Some problems we share as women, some we do not. You fear your children will grow up to join the patriarchy and testify against you, we fear our children will be dragged from a car and shot down in the street, and you will turn your backs upon the reasons they are dying. (Audre Lorde, cited in Katz 2003: 166)

In the process she presents a rather misplaced and perverted construct of that reality. Lorde's statement, which might apply equally to Palestinian women and Black South Africans in the apartheid era, is twisted by Katz, and Lorde's political position is emptied of its meaning. Katz claims that the two cases – blacks in largely white America (Lorde's context) and Ashkenazi settlers in largely Arab Palestine – are different inasmuch as Palestinians were the majority while the Zionist settlers were in the minority. With this she insists that women of the two 'nationalisms' were 'equally in danger' and 'equally threatened'. Both, she contends, feared that their 'children... [would] be dragged from a car and shot down in the street'. Not only would the other women 'turn ... [their] back upon the reasons why they ... [were] dying, but also they would continue to act in ways that perpetuated the killing of their children. Jewish and Palestinian women who embraced nationalism sacrificed each other' (Katz 2003: 166–7). In this partial historical memory, Katz totally ignores the fact that in the United States the white settlers were armed and the black minority were not, and that in Palestine the European Jewish settlers were armed and the Palestinian majority were not.

Moreover, Lorde, like Mohanty (1987), is critical of the notion of sisterhood on the grounds that it is a Western, white and middle-class expression. In her critique of Robin Morgan's introduction to *Sisterhood is Global*, Mohanty observes that this concept of a global sisterhood was based on an assumption of shared experiences and interests across cultures. It erased issues of power, class and culture by suggesting that a common psychological and essential experience of being 'woman' made solidarity immediately accessible across national, class and racial lines (Mohanty 1987: 115–16). This is precisely what Katz does: erases the forces of power, race, class and the experience of Palestinian women under British and Zionist settler colonialism, and equates the colonized and the colonial.

Before we proceed further in analysing Katz's account of Palestinian and Jewish Ashkenazi women's histories, it should be noted that the positing of 'sisterhood' between Ashkenazi feminists and Palestinian women is not Katz's alone. The view is shared by other Israeli radical feminists, especially peace activists, who see their work in groups such as Women in Black and Women Against Occupation as contributing to solidarity with Palestinian women. While this may be true in the case of Palestinian women in the territories occupied in 1967, it has not in fact been obvious within the state, among Palestinian and Ashkenazi women, either in the past or today. If anything, the issues of representation, inclusion and solidarity between Ashkenazi feminists, on the one hand, and Arab Palestinian and Mizrahi women, on the other, remain highly problematic, with the Ashkenazi feminist movement holding the upper hand on all decisions. The three different communities of women, none of which is monolithic or homogeneous, continue to lead most aspects of their lives separately. Even at 'national' level, at events such as Israeli Feminist Association (IFA) meetings, there has been little effort to bring these groups together. The attempt by the IFA to introduce 'affirmative action' in their work has in fact been criticized as a tendency to create separate sections for Mizrahi, Palestinian and Lesbian feminists (Shadmi 2004; Lavie 2005).

It may be argued here that the ubiquitous power relations (economic, political and social) between Ashkenazi feminists, on the one hand, and Palestinian and Mizrahi women, on the other, are largely responsible for the absence of collaboration and solidarity among feminists in the two groups. What is particularly poignant here is the absence of solidarity and collaboration among the two most marginalized groups of women; Palestinians and Mizrahi Jews. A feminist epistemology that analyses the absence of solidarity and collaboration between the two communities whose experiences have more commonalities than differences is yet to be produced.[2]

Having said that, it remains true that historically and contemporarily Palestinian women have not viewed themselves as a self-contained category, separate from the wider context of colonialism and nationalist anti-colonial struggle of which they were and are an integral part, just like their male counterparts. 'Sisterhood', which negates race and class, remains an empty term. Katz's approach to feminism and nationalism is oblivious to Palestinians' lived experience as colonized subjects, of both British colonialism and Zionism, identified by her as equivalent to Jewish nationalism. The real and dangerous threat in this case is definitely not Palestinian nationalism, but rather Zionism as a racist settler-colonial project. In her review of Katz's book, Islah Jad makes a similar argument, suggesting that Katz uses gender to deconstruct colonizers, while ignoring the colonizers' gendered policies focusing solely on Palestinian nationalist discourse, with the implication that 'the main hindrance to equal gender relations was only Palestinian nationalism' (Jad 2004: 108). Katz's approach, framed within the white middle-class feminist identity-based paradigm, is largely responsible for the conflation of the personal with the collective, masking the wider context of colonialism and abstracting notions such as nationalism. For Katz and other Zionist feminists who identify with Zionism as a Jewish nationalist movement, underplaying its settler-colonial role of dispossessing and displacing the natives, such a conflation might not be problematic. In fact Zionism for them is taken for granted, and nowhere is the question of its settler-colonial nature and its consequences for Palestinian natives raised.

The history of Palestinian women's struggle and resistance since the 1920s, including the 1936 revolt, the First Intifada (1987) and up to the present time, provides ample evidence to the fact that women's national identity has always been prioritized over their individual or gender identity. For Palestinian women, both their personal and their collective identity are diametrically opposed to Zionism. They do not see their primary subjection under colonialism as separate from their overall national subjection.[3]

This is the crux of the problem with most Ashkenazi feminist literature: it situates its analysis within an imaginary construction of Zionism as Jewish nationalism, legitimizing Zionism as a Jewish national movement rather than critiquing and rejecting it as a settler-colonial project in Palestine (Katz 2003; Swirski 2000; Shalvi 2002, Bernstein 1998). It is not surprising, therefore, as both Swirski (2000) and Katz (2003) posit, that women (both Palestinian and Jewish) are equally oppressed by their respective nationalisms. The ramifications of equating the Palestinian anti-colonial national movement with Zionism as a colonial-settler movement are particularly significant in terms of understanding Palestinian women's agency and resistance. They also have a bearing on the proper understanding of the lived experiential lives of Mizrahi feminists who refuse to be identified with Zionism as their national movement (Shohat 1988, 1999; Lavie 2002, 2007).

To reiterate a point made in the first chapter, Middle Eastern feminist contributions to the study of gender and citizenship (including that of Ashkenazi feminists, who focus on religion, nationalism and familialism), while insightful and a contribution to further complicating the area of gender and citizenship, cannot be generalized. Cultural institutions are not free-floating agents within a state, any state; they are affixed to the state and operate as base resources for its cultural expression. This also suggests that post-colonial, post-modern and other forms of currently fashionable modes of analysis that seek to go beyond polarities and dichotomies, instead of addressing the political-economic reality of a particular epoch, tend to reject or obfuscate concepts like colonialism and settler colonialism, and usually pay little attention to issues of class and race.

A proper understanding of women's status and role in any geographical location must be historically situated and examined in its specificity. More importantly, women's experiences of subjugation in such contexts must be captured as they actually are, namely representing their lived reality, and not as constructed or imagined phenomena. To account for such a reality, the following exploration discusses women's historical experiences, with an emphasis on the two most marginalized women groups: Palestinians and Mizrahis. Using historical materialism as an analytical framework to capture this reality, this chapter contributes to a better understanding of the history of women's subjugation.

Women and the Family in Palestine's Predominantly Agrarian Social Structure

Although gender relations and women's status are intrinsically linked to the institution of the family, the latter is neither a fixed nor an immutable concept. The Arab family, including the Palestinian one, is not what Orientalist literature on Arab women describes as 'traditional and patriarchal ... defined and regulated by Islamic law that has remained unchanged throughout the centuries' (Tucker 1993: xv) – a position emphatically expressed in Swirski's work (2000). The family, instead, constitutes a concept and a structure that lend themselves to history and change, changing in the process its internal dynamics. This is particularly true in our context of British and Zionist settler colonialism.

Until the early twentieth century, the Palestinian family served as a fundamental social organization and a basic unit for production, reproduction and consumption. It also functioned as an important nexus for organizing and rearranging social–gender relations, commanding in the process a degree of social, economic and political power over its members and in relation to society at large. The significant status of the family at this historical juncture was achieved as a consequence of the vital role it played in the production process. The family, in its traditional extended form known as the *hamula*, was organized around the then-existing land tenure system. In this system, two major categories of landed property, the *amiri* and mulk, dominated Palestine's pre-capitalist agrarian social structure. The mulk, or privately owned land, began to gain prominence and visibility with the decline of the Turkish Empire and its legal moves to privatize land ownership through the promulgation of the 1858 Ottoman Land Code and the Land Law passed in 1876. Cultivation on mulk land was performed by tenants in a system known as muhasasah, or share-cropping. The amiri (not the miri, which is used in most official documents to refer to state land)[4] was the predominant form of land tenure in Palestine. In the amiri land system the majority of peasants (fallaheen, masculine plural; fallahat, feminine plural) lived on and off of the land. As Doreen Warriner (1936) observed, each hamula ideally lived on a single allotment, with land being distributed by the head at intervals of three to five years in order to account for demographic change (such as deaths and new births within the family). In general, the hamula would live in a single village, but sometimes hamula kin would be spread out over several villages, while in other villages we find a number of small hamulas residing in the same village. The amiri land tenure system, a peasant form of production, characterized the living and working conditions of the overwhelming majority of Palestinians at this time. Production on amiri land was usually conducted by the whole family/hamula, with women, men and children taking part in the production process. As such, up until the late nineteenth century production was largely for consumption within the hamula, with a small surplus produced to pay the peasants' rent and land dues, traditionally expressed as the ushor (tithe). In theory, the ushor meant paying a tenth of a peasant household's total production, but in reality a much higher rate was extorted from the fallaheen, especially after the introduction of the land laws. However, the transformation from Ottoman colonial rule, in which levies were largely in kind, to British colonial rule, in which they were exacted in cash, took a variety of forms; this transformation, accompanied by violent collection measures, did in fact mark a crucial turning point in the lives of Palestinians. The introduction by the British of a new taxation system had a massively negative impact on the overwhelming majority of Palestinians. To defray its colonial administrative costs in Palestine, the British government drastically altered the existing Ottoman system of taxation, imposing exorbitant fees and taxes on an already impoverished peasant population (Abdo and Yuval-Davis 1995; Abdo 1989). Moreover, unlike the case during the Ottoman period, when many peasants were able to avoid or evade rules and regulations, at least in some form and for some time, this was for the most part not possible under British colonial rule. A full account of Palestinian living conditions during this historical epoch has been presented elsewhere.[5] For the purpose of this chapter, and in an attempt to contextualize Zionist settler colonialism and its ramifications for indigenous Palestinians, an analysis of the main forces of oppression endured by Palestinians is in order here.

To begin with, and despite the violence used by tax collectors under imperial rule, the Ottomans did not legalize the confiscation of peasant farmers' land, or enforce their eviction. In contrast to this, the organization of violence under British colonial rule was systematic and widespread. The British introduced and implemented new land and taxation laws as a means to further privatize the land and generate more revenue to cover colonial administrative costs. The tithe, the major source of taxation revenues for the Ottomans, was replaced in 1924 by a fixed amount to be paid in cash only, and not as levies in kind as under the Ottomans. During the British colonial period, state taxes were levied on top of all other land dues, including the newly introduced *tabu* (land registration) fees as well as other tenancy obligations. Furthermore, as revenues from taxes appeared to be insufficient to defray colonial administrative costs, the state moved to change both the magnitude and the means of tithe collection. The tithe in its old form was abolished and a new tax collection system was put in place, called the Commutation of Tithe Ordinance (1924); this established a flat-rate tax of 12.5 per cent of the *fallah*'s annual gross income. This ordinance established the commuted tithes for all villages at a fixed aggregated amount, to be paid annually, and for the first time tribes were included in the payment of such taxes.[6]

The inability of indigenous Palestinians to the pay the *tabu* land registry fees and other exorbitant taxes led the colonial government to enforce increasingly stringent penalties to guarantee the collection of these levies. Punishments included extrajudicial measures aimed at forcing the *fallaheen* to oblige: collective punishment; arbitrary imprisonment of all available male members in villages where one or more members had failed to pay taxes; confiscation of crops; raiding homes and destruction of furniture; the spilling of olive oil over rice and flour; harassing of women and children; and beating women who, more often than not, resisted the incursions. These extrajuridical measures were particularly evident during 1929 and were used as means to quell the widespread Palestinian peasant revolt at the time (see Abdo 1989: 110–15).

By the early 1920s, most reports suggest, the overwhelming majority of Palestinian peasants were impoverished and living in very harsh conditions. The political, judicial and extrajudicial measures imposed by the colonial administration had slowly yet progressively resulted in the further impoverishment of the *fallaheen*. This increasing impoverishment enabled the Zionist national project, inasmuch as more and more Palestinians were forced to pawn their tracts of land to members of the landowning class, both local and non-Palestinian. The effects of this obdurate treatment at the hands of the British were felt disproportionately among the most marginalized members of Palestinian society, namely women and children. The methods used to forcibly alter Palestinian social production and reproduction closely resemble the case of the colonial settlement of New England studied by Carolyn Merchant in her *Ecological Revolutions* (1989). An ecological revolution occurs whenever a native (typically mainly agrarian) social mode of consumption is replaced with a settler-imposed system of ecological tenure, forcibly and negatively re-creating the social orders and consumption patterns of the settlers. The speed at which the European-Jewish capitalist reordering of consumption was accomplished in Palestine was remarkable given the increasing economic desperation of the already impoverished indigenous population.

Between 1920 and 1947 it was reported that about 1,700,000 dunams (1 dunam = 1,000 square metres), or about 26 per cent of the total cultivable land, was expropriated from the indigenous direct producers (Shaw 1945–46). An earlier British official document, the Simpson Report, found that 60 per cent, or 1 million dunams, of indigenous Palestinian land had already been transferred to the ownership of the Zionist settlers between 1920 and 1930 (Simpson 1930: 16).[7] It is clear from this historical evidence that, with the help of the British colonial government, Zionist settler colonialism in Palestine established itself through the expropriation and alienation of tens of thousands of Palestinian *fallaheen* and *fallahat*.

The claim that the land acquired by the European-Jewish settlers was peacefully transferred to them through purchase or market forces, as in the patently false official Israeli version, is also presented in the writings of Ashkenazi feminists (Katz 2003: 55; Mayer 1994: 3). Elsewhere I provide a detailed account of the poverty of such ahistorical analyses, which falsify Palestinian history in order to justify the Zionist seizure of land (Abdo 1989: 140–50). The following quotation from the 1937 Peel Commission report exemplifies the pauperization of former Palestinian peasants, who, no longer holding land, were unable to find work and as a result ended up crowding the streets of large cities such as Jaffa:

> Thousands of unskilled workers in Jaffa cannot afford a house
> to sleep in – they sleep in tin huts or in the open. For 18 years
> past, hardly a single house has been built for the labourers or the
> poor; the municipality does not build them and no one feels that
> it pays to build for them commercially.... I am not exaggerating
> if I say that in some seasons in Jaffa, when the oranges are being
> loaded, some 10–15 thousand people live in the city and its suburbs
> without a single proper latrine.... Thousands live in tin huts
> without the most elementary accommodation and without any
> water supply except what they can carry in small jars from a far
> distance. I observed that in many of the hut-colonies, they hardly
> use more than a cubic metre of water a month. (Peel Commission
> 1937: 299)

The experience of Palestinian *fallaheen* and *fallahat* under British and Zionist colonial rule resembles what Marx has termed 'primitive' or 'simple accumulation', the process that uproots and pauperizes peasants through the use of legal and extrajudicial measures aimed at the development of a capitalist-based mode of production requiring 'free' labour power. Within the Palestinian context, this process did indeed 'free' a large section of the peasants (including women) from their land, transforming them into proletarians. Simultaneously, this process of proletarianization also alienated the indigenous inhabitants from their land, making it available for the use of capitalist or other owners, including local and absentee landlords as well as Zionist settlers.[8]

Unlike in the Western European countries, especially Britain, where expropriation turned peasants or farmers into a mass of wage labourers required by the emerging capitalist relations, in the Palestinian case the Zionist colonial project had a different end in mind: turning Palestinian land into exclusively Jewish land and employing only Jewish labour to work it. At the outset, the Zionist settler-colonial movement was interested in 'creating facts on the ground'. This demographic and geographic policy is exemplified in the policy of 'Stockade and Tower' introduced by the Jewish Agency in 1937: filling settlements with settlers.[9] This policy was no different to the subsequent Israeli state's land policies throughout its history to the present day. The implementation of these policies was carried out through the promulgation of a set of legal measures introduced and enforced – very often through the use of physical violence – to ensure the exclusion of indigenous Palestinians as agricultural labour on land under Zionist (Jewish) control. Such legal measures were expressed in the three Zionist slogans: *kibbush ha-adamah* (conquering or colonizing the land); *kibbush-ha-avodah* (conquering labour); *kibbush ha-shouk* (conquering the market). The policies were enshrined in all Zionist institutions, particularly the two most influential ones: the Jewish National Fund (JNF), the aim of which was to buy Palestinian land for the 'Jewish home', and the Histadrut, which became Israel's only labour organization (Abdo 1992). The implementation of these slogans in policy, adhered to throughout pre-1948 Palestine, continued until 1964, when the Histadrut began to accept Arabs/Palestinians as legal, liable to pay dues and receive health benefits.

Defenders of the Zionist slogan of 'Jewish only labour', land and market often use the argument that ideology for Zionism was and remains more important than the economic basis upon which most settler colonial rules are established. In his early writings, Baruch Kimmerling (1983) argued exactly that, by suggesting that the Zionist or Jewish movement was different to other settler colonial movements, such as French colonialism in Algeria, as the former did not exploit the labour of indigenous Palestinians but brought its own Jewish workers and used them as labourers. This analysis of Zionism, which seems to valorize ideological and political values over the economic efficiency of exploiting Arab labour, thereby rendering the Marxist notion of simple accumulation not entirely relevant, is only partially true. The Zionist settler-colonial movement prior to the founding of the state, and Israeli state practice after its founding through to this day, have been able to utilize this ideology as a strategic ploy: to Judaize Palestine by confiscating indigenous peasants/farmers, build as many settlements as possible, and change the demographic shape of the country by importing Jewish settlers/immigrants. As for the Zionist labour market, which constantly needs cheap labour power, especially in the agricultural and construction industries, at different times, and despite the 'Jewish only labour' principle, it employed indigenous and other Palestinian cheap labour. It also imported 'foreign' Jewish and non-Jewish workers from Africa and Asia to work in these two sectors. In the 1920s, for example, around 20,000 Yemenis believed to be Jews were brought in as cheap labour power in order to replace indigenous Palestinian labour employed in the Jewish construction and agricultural industries.[10] This process was continued by the early Israeli state, when in the early 1950s hundreds of thousands of Mizrahi (Arab) Jews were brought into the newly established country, to be followed in the early 1990s by further hundreds of thousands of Jewish Russians from the Soviet Union. Yet, as will be seen later in the book, after 1964 and the lifting up of the Histadrut's policy of 'Jewish labour only', tens of thousands of indigenous Palestinian workers were employed, primarily in the agricultural and industrial sectors, to be joined following the occupation of the rest of historical Palestine (1967) by some 150,000 Palestinian workers who were annually given work permits by Israel. To all of this must be added the hundreds of thousands of 'foreign' non-Jewish workers who throughout the late 1990s and early 2000 were also brought in as cheap labour, especially from Asia, the Philippines, China, Korea, Africa and Romania.

The geopolitical and strategic role of the Zionist settlements, which evidences its settler-colonial nature,[11] has never been an issue in the majority of the narratives of this history that appear in Ashkenazi feminist literature. Quite the contrary, Ashkenazi feminist narratives have abstracted Zionism from its materialist basis, treating it as a part of the natural process of emergence of the 'national home' as the culmination of the Jewish nationalist movement.

Women and Labour in Agrarian Palestine

The overall economic policy and political controls established during the period of British colonialism, strengthened by the political and economic agenda of the Zionist settler project, have left their imprint on social and gender relations as well as on the structure and functions of the Palestinian family/hamula. It is possible to identify two general tendencies that have had a simultaneous effect on gender relations during this period: the first was expressed in the loss of land and direct access to agricultural labour, which also meant the loss, albeit partial, of the traditional public sphere that peasant women have traditionally occupied (see Merchant 1989); the second was expressed in the development of a capitalist sector outside of, separate from and exclusive of the indigenous inhabitants – that is, the introduction of a new public sphere for Jewish settlers only.

These changes also led to the emergence of large-scale pauperization of Palestinian peasants, their eventual proletarianization, and the development of the phenomenon of labour migration among Palestinian males and in some cases even small nuclear families. Loss of land also meant that an increasing number of women lost their traditional work in agriculture as tillers and cultivators, especially during the seasonal work of cultivation in which many women and children were involved. In addition, women lost other forms of agricultural-related labour such as farming, picking oranges and olives, collecting firewood, tending and grazing, as well as subsidiary tasks including milking, processing milk and yogurt-making. The large-scale economic ruin in Palestine removed a large number of *fallahat* from their traditional sphere of direct agricultural production.

Palestinian women's labour in direct agricultural production suffered an additional severe decline due to the further capitalist development of the Zionist settler movement and their takeover of traditional Palestinian agricultural sectors, especially the citrus and olive home industries, which they turned into large-scale profit-making concerns. Olive oil production was one of Palestine's main traditional cottage industries, and one in which women were directly employed. Women and children, especially in the Galilee and the Jabal Nablus areas, were heavily involved in the picking of olives, the processing of olive oil, the production of olive oil soap, and the marketing of these commodities. With the emergence of Zionism as a European-Jewish settler movement, large-scale mechanized production of oil, with the subsidiary products of soaps, perfumes and a variety of oils, gradually led to the demise of Palestinian influence in the industry, leading in the process to the devaluation of women's labour in this economic sector.

As in the case of the olive oil industry, economic privations were felt throughout the coastal plain within the economic sphere of citrus production, which had constituted another major means of survival for many Palestinian families; a large number of women were traditionally employed in the picking, packing and exporting of citrus fruits.[12] As in the central and northern districts, on the coastal plain the Zionist takeover of large tracts of land – especially in and around the city of Jaffa – the expulsion of indigenous people and their repalcement with Jewish settlers has drastically change the face of the citrus (mainly orange) industry. The capitalist mechanization of the citrus industry, the continued confiscation and appropriation of Palestinian land in and around the port city of Jaffa, the eventual destruction of the city and the further development of the new city of Tel-Aviv, have led to the demise of the Palestinian citrus industry. Eyal Sivan's 2009 documentary film *Jaffa: The Orange's Clockwork* provides a brilliant account of the process whereby the traditional Palestinian orange industry was turned by Zionism into its main commercial product, the sale of Jaffa oranges as an all-Jewish enterprise.[13]

It is worth noting here that the marginalization and devaluation of the olive oil cottage industry was felt not only at the economic level of women withdrawing from the public sphere of production, but also at the cultural and symbolic levels. In economic terms, this sector was labour-intensive and therefore depended almost exclusively on female labour power; since it was largely a home industry, this meant that women had no choice but to be heavily involved. Moreover, women in this sector participated not only in the production process, but, as mentioned earlier, also in the exchange, circulation and sale of the products. The sight of *fallahat* selling *makbous* (processed olives), as well as olive oil and soap, in urban areas in the Galilee (especially in Nazareth) was still common during the late 1960s and early 1970s.

The olive tree has always been a potent cultural symbol of Palestinian nationalism. Olive oil was – and to a large extent has remained – a major food staple and it concomitantly gained cultural and symbolic meaning. The Christian symbolism attached to the wood of the cross was adopted within Palestinian culture, turning the olive into a sacred medicinal or therapeutic remedy used by many women, especially village dwellers, for a large number of ailments; for example, a child with an ear infection might receive a drop of warm oil in the ear, and a child with a stomach ache might have her belly rubbed with warm oil. As olive oil soap was the only kind available for many generations, it transcended the realm of simple commodity and acquired mythical values associated with traditional use. Long after the introduction of chemically produced soaps, olive oil soap continues to be considered as possessing therapeutic properties for many different kinds of skin and hair problems. Now olive soap is sold in European and North American markets as a specialized niche product with important curative qualities.

As with the harvest of an important crop in most agrarian cultures, *Mawsem al-Zaitoun*, the olive season, acquired a special relation to gender formation, functioning as a public space for women's social gatherings. In pre-Israel times, women who owned or rented olive fields located at a distance from their places of residence often spent the whole season in the field mingling with other villagers. In the Ottoman province of Greater Syria, of which Palestine was a part until the British takeover, this season was looked upon by young women as potential opportunities for matchmaking.[14] The gradual destruction of both the citrus and the olive sectors of the economy, alongside the widespread loss of land and the economic ruin of the peasantry, had reduced for the first time – and in some cases entirely eliminated – women's public productive role, making them heavily dependent on male wage labour (if and when such labour was available).

Throughout the British and Zionist settler-colonial period, the landless Palestinian proletariat were largely excluded from European Jewish industry. Their exclusion, as noted above, was institutionalized through the main Jewish labour/capital organization, the Histadrut, an establishment that employed racist policies vis-à-vis Palestinian citizens until 1964. The only large-scale source of employment for landless Palestinian proletarian men during British rule was the government sector, specifically in the Iraq Petroleum Company (IPC) and the railways.

Outside of the seasonal employment in agriculture, in which some Palestinian women also worked, those desperate for income to feed their families found themselves accepting highly exploitative jobs which were largely shunned by men and Ashkenazi Jewish women, such as in the tobacco industry. Evidence from the British-owned tobacco company in Nazareth suggests that during 1931–38, this factory employed some 400 workers, the overwhelming majority of whom were Arab women, children and elderly men. The working conditions and wages paid to these workers were described as appalling. For example, the average wage for cigarette packing among Palestinian women workers during the years 1931–38 was estimated at about 95 mils per day (100 mils = 1 Palestinian lira or pound) as compared to 200 mils per day paid to Jewish women doing the same work.[15] Another report on the same factory revealed that the length of the working day for Arab Palestinian women averaged thirteen hours, for which they received 50–70 mils (testimony of George Mansour, Secretary of the Arab Workers' Association, cited in Peel Commission 1937: 299). Moreover, statistics on tobacco work for the years 1931–33 show that the daily wage of an Arab woman in tobacco leaf sorting averaged 70 mils for a ten-hour working day, compared to 130 mils paid to a Jewish woman doing the same job for eight hours (Budeiri 1979). Although these wage rates demonstrate the presence of a racialized system of pay for Arab and Jewish workers, the findings of the Commission are also explained in part by the strong role of the Histadrut in its efforts to create jobs for Jews – which is to say in its protection of Jewish labour as expressed in the slogan 'Jewish only labour'. The Arab Labour Association, also in existence at this time, was largely concerned with the labour of the male Arabs who comprised the majority of its members, thereby leaving female labourers vulnerable to British and Zionist labour policies.

These privations were a fundamental fact of life for the overwhelming majority of Palestinian women under British and Zionist colonialism. They were an expression of the primary contradiction of the epoch: between the living conditions of the indigenous poor peasants and proletariat, on the one hand, and those of the capitalists and landowners (local, absentee, but more importantly Zionist), on the other – that is, between the lives of the colonized and of the colonizer. To twist this reality and suggest that the main contradiction was between women and men, or between women and their traditional culture or even their nationalist elite, as most Ashkenazi feminists contend, entirely ignores the historical evidence. This is not to suggest that conflict between the genders was not present in Palestinian society, as the dialectic alienating women from their labour is omnipresent in human relations in varying degrees of severity. However, the claim that intra-Palestinian concerns dominated women's thought processes on an equal or greater level than ethno-national concerns is a clumsy smokescreen used by Ashkenazi feminists to obfuscate history and legitimize the theft of Palestine from its indigenous population. It is clear from this discussion that Ashkenazi feminist writers have in fact strengthened Jewish patriarchy through their legitimization of Zionism as the Jewish national movement and the failure to challenge Israel as a Jewish state.

The above presents only a fraction of the material history of Palestinian women's lived experiences prior to the Zionist ethnic cleansing of Palestine that enabled the establishment of the State of Israel. This process did not stop there, but rather intensified further with Israel's policies of ethnic cleansing and cultural genocide referred to as the *Nakba* (Arabic for catastrophe) by its autochthonous Palestinian victims. A more detailed discussion of this idea will be presented later in this chapter. But before leaving this account of Palestinian women's experiences under British and Zionist colonialism, we will explore one more significant change that occurred at the familial–cultural level and had a strong impact on gender relations.

The British colonial government was heavily involved not only in the economic transformation of Palestine and the Palestinians; it also intervened in the political and cultural process, with significant consequences for gender relations. The *hamula*, which has undergone major changes as a result of peasant expropriation and proletarianization, was also heavily targeted by the colonial state. Recognizing its role as a social and political mechanism, the British, in a bid to further control the peasants, guarantee tax collection and help quell Palestinian resistance, invented the *mukhtar*. The term *mukhtar*, which existed before the British, designated the elder male in the *hamula*, or kin-related *hamayel* (clan or tribe), chosen to represent the community's social, economic and political interests. Considering the fact that many, if not most, Palestinian villages traditionally and until the late 1940s were made up of one *hamula* or several kin-related *hamayel*, the appointed mukhtar became the village head as well. With this practice, the British not only destroyed the participatory traditional system but reinvented the role of the mukhtar – from a figure representing his clan's interests to one largely serving the government. It is important to note that, although the phenomenon of the mukhtar has usually been studied within the context of the Israeli state (e.g. Nakhleh 1977; Zeidani 1995), it was largely invented by British colonial rule. This process of reinvention is somewhat similar to the practices of other colonial and settler-colonial regimes, such as that of timars in India under British colonialism, and the tribal chiefs appointed by the government in the context of Canadian settler colonialism.

In 1930 the British government appointed a large number of mukhtars from within their native villages, some from among the existing *hamula* or village heads and others from outside. According to one British report, the number of mukhtars appointed during that period greatly exceeded the actual number of villages: as compared to approximately 550 villages known to have existed in Palestine in 1932, the number of appointed mukhtars was estimated at 1,344 (Stein 1984: 57). According to the same account, the majority of the mukhtars were appointed in the Northern District (the Galilee), an area which was densely populated and where peasants were known for their resistance to taxation and to British rule at large (57). This process sowed the seeds of further oppression of women and the breaking down of the *hamula* structure.

For at least the first two decades after the foundation of the State of Israel in 1948, the role of the mukhtar changed dramatically: he assumed responsibility for keeping law and order in the village, and for providing political allegiance to the existing ruling party or government. For example, since the Labour Party – the ruling party in Israel until the late 1970s – needed the votes of the fast-growing Palestinian population in order to maintain its rule within the formal democratic system, a major task performed by the mukhtar, as Zeidani (1995) indicates, was to gather the votes of the village and ensure 'Arab loyalty' to the government.

The political power of the mukhtar accorded him a position of social power. All social events in the village needed his approval and blessing, including marriages, divorces and so on. The mukhtar, in the early years of the state, also served as a reference and a resource for resolving conflicts within or between villages, and his rulings were generally accepted by the villagers. Family problems, including gender-based violence, were also taken to the mukhtar for arbitration. In other words, his was the role of a local colonial administrator or governor (Rosenfeld 1968; Nakhleh 1977; Zeidani 1995). The replacement of the traditional leadership role by the il-legitimately appointed mukhtar (in terms of local tradition) came to further entrench patriarchy within the Palestinian family. This was the reality on which the Zionist settler-colonial movement imposed itself as a project with ambitions of empire. It is also the reality that Zionist feminists have obliterated, obfuscated or totally ignored. One's identity as a progressive, critical and anti-colonialist feminist must clearly be positioned within an anti-racist, anti-apartheid and anti-Zionist politics and cannot hide under the rubric of nationalism or culturalism. This position will become clearer in the following discussion, which explores Zionist Ashkenazi feminists' perspectives on Mizrahi Jews in Palestine.

Ashkenazi Women and Benevolent Colonialism

The history of Ashkenazi Jewish women in Palestine, often presented in the context of Zionism as the Jewish national movement, is entangled with the Zionist colonial project as an outside force, on the one hand, and the Palestinians as the indigenous people of the land, on the other. Yet, as Smadar Lavie observes, this history is also intertwined with that of the minority Mizrahi women who lived (being immigrants or otherwise brought into Palestine) during that period (Lavie 2007). In other words, any history of Ashkenazi women that does not take account of the context of the colonized Palestinians and the colonial European Jewish (Zionist) settler movement will necessarily be misleading.[16] Though an apparent recognition of such can be found in some Ashkenazi feminist accounts, there is a tendency to obfuscation through trivialization, oversimplification and decontextualization.

The European Jewish colonial project in Palestine, which brought with it a ready-made-in-Europe narrative of Palestine and the Palestinians, continues to be adopted either partially or wholly by mainstream Jewish feminist writings. Eurocentric in essence, this narrative presents the hegemonic Zionist vision, which saw the indigenous population not only as part of 'the exotic natural environment' – as the populations of other colonial societies were often perceived – but also in terms of the Orientalist vision of biblical times (Shohat 1988: 29). Zionism constructed the myth of Palestine as sparsely populated: 'a land without people for a people without land'. As Frenkel and Bichler inform us, this slogan was constructed along the following lines:

> A group of pioneers strongly committed to the Zionist ideal arrived first in Palestine in the late 19th century.... They found the country wild and unpopulated.... They started from scratch to work the land and prepare it for successive pioneers.... More pioneers followed and all began to dry swamps, revive their culture....
> (Frenkel and Bichler 1984: 14)

This is the kind of historically false narrative that is often adopted by mainstream Ashkenazi feminism. The Ashkenazi liberal and radical feminist narratives of European Jewish women's history in Palestine employ notions adopted or developed by the Zionist settler project, with no critical perspective on the settler-colonial and racist nature of the movement. For example, the use of the notion of *Yishuv* to refer simply to Jewish agricultural settlement is oblivious to the fact that such settlements were erected on Palestinian lands after the expulsion of the indigenous inhabitants. To put it differently, *Yishuv* is but a euphemism for the settler-colonial nature of the Zionist movement. Similarly with a whole set of recently constructed Hebrew terms, such as *alia* (ascendance), which, used to describe European Jewish immigration to Palestine/Israel, is imbued with a sense of spiritual power and reward for settlers; likewise, the term *halutzot* (female pioneers). All such terms are deployed to boost the morale of the female settler, not only asserting her belonging to the land of Palestine/Israel, but also constructing her as its righteous proprietor.

This terminology is of a piece with the Zionist settler-colonial slogans of *kibbush ha-adamah*, *kibbush ha-avodah* and *kibbush ha-shouk* mentioned earlier in this chapter: terms that were and continue to be used by the Histadrut and the JNF (later Hebrewized as *Keren Kayemet L'Yisael* – literally 'The fund for the establishment of the State of Israel') in the project of building a 'Jewish home' or a state on Palestinian land. To continue to use such terms uncritically or to justify them as essentially necessary expressions is not just historically wrong; it is also logically incoherent and morally repellent. How exactly did these Ashkenazi women – namely, the *halutzot* – partake in the development or rather de-development of Palestine?[17] We are never told the answer to this crucial question; nor is the reader told whose land these 'pioneers' settled on, or at what cost and to whom. If it is acknowledged that Palestinian land was not empty and that Palestinians were not seeking Western salvation, the question begs to be asked: who was displaced and replaced by Jewish settlers when the lands of Palestine were freed?

In *Women and Gender in Early Jewish and Palestinian Nationalism*, Sheila Katz (2003) sets out to establish her theory that nationalism is women's main enemy, and that Palestinian and Jewish women's true emancipation is possible only through their struggle against this patriarchal force. The author tries to demonstrate the presence of 'good' or 'sisterly' relations between indigenous Palestinian women and Zionist settlers, and asserts that such relations would have been much stronger if both renounced their 'male' nationalisms. However, by evading the Zionist settler-colonial role in displacing, impoverishing and alienating indigenous women and men from their only means of production, the author ends up trivializing and oversimplifying the entire history and thereby directly enables the promulgation and expansion of the militarized Jewish male identity. In her constructed imagining of 'sisterhood' between Jews and Arabs, Katz actually effects the weakening so-called sisterhood, even among Ashkenazi women.

Using data based on upper-class Zionist women's diaries, travel documents and European Jewish missionary observations, Katz presents the reader with examples of good 'neighbourly' relations between women working the land, the *fellah* (the Hebrew version of *fallah*), 'agricultural labourers', 'domestic workers' and the benevolent European Jewish upper-class women who 'document' and 're'-present such relations. While reading these narratives, the reader cannot fail to notice the colonially benevolent paternalism of these settlers and their concern over how to 'modernize' or 'civilize' the 'backward' women of the Other. This vision is evident in Katz's reference to the then-existing discourse on education and the need to 'civilize' the 'uncivilized' and 'traditional' Palestinians and other Arabs or other Jews, such as the Yemenis. It also informs her reference to the need to teach these women 'social hygiene', such as cleanliness, proper childcare and how to look after their health (Katz 2003). It in fact makes little if any difference whether such terminology is that of the author herself or that of the upper-class Zionist women who used the services of female Others on their appropriated land or as domestic workers. Nowhere does the author embark on a serious critique of these issues. Instead, they are introduced uncritically as being representative of the prevailing discourse of the time.

Katz's book includes a number of anecdotes of 'neighbourly' relations between European Jewish settlers and Palestinian women. Such individual stories are not difficult to find. The recent collection of oral history of Palestinian women in pre-1948 Palestine contains several references to neighbourly relations between Palestinian Arab women and Jewish settlers, especially settlers living in and around Arab villages and towns.[18] Moreover, in Ibtisam Maraa'na's film *Paradise Lost*, one of her protagonists (her own mother) speaks positively of her European Jewish employer in whose house she worked as a domestic servant. But this relationship is well contextualized in the movie, with the film-maker and her mother well aware of the power and colonial relations that governed domestic working conditions in Ashkenazi homes. To assert the socio-political equality of Arab and Jewish women based on a smattering of anecdotal evidence is tantamount to negating the ill effects of antebellum slavery in the American South because a handful of white Southern women had good post-bellum relations with their black female domestic servants.

Logically defensible historical analysis, however, is not what one finds in Katz's references to Palestinian–Zionist 'neighbourly' relations. Katz, relying almost exclusively on Katznelson-Rubashov's book *Divrei Ovdot* ('Words of Female Workers') (2002) – translated into English as *The Plough Woman: Records of the Pioneer Women of Palestine* – presents a racist and profoundly misleading narrative. This latter book is considered a classic on the subject of pioneer Zionist women, and hails settler women as 'keenly motivated by the vision of creating a future Jewish homeland, an egalitarian society that would foster and celebrate individual growth, sustain family life, and provide a secure future for all'. Aiming to explore issues such as Zionist women's arrival in 'Eretz Israel', children, their work, social relations and the like, the study is only superficially apolitical. One searches in vain to find any information on the background of those identified as 'women field workers', the *fellah*. With diaries written by Katznelson-Rubashov, who became Katznelson-Shazar after marrying Zalman Shazar, Israel's third president, one wonders what quality it is that makes such a book a classic other than its utility for mythologizing Israel as a peaceful, democratic and open-minded polity.

Ashkenazi Jewish *halutzot* are generally presented by Zionist feminists not as settlers or part of the Zionist colonial project, but as agricultural workers in Palestine. Margalit Shilo's sympathetic review of Kaznelson-Rubashov's book has nonetheless questioned what she refers to as the 'intention of the editor of the English translation of the book to credit all the pioneer women with the achievement of the very few', adding: 'as far as I know the only place where women pioneers actually ploughed the land was in Sejera (Hebrew for the Palestinian village of al-Sajarah). Most of the women who contributed to this volume struggled mainly with traditionally feminine work: cooking, cleaning and caring for children (Shilo 1992).[19]

Had Katz adopted a critical approach to Kaznelson-Rubashov's narrative she might have realized that Sejera/Al-Sajarah was the birthplace of the late world-renowned artist and social critic Naji al-Ali, and the home of many other Palestinian women, men and children, all of whom were evicted from this village to make room for the 'pioneers'. Historical accounts like the one presented by Katz are narratives of evasion and denial; they tell of exploitation and oppression of Palestinian (and Jewish) women, but make no direct reference to the Zionist expropriation of Palestinian land, its destruction of the peasant economy and the privation of indigenous Palestinians. To erase the role of a Palestinian *fallaha*, situated in an overwhelmingly agrarian society, and superimpose a European Jewish settler originating from predominantly industrialized Europe erases the long history and identity of the indigenous Palestinians. It also masks the role of other agricultural workers, namely the Yemeni Jews, brought to Palestine to replace indigenous Palestinian labour power.

Finally, as members of the Zionist settler movement, Ashkenazi women, to a large extent, were aloof from the poverty, poor education, displacement and colonization which shaped the experiences of Palestinian women. They lived in separate settlements with little or no contact with indigenous Palestinians, except for the sporadic use of them as domestic labour or agricultural workers. Ashkenazi women received a full education, both from the colonial government, whose concern was urban education, and from the Zionist movement, which established its own Jewish school system. They also enjoyed full health and other social services courtesy of the Zionist movement, which under British colonialism was able to establish a state within a state. The Zionist settler project, together with the urban-biased approach of the colonial regime, undoubtedly resulted in a further widening of the gap between Palestinian Arab women and European Jewish or Ashkenazi women; it also widened the gap within Arab culture between the urban Christian minority and that of the Palestinian Muslim majority, most of whom resided in villages.

In the absence of a political-economic analysis of Ashkenazi women's history in pre-Israel Palestine, it is hard to gauge the public role of European Jewish female settlers. From what has been so far discussed, it is clear that the British and Zionist policies of labour, health and education were primarily concerned with male and female European Jews, in the process setting the historical precedent for a differential status of Jews as compared to the inferior status of non-European Jews, mostly Palestinians. This historical factor has also been ignored by Ashkenazi feminists. It is true, as discussed in Chapter 1, that Ashkenazi women were not placed in high or elite positions in the Zionist army, but it is known that female Zionist settlers were involved in Jewish terrorist organizations such as the Irgun, led by Menahem Begin, who in the late 1970s became Israel's prime minister, or the Haganah (later incorporated into the Israeli army). Zionist feminists such as Katz who have written and continue to write about the *halutzot* should be aware that shared gender does not make women a class in themselves.

To claim that if Jewish and Arab women were only to renounce the patriarchal structure of their nationalism then peace and justice would be achieved is not just simplistic but delusional. As the account below demonstrates, some Ashkenazi female settlers were actively involved in massacring women, men and children. At the time Katz wrote her book (2003), a large body of literature by Israeli, Palestinian and other historians and social scientists on the dynamics of this period was already available to the public. Her decision to ignore this literature is in itself a political statement: by opting for an erroneous set of reported facts she has produced an account that is untenable, lacking as it does historical and contextual validity. The gravity of the Zionist targeting of Palestinian women during the Nakba is exemplified in the following case of the Palestinian village of Deir Yassin.

The Deir Yassin massacre, which was to become a prominent chapter in the collective memory of Palestinians, has received a great deal of attention by Palestinian, Jewish and other authors, including Hadawi (1970), Khalidi (1992), Kark and Oren-Nordheim (2001), Morris (2004) and Segev (1998), among many others.

The following graphic description of the massacre, based largely on eyewitness accounts of the massacre reported by a British official and by Jacques de Reynier of the International Committee of the Red Cross, is a reminder of the deeply racist and hate-mongering attitude towards indigenous Arabs held by the Zionist settler movement in Palestine. The massacre at Deir Yassin took place on 9 April 1948: in total some 250 people were shot dead and many more wounded. According to Martin (2004), of the 250 killed, 25 pregnant women were bayoneted in the abdomen while still alive; 52 children were maimed in front of their mothers, then slain and beheaded; their mothers were in turn murdered, their bodies and sexual organs subsequently mutilated; 60 other women and girls were also killed and mutilated. Quoting British Army officer Richard Catling, who was present at the scene, Martin writes:

> There is ... no doubt that many sexual atrocities were committed by the attacking Jews. Many young school girls were raped and later slaughtered.... Many infants were also butchered and killed. I also saw one old woman ... who had been severely beaten about the head with rifle butts. (cited in Martin 2004)

The involvement of Ashkenazi 'female pioneers' in this massacre has a direct bearing on Katz's abstract and ahistorical notions of 'solidarity' and 'sisterhood'. Jacques de Reynier, who met the 'cleaning up' team on his arrival at the village, had the following to say:

> The gang ... was young ... men and women, armed to the teeth ... and [had] also cutlasses in their hands, most of them still blood-stained. A beautiful young girl, with criminal eyes, showed me hers still dripping with blood; she displayed it like a trophy. This was the 'cleaning up' team that was obviously performing its task very conscientiously. (cited in Martin 2004)

These accounts of one of many massacres committed by the Israeli state cannot be washed away by talk of 'women's solidarity' or gender alliance.[20] In the context of colonialism, the relationship between women is one of colonizers and colonized; overemphasizing gender and ignoring the fundamentally racist structure of settler colonialism and the power relations involved are tantamount to complicity in the colonial-settler project.

Moreover, no feminist account of the history of pre-Israel Palestine or of the Zionist movement can be taken seriously if it overlooks the forced expulsion of 80 per cent of the native inhabitants of Palestine, pays no heed to their killing, torture and rape, and disregards their suffering – especially today, given the mounting evidence testifying to such atrocities provided by a growing number of Palestinian and Jewish researchers. For the historical accounts of Ashkenazi feminist women, such as Katz, to ignore the evidence of brutal female enablement of and complicity in the operation of the patriarchy of Zionism is morally reprehensible and politically untenable.

Mizrahi Women in a Historical Perspective

It is important to note that in this study the term 'Mizrahi' is not used to identify a unified or homogenous identity; rather, it here refers to a multiplicity of identities, social and class positions. While the overwhelming majority of Mizrahis originated from the Arab and/or Muslim worlds, differentiations between the various 'ethnic/cultural' groups, and indeed within each group, are manifested in various domains, at work, in education, with regard to public presence and involvement, as well as in terms of access to knowledge. Differentiation among women from the 'same' background (say, Arab or Muslim) is also determined by class and social status. Having said this, in a manner comparable to the book's treatment of Palestinian indigenous populations the term 'Mizrahi' will be used to refer to a general category of a racialized and marginalized group of citizens. The designation 'Mizrahi, rather than the terms 'Oriental' or 'Sephardic' Jew, used in official Israeli literature, draws attention to the ethnic and racialized differences that have marked Arab Jews as the Oriental Other to Israel's founding Zionist leaders, who were Ashkenazis – European Jews.

The expansionist nature of the Zionist settler-colonial regime has expressed itself in two types of immigrant: those required for demographic reasons and military functions, and others deemed necessary for basically economic reasons. The former are usually selected from the preferred or desired category: European, white Ashkenazi Jews. They were, and are, well taken care of, being seen as the reproducers of the nation 'proper'. The second category of immigrants is the less (or rather un-) desired category deemed necessary for the capitalist colonial project. They have generally been brought in as the undesired, inexpensive, seasonal and largely casual labour required by the erratic logic of capitalism, especially in its Zionist context of racialized policies against indigenous people. The Yemeni Jews of the early settler-colonial project belong to this category.

As noted earlier, in the 1920s over 20,000 Yemeni Jews were brought to Palestine by Hapoe'l Ha-Tzai'r (Young Workers of the Socialist Zionist Party), which had been delegated to travel to Yemen with the mission to persuade them to emigrate. These Arab Jews were brought in as agricultural labourers to replace local Palestinian workers, who were thus rendered unemployed (Kimmerling 1983: 34). By the late 1940s, the number of Yemeni Jews in Palestine was estimated at 40,000 (Lavie 2007: 2). Common to the lived experiences of most Arab or Muslim Jews are generally dilapidated living conditions and living in abject poverty. Even Katz does not fail to see this when writing about Arab, especially Yemeni, Jews, whom she describes as

> living in mud-hut villages, with appalling standards of sanitation … sitting listlessly on their doorsteps for hours and even days at a time, not worrying about the flies on the baby, not interested in the dirt in the house and yard, not even caring about work. (Katz 2003: 118)

Yet, although she includes a brief description of their lives, Katz fails to analyse or explain the reasons for their miserable living conditions, which is curious given that they were brought to the country by an arm of the Jewish Agency! In contrast, Mizrahi feminist scholars, such as Smadar Lavie, provide a comprehensive picture of Arab Jewish lived reality in Palestine. Lavie explains how Yemeni men were brought in to work as seasonal agricultural labourers and used as a reserve army of labour to satisfy the growing European Jewish capitalist sector. Yemeni women were also semi-permanently attached to the workforce, working partly in agriculture and partly in domestic service. In her account of these women, Lavie opts for the politicized term 'domestic servants' in opposition to the 'economically correct' and politically neutral concept of 'domestic labourers'. On this she says:

> The Ashkenazi Zionist apparatchiks, whose wives were busy with public charities, favoured Yemeni women as cleaners and launderers. They called them Rumiyyas, after the fragrant herb *rùmiyya*, used by Yemeni Jews for the *havdala* ritual ending the sacred Sabbath and demarcating the beginning of another week.... Aside from the severely disabled and the very old, the whole Yemeni family went to work outside the home. (Lavie 2007: 13)

As Lavie observes, seasonal labourers who went to work in the Ashkenazi colonies often lived in the fields without a roof over their heads, while others lived in barns and slept with the domestic animals. None was allowed to live inside the zones of the colonies. Moreover, the *yishuv*, she adds, 'relied on child labour by Yemeni girls, and less frequently, by Palestinian girls' (2007: 14). The working day for these females is described as long, and they usually were not entitled to even one day off per week. Lavie's use of the term 'domestic servants' denotes the dreadful working conditions of these women, who were regularly beaten by their male and female Ashkenazi employers, and also raped by the men (2007: 14).

As with indigenous Palestinians, Jews from Arab/Muslim countries are depicted in the Zionist narrative as 'natural labourers'. A common Ashkenazi term for a working Yemeni girl was *behemàt bayit ktanà* (a little domestic beast) (Lavie 2007: 15). Their small size and relative weakness undoubtedly served the interests of Ashkenazi capitalists (especially farmers), who got away with overworking them, keeping them under tight control, and more generally exploiting them – hence their reputation as 'natural labourers'.

The settler-colonial racialization and subjugation of Mizrahi Jews was neither incidental to, nor a fleeting occurrence of, the economic conditions at the time. There is an increasing body of work, especially by Mizrahi women, describing the poor social and economic conditions of Mizrahi Jews in general and Mizrahi women more specifically during the two decades following the establishment of the State of Israel (e.g. Shohat 2002; Nimni 2003a; Dahan-Kalev 2003). The overwhelming majority of these studies paint a rather appalling picture of the way these Jews have been treated by the Israeli state. One major critique launched by Mizrahi feminists against Ashkenazi feminism targets the latter's attempts to depict Zionism as the national movement of all Jews. In most Mizrahi literature, including feminist work, a clear line is drawn between Zionism and Jewish nationalism. Whereas Zionism is seen as an exclusive movement of the Ashkenazi, the category 'Jewish' is understood to be a differentiated one made up of various ethnicities and cultures and not a unifying concept or an expression of a national identity.

The debate around the relationship between Zionism and Jewish nationalism is best articulated in the growing literature on post-Zionism (Kovel 2007; Nimni 2003a, 2003b; Lavie 2005, 2007; Hever et al. 2002). This debate challenges the claims that Zionism represents a nationalism for all Jews and that all Jews are Zionists. For most Mizrahi scholars, including feminists, Zionism represents the position of only some European Jews, who brought the ideology and movement from the West and implanted them in Palestine; further, it only speaks for them. This scholarship also challenges the myth constructed around Mizrahi immigration from Arab countries. Thus, in contrast to the Zionist narrative, which constructed Arab (Mizrahi) Jews as refugees who fled their countries because of pogroms and persecution, Mizrahi literature on these issues presents a radically different story. In post-Zionist and anti-Zionist literature we learn that, in reaction to the establishment of the State of Israel, the destruction of Palestine, and the ethnic cleansing practised against Palestinians, riots (rather than 'pogroms') did erupt in most Arab countries and anger was vented against Jewish nationals in these countries. In various cases, especially in the case of Iraqi Jews, scholars have also emphasized the point that the Jewish (Zionist) Agency was actively involved in recruiting Arab

Jews. Mention is made of the use of force and violence by Zionists in efforts to force these communities out of their Arab home countries. Shohat (2003), Nimni (2003a) and Dahan-Kalev (2003), for example, provide ample evidence of Zionists who left Israel for Iraq in the 1950s with the purpose of recruiting Iraqi Jews for immigration to Israel. Recruitment, it is reported, was conducted through the use of force and violence, such as placing bombs in synagogues, to spread fear among the Iraqi Jewish community.

Referring to his own experience as a Zionist agent recruiting Iraqi Jews for the newly established State of Israel, Naeim Giladi, in his article 'The Jews of Iraq', documents the violence used by the Zionists to cause them to leave Iraq for Israel. He observes:

> About 125,000 Jews left Iraq for Israel in the late 1940s and into 1952 ... most because they had been lied to and put into a panic by what I came to learn were Zionist bombs. But my mother and father were among the 6,000 who did not go to Israel. (Giladi 1988)

In a political statement expressing his position and reasoning, the author notes: 'I write this article for the same reason I wrote my book: to tell the American people, and especially American Jews, that Jews from Islamic lands did not emigrate willingly to Israel; that, to force them to leave, Jews killed Jews' (Giladi 1988).

The racialized positioning of Mizrahi Jews within the newly established State of Israel has marked their history and experience of citizenship in the Jewish state. Mizrahi Jews, especially women who in their countries of origin were Arab citizens, became in Israel orientalized and othered through a set of institutional policies and practices which subjugated them economically, socially and educationally. Living conditions for Mizrahi Jews, especially women, at least in the first two decades of the state, were downright appalling. The immigration policies Israel enacted towards the Mizrahis were not open-ended, but calculated, with the aim of controlling this population. Zionism needed (Arab) Jews for several reasons: demographically, they were needed to legitimize the state as Jewish;

geographically, they were necessary for the Judaization of the land; economically, they were needed to supplement and strengthen the emerging market; and, finally, Mizrahi Jews (especially males) were needed to shore up Israel's military power. In fact, due mainly to natural population increase among the group, by the early 1990s Mizrahi Jews accounted for the majority of the Israeli Jewish population. Nonetheless, such needs were not translated into an equitable treatment of these Jews or in their absorption as desired nationals. Quite to the contrary, Israel ensured that through well-calculated immigration and absorption policies Mizrahi Jews would not 'threaten' the white, European character of its *Sabra* nationals, seen as the founding fathers – and mothers – of the state (Shohat 2002; Ghanem 2003).[21]

Mizrahiyout: Between Cultural Erasure and Resistance

The terms 'Mizrahi' and 'Mizrahiyout' have become the subject of a major debate among Israeli scholars. The terms did not constitute the 'original' identity of Jews from Arab/Muslim countries, but rather developed out of their specific socio-economic, political and cultural experiences after arriving in Israel. As noted above, it was the change in living conditions of these Jews, from their former status as ordinary people in their countries of origin, practising their religious customs in an Arab culture, to becoming Others in Israel which led them to adopt these terms as a form of political identity. The terms were developed to counter Israel's official term, 'Orientals', which has served to orientalize them. The following brief history of Mizrahi settlement in Israel illustrates the Israeli policies and practices that orientalize Arab Jews and the countering of such policies through the adoption of 'Mizrahiyout' and 'Mizrahi' as a political identity.

As early as 1951, a special settlement plan was devised to accommodate the large numbers of Mizrahi immigrants arriving in the newly established state. The architect of the plan was none other than Ariel Sharon, who at the time served as the director of the

Planning Office. Sharon devised a plan which aimed at settling and populating the spaces that the Zionists had emptied of indigenous Palestinians but that remained uninhabited by Ashkenazi Jews. By that point, Ashkenazi immigration to Israel from Europe had waned, and Ashkenazis had already occupied major towns in the centre and north of Palestine/Israel. Settlement policies devised for Mizrahi Jews, as Safadiyyah and Yiftahel (2003) observe, were easy to implement since the state could direct the newcomers to special towns not yet populated but in the process of being developed. These *ayarot pituah*, or 'development towns', were to be the destination of Mizrahi Jews (Safadiyyah and Yiftahel 2003: 51; Khazzoom 2005: 117; Tzfadia and Yiftachel 2001, 2004).[22] However, before moving into such development towns, which would be their permanent place of residence, Mizrahi Jews were first sent to live in what were known in Hebrew as *ma'abarot*, or transit camps. In addition to Mizrahi immigrants these camps would also temporarily house several groups of Ashkenazis (e.g. from Romania and other countries in central and eastern Europe). Living conditions in the camps, most Mizrahi scholars concur, were appalling and alienating, particularly for women, who struggled to keep their families together and survive in deplorable conditions. For several years the *ma'abarot* were the place of residence for the overwhelming majority of Mizrahi Jews (Motzafi-Haller 2001: 703).

Even after the Mizrahis had moved to their permanent place of residence in the development towns, living conditions were not much better, for their new homes were found to be largely deficient. Such towns included Ber Sheva (Hebrew for Bir el-Sabea'), Ashkelon (Hebrew for A'skalan/Al-Majdal) and, later, the settlement of Sderot in the Naqab (Negev) area. The concentration of Mizrahi Jews, especially in the southern part of Palestine/Israel, as Udi Adeeb[23] (2003) observes, was designed largely to serve a specific political purpose: to settle Mizrahi Jews in separate or segregated areas far from Ashkenazi centres and to populate the areas around Israel's borders, specifically with Egypt. Commenting further on this phenomenon, Adeeb suggests that the Ashkenazi administration settled Mizrahis in peripheral locations and in villages and homes deserted by the Palestinians from 1948 on in order to minimize a perceived Mizrahi threat to Ashkenazi resources. Settlements in Israel, he argues, 'constitute important factors in the Zionist colonial policies of divide and control. Instead of creating a united Israeli identity, settlement policy played a role in dividing citizens and sustaining inequalities' (Adeeb 2003: 53–4).

The development towns suffered from a lack of adequate funding for social services. Such towns could not provide sufficient employment; nor did they enjoy proper services such as education, housing or health services. Moreover, in addition to their geographical exclusion from Ashkenazi centres, the large numbers of Mizrahi Jews sent to live in development towns – in which they comprised 90 per cent of the population – suffered cultural, political and economic marginalization, and became highly racialized (Ghanem 2003; Adeeb 2003; Khazzoom 2005). A comprehensive account of the state of education among Mizrahi Jews, especially women, is provided in Chapter 4; however, it is important to note here that the orientalizing mentality that the Zionist state adopted towards the Mizrahi community was embedded in the official strategy of education initially designed and implemented within this community. Hence the introduction of pre-vocational training, largely designed for *ayarot pituah*. This educational strategy aimed, first, at schooling girls to become future housewives, confining them to what Yonah and Saporta refer to as the 'private patriarchal order' (2006: 89). Second, educational programmes delivered by schools in the development towns were aimed at training Mizrahi women to manage a household efficiently, economically and hygienically, and they would therefore need to 'acquire a basic knowledge of sewing for personal and family needs, cooking, baking, rational nutrition, household maintenance, ... infant care, growing vegetables, landscape gardening, and managing a chicken coop' (Yonah and Saporta 2006: 84). Embedded both in this strategy and in the Ministry of Education, the institution which implemented it, was the assumption that Mizrahi girls should prepare for gendered roles in keeping with their traditionally defined ones. Finally, this strategy also had the parallel economic agenda of 'producing and reproducing Mizrahis as proletariat' (Yonah and Saporta 2006: 85).

Feminist literature on migration recognizes the advantages and disadvantages it potentially has for women's status. Some work also understands the possibility or potential that migration can have for empowering women. This, however, is not the case with Mizrahi, especially Iraqi women who migrated or were otherwise brought to Israel. According to one Mizrahi feminist scholar, Iraqi women's migration to Israel has resulted in feelings of alienation and experience of racism, and in the erosion of the (Arab) cultural and traditional rules and roles that were empowering for women. The transition in this case, Aziza Khazzoom writes, 'was from high positions women held in Iraq to the feeling of inferiority in Israel' (Khazzoom 2005: 214–15). To put it differently, the act considered by the Zionist movement as *Aliyah* (ascent), an overall improvement of living conditions of world Jewry perceived to be 'homeless' or without a unifying national identity, in the case of Mizrahi Jews turned out to be more of a *Yeridah* (descent) in terms of their overall treatment by the Ashkenazi establishment in Israel.[24] Mizrahi women's ethnicization and racialization upon their arrival in Israel meant downward mobility from the status of full citizenship they had held and enjoyed in their original Arab countries.

The deplorable life conditions in the development towns, Adriana Kemp notes, resulted in many attempts by Mizrahis to leave these settlements and move to the big cities in search of a better life (2004). According to this author, already by 1951 a stormy debate among Mizrahis had developed about their officially designated place of settlement and their move to the development towns. In the early 1960s, as Adeeb writes, a movement against Mizrahi racialization known as the 'Black Panthers' was already in existence (Adeeb 2003). However, given the political nature of the debate and the movement, the state used force to quell the initiative and discipline Mizrahis, keeping them in their place (Kemp 2002: 38–9).

It is important to note that when the state was confronted by Mizrahi challenges concerning their structural racialization and sub-standard living conditions, the state justified its policies as 'temporary'. This explanation, as Benjamin and Barash argue, was 'supported by both the emergence of a "Mizrachi"[25] middle class that has been able to provide decent education for the next generation, especially among Mizrahi men who were integrated into all ranks of the army (including the chief-of-staff – true for 2002), politics (including the President of Israel), and the financial elite' (Benjamin and Barash 2004: 267). In this context, the authors write, 'arguments on discrimination against, or racist treatment of Mizrachi Jews, are often dismissed and silenced because they are inconsistent with the Zionist theme of a unified Jewish–Israeli collective' (2004: 267–8).

The official state position on the racialization of Mizrahi (specifically women) as a temporary social problem to be dealt with at an indeterminate future date was a position also adopted by Ashkenazi feminists, as Motzafi-Haller observes (2002). Ashkenazi women, she argues, 'feared the traditional nature of the Mizrahi women will bring down their modernity. They more specifically feared such traditional culture would be passed on to their children' (2002: 700–701). In the early years of immigration, the author notes, 'Ashkenazi women suggested a strong missionary-like zeal that called for acts of intervention by the state to prevent what was defined as the "cultural retardation" of Mizrahi children caused by their own mothers' (2002: 703). She adds, 'Mizrahi children, referred to as *teunei tipuah* (Hebrew for children in need of special care), were deemed to need to be rescued from the 'cultural backwardness of their families' (2002: 703). Although up until the late 1970s Ashkenazi feminists were 'concerned' with 'modernizing' Mizrahi women, in the past two decades the former seem to have adopted a new strategy: that of silence. 'Mizrahi women', Motzafi-Haller has posited, 'have simply dropped out of the range of research and academic interest' (2002: 704).

In the growing Mizrahi feminist literature on Arab women's histories, the work of Ella Shohat has undoubtedly been pioneering, contributing substantially to an alternative epistemology of the Mizrahis. This is particularly evident in her 'Sephardim in Israel:

Zionism from the Standpoint of Its Jewish Victims' (Shohat 1988). In this article, Shohat employs an anti-colonialist feminist approach that emphasizes similarities between Mizrahi Jewish women and Third World women, while identifying Zionist feminists as part of the First World, highlighting the racialized and racist policies of Zionism and the State of Israel towards its Mizrahi Jewish citizens. Shohat advances the thesis that Zionism is an orientalizing movement aimed at robbing Mizrahi women (and men) of their Arab/Islamic culture, erasing their identity and portraying them as 'brutal and cultureless creatures whose objection to Zionism lacks rational grounding' (Gerber 2003: 23; Shohat 1988: 1–2). In other words, she likens the relationship between the state's treatment of Ashkenazis and of Mizrahis to that of the relation between First and Third Worlds (1988: 2-3). Similar arguments are also made in her 'The Invention of the Mizrahim' (1999).

Particularly poignant in the narratives found in Mizrahi feminist literature are women's personal experiences as schoolgirls, and as mature women joining the Jewish social/public sphere of the hegemonic Ashkenazi culture. Referring to her own experience as an Arab/Iraqi Jew, Shohat emphasizes the split identity she was forced to live: a familiar or 'normal' identity which characterized her life in the private domain (at home), and an imposed 'Jewish Israeli' one when leaving the house to go to school or mingle with other (Ashkenazi) Jews (Shohat 2002). At home, she recounts, she lived a normal life, speaking Arabic with her grandparents, and was known as Habiba, her original name. Yet, when she left the house, for example to go to school and mingle with Ashkenazi Jews, she was forced to go through a different process of socialization, using her imposed Jewish name (Ella) and denying her Arab roots, identity and culture in order to fit in within the unfamiliar Ashkenazi environment. 'My first public performance of the Hebrew language', Shohat relates,

> was not a textbook example of the 'normal' linguistic development of a child. I vividly remember my first anxious days in kindergarten, when I was less terrified about the separation from my mother than about what Arabic words would slip into my Hebrew. (2002: 265)

Living two distant and distinct identities – one as an Arab and another as an Israeli Jew – became quite a burden to children like Shohat: 'Like so many Sephardi–Mizrahi children, I just wanted to be transparent, without that dark, opaque Arab history, unburdened by the Arabic culture. I soon learnt to pretend not to speak Arabic and to speak a Europeanized Hebrew' (2002: 264).

The stories and narratives told by various Mizrahi feminists reflecting on their childhood and adulthood experiences of alienation, cultural erasure and social estrangement make fascinating reading – albeit that they are filled with bitterness, disappointment and anguish. One such telling narrative is that of Henriette Dahan-Kalev. In 'You're So Pretty – You Don't Look Moroccan' (2003), she reflects on her experience as an Arab Jew who was forced to internalize institutionalized racism directed against her and her community. The crux of the matter was that her education depicted Arabs, including Arab Jews, as 'Orientals', 'poor', 'uneducated' and 'backward' compared to the 'developed', 'cultured' and 'modern' European Jews, so, Dahan-Kalev writes,

> Who was I to doubt these truths? In a sense, I did not exist, whereas these fictitious truths did exist – they had been propounded by the members of the intellectual elite of society.… This discourse stimulated the minds of subsequent thinkers, all of whom, in turn, nurtured the myth of primitivity versus modernity. (2003: 174)

Feeling powerless within an orientalizing discourse and a racializing reality, Dahan-Kalev recounts: 'I conformed … this discourse functioned as a massive system of exclusion, filtering out those of us who failed the Ashkenazification test, a system essentially fertilized by philosophical, literary, ethical and educational authorities' (2003: 175).

While this narrative and similar ones depict Mizrahi women's childhood anxiety and confusion about their culture and identity, other narratives related to their experiences of adulthood are also present. Despite major changes in Israel's policies, which aimed at integrating Mizrahi Jews into the mainstream (Ashkenazi) Jewish economy and polity, as Benjamin and Barash note, social relations between Ashkenazis and Mizrahis did not alter drastically. In 'He Thought I Would Be Like My Mother: The Silencing of Mizrachi Women in Israeli Inter- and Intra-marriages', Benjamin and Barash (2004) compare the experiences of eleven Mizrahi women married to Mizrahi men and eleven Mizrahi women married to Ashkenazi men. Among their major findings is that the public silencing practised by the Israeli state and institutions against Mizrahis, especially women, is replicated in the private/domestic sphere in 'mixed marriages' between Mizrahi women and Ashkenazi men. In addition to patriarchy's gender silencing, which is practised in both cases of marital relations, ethnic, racialized silencing, they argue, is largely practised in the case of Mizrahi women married to Ashkenazi men (Benjamin and Barash 2004, 2005: 271).

In a section on 'Selecting a Husband', the authors note that in the case of Mizrahi women marrying Ashkenazi men, an assumption is often made that such a marriage will guarantee women a better and more liberated life than if the husband were of Mizrahi origin. Quoting one interviewee, they write:

> It is not an accident that I chose to marry an Ashkenazi man. After having a Moroccan boyfriend for five years, I wanted the opposite type. I wanted a more liberal and less chauvinist man and.... I thought that if I would marry an Ashkenazi man.... there would be more equality with housework.... My Moroccan boyfriend sometimes used to move the couch and tell me that there is dust here, which irritated me. With an Ashkenazi man, everything was going to be more equal. I felt like I was getting into a different league. (Benjamin and Barash 2004: 275)

Although the authors receive a variety of responses to the question on ethnic silencing, they observe that such silencing occurs both directly, especially through the intervention of Ashkenazi in-laws, and indirectly, through the husband's avoidance of issues of origin and ethnicity, deeming them meaningless and not worthy of discussion (2004: 279). Acknowledging the important insights such studies contribute to understanding Mizrahi women's lived experiences in

Israel, feminist studies on this community, as with Arab Palestinian women citizens, need to be better situated within the larger context of Israel's political, economic and ideological policies and institutions. Later, in Chapters 3 and 4, a more comprehensive account of the educational status and economic performance of Mizrahi women is presented. Depicted as 'traditional', 'uneducated' and 'breeding machines', Mizrahi women were the most targeted group in Ashkenazi literature. Suffice it to mention here that the deep pain and injury felt by Mizrahi academic feminists as a result of their loss of identity, cultural erasure and personal and collective devaluation have always occupied a central place in their epistemology.

Unlike Palestinian women who were geographically, physically and culturally separated and segregated from Jewish society and who were considered to be an undesired minority, Mizrahi Jews until at least the early 1990s made up the majority of the Jewish population and could not be easily ignored. The concept 'Mizrahiyout', which was officially introduced as a tool of racialization and othering of this community, was in fact reclaimed by Mizrahi feminists as a form of challenge and resistance to their experienced history of denial, cultural erasure and segregation. The term 'Mizrahiyout', as Motzafi-Haller observes, became a means of consciousness-raising among the community and a means to an alternative epistemological identity or self-representation.[26]

Having identified the racist, racializing and ethnicizing practices of Zionism and the Israeli state, practices that victimize both indigenous Palestinians and Mizrahis, it is important that Palestinian and Mizrahi women should not be seen as mere recipients or silent victims of their oppression. Women express resistance to their oppression in a variety of ways. In the case of Mizrahi women, they articulated their voices of resistance through critical feminist writings and narration of their own experiences. Through such writings, they also contributed to the emergence of a new epistemology that challenged their official, patriarchal and racialized construction. Such means were also used in the growing scholarly material produced by Palestinian feminists.

However, considering the specific violent and colonial history that Palestinians endured under British and Zionist settler colonialism, including Israel's racist and exclusionary treatment towards them as citizens with proud national aspirations, Palestinian women took a more active role in all of the national resistance movements, these movements having also marked their history from before the establishment of the state until the present day. Space precludes the provision of a full account of the role of Palestinian women in the resistance movements; such an account requires a separate volume. Nevertheless, discussion here cannot be complete without reference to Palestinian women's role in making their history, challenging their colonial oppression, and using all means to resist their colonizers. A reference to the role of agency deployed by Palestinian women citizens of Israel in resisting state land grabbing, economic racism and other forms of marginalization was made in the previous chapter. Palestinian women have formed an integral part of the resistance throughout their history, whether in pre-1948 Palestine or in post-1967 Israeli occupied Palestinian territory (OPT). A detailed description of their resistance in the first period, prior to the establishment of the State of Israel, especially during the 1936–39 revolt against the British colonizers, has recently been documented using the method of oral history. Three volumes of oral history interviews with Palestinian women covering all geographical spaces, concentrating on Palestinians, refugees and others, were published in Arabic by the Palestinian Women's Research and Documentation Centre (Abdel-Hadi 2007, 2008). A relatively large body of feminist literature has in fact been devoted to Palestinian women's role in the resistance in the occupied territories of the West Bank and Gaza, especially during the First Intifada.[27]

The discussion here about the history of women in Israel has demonstrated that a proper understanding of the status and role of women, in this case racialized and ethnicized Palestinian and Mizrahi Jews, is possible only if women's status and roles are historicized and contextualized in their proper historically specific material conditions. Such an understanding, it was also demonstrated, requires a feminist methodology that presents rather than re-presents their lived experiences. Presenting such a history must be grounded in a methodology which considers the cultural and the material context of a people subjugated under a settler colonial and racist polity, as in the case of Palestinian women, and that attends to a racializing and ethnicizing Zionist structure that obfuscates Jewish differences under the rubric of Jewish nationalism, as in the case of Mizrahi women's history. No proper feminist approach, it is argued here, can capture such realities without paying special attention to the main forces of oppression. It is at this level of analysis, this chapter argues, that Zionist Ashkenazi feminists fail to properly comprehend the history of Palestinian and Mizrahi women. In other words, feminists' reluctance to confront and challenge Zionism for what it is, rather than taking it at face value as the Ashkenazi feminists identified above have done, renders them somewhat complacent about Zionist atrocities. What marks truly progressive and critical feminists is a clear stance not only on gender patriarchy but also on class, race and anti-colonial principles. Anti-Zionism, as an approach used by some Ashkenazi scholars (see, e.g., the work of Ronit Lentin [2002, 2005, 2008], Ilan Pappé [2004, 2005] and Uri Davis [2003]) and Mizrahi scholars (e.g. Ella Shohat [1988, 1999] and Smadar Lavie [2002, 2005]), must constitute an integral part of feminist analysis of women's citizenship in Israel.

THREE

Women and Economic Citizenship

Same but Different: Palestinian, Mizrahi and Ashkenazi Women

IT IS GENERALLY acknowledged that females are more disadvantaged economically than males and that gender discrimination in the labour force is part of this phenomenon. This holds in the case of Israel. However, due to the racist character of the Israeli state, the different groups of women identified in this study – Ashkenazi, Mizrahi and Palestinians – are also differentially discriminated against. Mizrahi women, who bear the legacy of the ethnic/racial discrimination that marked the early decades of their immigration, are still largely to be found in a lower economic position than Ashkenazi women. As for Palestinian women, they have come to occupy the lowest rung in terms of economic rights, facing national and racial discrimination at all economic levels.

The focus in this chapter is an analysis of one citizen group, Palestinian women. There are two primary reasons for this. The first concerns Mizrahi women. On the one hand, it is important to reiterate that in all Israeli official statistics and reports Jews appear as one category; no distinction is made between Ashkenazi and Mizrahi. On the other, structural and institutional changes in the last three decades, which saw greater integration of Mizrahis (especially males) in the Israeli military and politics and the emergence of a sizeable middle class, has further reduced the distinction between the two Jewish communities. The official presentation of the composition of the labour force presents statistics that tend largely to demonstrate that the main distinction is between 'Jews' and 'non-Jews' or Palestinians. Notwithstanding this institutional mask, the relatively lowly position of Mizrahi women in the Jewish labour market will be accounted for in this chapter.

One of the main challenges in writing about women's economic citizenship rights in Israel, especially among Palestinians, is that in most credible economic analyses Palestinians are not presented as a unified national group. In line with the 'ethnocratic' character of the Israeli state, in Yiftachel's words (2006), or more properly the racist policies of the Israeli state,[1] Palestinian Arabs are divided into the 'ethno-religious' groups Muslims, Christians and Druze. Such divisions will be adopted and placed within a critical context.

General Economic Features of
Palestinian Citizens in Israel

It is commonly acknowledged that Palestinian citizens are the poorest sector in Israel. Daniel Gottlieb and Suleiman Abu Bader, who authored a report on poverty in Israel for the Jerusalem-based Van Leer Institute, found that the economic gap between Arabs and Jews in Israel has widened over the past decade. The authors found that in 2006, 56 per cent of 'Israeli-Arabs' (Palestinian citizens) lived under the poverty line, as opposed to 36 per cent ten years previously. This compares to a rate of poverty estimated at 17 per cent for the Jewish population (Branovsky 2007). While there is insufficient data on the sectors most affected by poverty among the Palestinians, it is no surprise to learn that children, youth and, particularly, divorced and single women are among those hardest hit. The report presents a gloomy picture of the economic effects on children. According to the data, 78 per cent of Arab children residing in central Israel were living below the poverty line in 2006. The high rate of poverty recorded in this part of the country references the so-called mixed cities of Haifa, Acca (Acre) and Jaffa, where most Palestinians continue to reside in largely underdeveloped Arab quarters. The Van Leer study has confirmed the deplorable conditions of certain sectors among Palestinian women, namely those living in the South, the Bedouins, among whom the scale of poverty is estimated at about 70 per cent (Branovsky 2007).

As for employment and unemployment rates of the most marginal within the marginalized, the Van Leer report estimates that only 7 per cent of Bedouin women living in unrecognized communities are employed, while the number of women in the recognized Bedouin towns is not much better, coming in at 10 per cent (Branovsky 2007). The report – in common with an increasing number of studies and reports coming out of Israel – documents the deplorable state of Palestinian citizens' lives and recommends aggressive state intervention to ameliorate the conditions of poverty and deprivation, conditions that this chapter will document.

Poverty continues to be the lot of most Palestinian citizens in Israel, a situation that is attracting global attention and concern. The issue, for example, has become a major concern for the Organisation for Economic Co-operation and Development (OECD) as it considers Israel's request to join. In its 2009 report on Israel's economy, the OECD expresses deep concern about the high poverty rates prevalent among Palestinian citizens. The Organisation links such rates directly to what it believes to be Israeli 'discriminatory policies against this group of citizens' (OECD 2009: 5; see also OECD 2010a: 41, 2010b). According to this report, which is based on official Israeli statistics for 2009, among other international sources, 'just over 20% of households [in Israel] are below the relative poverty line compared with an OECD average of 11%'. The report adds that 'Poverty is concentrated among the 20% of the population who are Arab-Israelis whose poverty rate is around 50%' (OECD 2009: 6).

The 'peripheral' status of Palestinian citizens in the midst of a Jewish-centred economy and polity is expressed in all spheres of life. Palestinians are geographically, economically and politically separated, or rather removed, from the Jewish centre of the country or state. This racial separation is reinforced institutionally and structurally through a variety of plans and policies. A 2010 short documentary produced by ADALAH entitled *Targeted Citizen* argues that Israel's racialized separation of Palestinian citizens is targeted, planned and institutionalized. The documentary accounts for some of the important procedures used by the state against its Palestinian citizens. Among the evidence provided we find: home demolitions of Arab citizens; police violation of Palestinian civil rights activists; and the confiscation of the overwhelming majority of Arab land, leaving only 2.5 per cent for the Palestinians, who make up 20 per cent of Israel's population. Mention is also made of the fact that over 60,000 Palestinian citizens are currently living in 'illegal villages' lacking infrastructure and all amenities, including heat, running water, schools and health-care services, while many thousands are living in 'unlicensed' homes, awaiting demolition orders. Furthermore, the report notes discrimination in budgetary allocations to Arab cities and villages and the fact that throughout the sixty years of Israel's existence not a single Arab city or town has been built, in contrast to the construction of over 1,200 new Jewish towns and settlements.

Official Israeli statistics on employment and unemployment among Palestinian women vary widely, depending on who constructs the categories and for what purpose. A major concern regarding official data on Palestinian women's participation – or lack thereof – in the labour market is which working women are considered 'employed', and therefore included in state/official statistics, and which are considered 'unemployed', and thus excluded from statistics on female labour participation.[2] However, Israeli statistics, it is argued here, do not account for all Arab women in the labour force. According to Nabil Khattab,

there is a reasonable basis to believe that the Arab female labour market participation is underestimated by official statistics due to unreported paid jobs such as housekeeping, unskilled workers in agriculture and in local small textile manufactures. (Khattab 2002: 93)

In official discourse, a lack of jobs in the Arab sector as well as in the Israeli Jewish economy, the 'bi-ethnic' market, combined with other socio-cultural factors, is sometimes suggested as the primary reason why many women do not seek employment, rendering them part of the category of 'discouraged' workers (Stier 2002). This is particularly true with regard to married women, who are reported to be three times less likely to be in the labour force than unmarried women (Khattab 2002: 102).

Jewish women, especially Ashkenazis, are heavily represented in government positions such as daycare centres, colleges, hospitals, transportation and so on; Arabs in general, however, are deprived of such amenities, further reducing the scale of women's labour participation. Reasons advanced in academic and official state circles for explaining Palestinian women's low rates of labour participation, and the related issue of widespread poverty among Palestinian women, are often based on cultural/religious rather than structural and institutional factors. In such explanations, Palestinian Arab culture, patriarchy and religion are blamed for women's low status in general and the low rates of labour force participation more specifically. Although cultural factors, including family patriarchy and the traditional gender division of labour, present limitations to women's public presence and labour force participation, the significance of this factor tends to be exaggerated. The Orientalist racist perspective held by the colonial-settler state regarding its 'non-Jewish' Palestinian citizens is one thing, but the internalizing of this belief and its presentation as an important factor – especially by radical Arab and Jewish academics – is quite another.[3] It is the structural and institutional forces, this chapter argues, that present the primary impediments to women's economic involvement and labour force participation. Before proceeding further, a contextualization of the debate on Palestinian women's labour economic participation is required.

The debate on Palestinian women's labour force participation

Most Israeli economic and labour studies, including those by Palestinian scholars, tend to accept the presence of two separate economies and markets without challenging the very racist policies and politics which led to their formation and continued existence. While progressive scholars understand the strength of the Jewish market (referred to by most as 'bi-ethnic') and lament the poverty and underdeveloped state of the Arab market (referred to by some as 'mono-ethnic', and by others as an 'enclave'), they take economic separation as a given. In fact, some authors go so far as to suggest that the presence of two separate labour markets, and especially of the mono-ethnic or enclave market, is more conducive to Arab women's labour participation. For example, Semyonov and Lewin-Epstein argue that the mono-ethnic market 'ensures that women conform to their cultural norms of working within their community' and that it 'protects women from discrimination present in the Jewish dominated labour markets' (Semyonov and Lewin-Epstein 1994: 58). Khattab agrees, asserting that the enclave market serves as a space for women to develop social capital (Khattab 1994: 94).[4] While he locates the basic problem of the enclave model in the lack of resources provided by the government, it provides, for him, a relatively exploitation-free space for women. Following a largely ethnic-based approach, Khattab also differentiates between the different religions/ethnicities among Palestinians, arguing that Christian women have more social capital and a stronger presence in the labour market than do Druze or Muslim women. According to him, 'the ethno-religious identity is one of the basic factors for the dismal participation of women in the Israeli labour market, as it determines the social, demographic, economic and cultural mobility of ethnic Arabs' (Khattab 2002: 103). However, the ethno-religious approach fails to explain why, for example, Christian women are more 'modern' and constitute the largest labour force participation, while Muslim and Druze women fare badly in this domain. What are the lived experiences and circumstances, both historical and contemporary, which place Christian Arabs in a more advantageous position than Muslims?[5]

The structural circumstances within which Palestinian women found themselves from the onset of the Zionist settler movement and continue to endure under the Israeli state constitute the primary factor in their low status. This pertains whether they are members of the so-called enclave labour market or the 'bi-national' or Jewish market. To begin with, within the enclave or the apartheid Arab market, this chapter will argue, Palestinian women occupy primarily 'feminine' positions such as teaching, nursing, social work, secretarial or similar low-level administrative jobs in small offices; such jobs represent an extension of their role in the private/domestic sphere. Most women working in this sector are married, compared with the small number of Palestinian women who are employed in the bi-ethnic or 'the Jewish Market', who tend to be single and deemed highly educated.[6] These kinds of employment, contrary to the arguments presented above, do little to improve women's human and social capital, since such work does not necessarily introduce new challenges, knowledge and skills for the women involved.

There are few or no grounds to suggest that women working in the enclave Arab sector are protected from exploitation. There is no support for the view that patriarchy within the Arab sector is more woman-friendly than its Jewish counterpart. Throughout the history of local Arab municipalities and village councils, women's work and representation have been, to say the least, dismal, and women employed in local councils often tend to occupy low-level jobs. While more studies are needed to determine the nature of female employment in the growing retail industry in the Arab sector, an initial investigation in some of the clothing stores in Nazareth suggests that most women employees (salespeople, cashiers, cleaners and so on) are highly exploited. The overwhelming majority of female workers in the sector are employed on a part-time basis and receive below-average wages in jobs with no labour or social security.[7]

More importantly, references to the 'absence of exploitation' of Palestinian women employed in the Arab sector ignore the tens of thousands of women who up until the early 1990s were employed in unskilled or semi-skilled jobs, for example in the textile industry. These workers were triply exploited on the basis of gender, class and race. Between the 1970s and early 1990s, a large section of Palestinian women citizens were employed as blue-collar workers, largely in the textile industry that was established in the Arab sector in large cities (Nazareth, for example) and in villages, especially in Druze villages in the north. Agricultural labour was another sector that absorbed a sizeable number of Palestinian women. But since the early 1990s, a new economic trend has developed in the country. Israel began importing foreign labour by the early 1980s, with the aim of reducing the economy's dependence on Palestinian labour from the Occupied Territories. This move was also facilitated by the Oslo Accords, which enabled Israel to integrate itself deeply in the then-emerging neo-liberal global economy. This included the targeting of cheap labour power through flexible labour strategies. It is important to note that Israel's drive to tap into the larger global market, in addition to the regional (Middle Eastern) market, could not have succeeded without the strong role played by the Oslo agreement, which basically enabled the state to eliminate the Arab boycott. By the end of the 1970s/early 1980s Israel's mode of accumulation began to experience a shift: from one based on the Fordist mode to the more flexible 'post-Fordist' model. The flexible nature of the Israeli economy reached its peak in the late 1990s and the early 2000s with the influx of foreign, primarily non-Jewish, workers into the country. The first wave of migrant labour to Israel can be traced back to the 1967 occupation of the West Bank and Gaza Strip, when Palestinians from the Occupied Territories were allowed to work in Israel in the construction and agricultural sectors. By the 1980s, the non-citizen Palestinian labour force (from the OPT) comprised about 8 per cent of the Israeli labour force (Raijman and Semyonov 2004: 781).

Due to the restricted mobility imposed on the Palestinians in the OPT after the First Intifada of 1987, the number of migrant labourers declined and a labour shortgage was declared in the economic sectors they used to occupy. In an attempt to find a temporary solution, the state (through the Ministry of Labour) issued work permits and allowed foreign labour migrants to enter and ease the shortage. By 1987, 'the number of permits accorded by the Israeli Ministry of Labour was 2,500, and it increased gradually up to 9,600 in 1993 when Israel had begun importing large numbers of overseas foreign workers mostly from Rumania (construction sector); Thailand (agriculture sector) and Philippines (geriatric care, nursing and domestic services)' (Raijman and Semyonov 2004: 282). By 2001, of an estimated migrant labour force of 240,000 in the Israeli labour market, 60 per cent were classified as 'illegal workers' and had no permits (282).

It is not, surprising, therefore that by the mid-1990s almost all plants that had been employing mainly women (especially in textiles) were closed and production moved out of the country. It is interesting to note that some authors attribute this development to globalization without explaining exactly what the term means, as with Drori (2000). The fact is that, largely as a result of the Oslo Accords and its consequent normalization of relations with Egypt and Jordan, most of these industrial complexes were moved from the Arab sector in Israel into border areas (especially Jordan and Egypt) where labour power is cheaper, not organized or unionized, and where workers' rights can be trampled on.[8] The textile industries that had employed a large number of Palestinian women, Michal Schwartz writes, was shut down, and they 'reopened in Jordan, Egypt, Romania, and China, where the minimum wages are much lower than in Israel' (Schwartz 2006: 2). Nursing came to be staffed by workers from the Philippines, while agricultural positions were filled by Thais. All this resulted in increased unemployment and the rise of poverty among the Arabs (2). A full account of the triple exploitation on the basis of gender, ethnicity and race, and of the role within patriarchal Arab society that these textile workers occupy, is given in the section on the racially segregated Arab labour market below. What is important to emphasize here is that culture, religion and education cannot be used as sufficient or legitimate means to explain Palestinian women's low labour market participation, especially when we realize that the overwhelming majority of women workers in the textile industry were from among the Muslim and Druze communities.

Finally, Palestinian women, especially those residing in remote villages, and in the Naqab or in the 'unrecognized villages' specifically, who also happen to be overwhelmingly Muslim, constitute a particularly disadvantaged population. Even if jobs are found in and around these localities, for these women the Hebrew language – the official language in all government jobs – presents an obstacle. Moreover, heavy domestic responsibilities and the traditional patriarchal family, on the one hand, combined with the absence of affordable and sufficient daycare centres, of public transportation, and of infrastructure, not to mention government offices and human resource centres, on the other, place additional constraints on and obstacles to Palestinian women's participation in the labour force. These factors must be recognized and not ignored, as is the case in the overwhelming majority of male-oriented economic studies.

Female education and labour force participation: a critique

Official studies emphasize education, or the lack thereof, as the major reason for women's (and especially Muslim women's) low rate of labour force participation (Khattab 2002, 2005; Swirski and Konor-Attias 2007). For example, Swirski and Konor-Attias's study (2007) found that those with less than twelve years' education are highly represented in low-income jobs, estimated at 31.6 per cent. However, the group with the smallest proportion of low-wage and the largest proportion of high-wage jobs is those who have had sixteen or more years of education, estimated at 14.8 per cent. This group also has the largest proportion of wage earners in the top percentile – 2.9 per cent (Swirski and Konor-Attias 2007: 22).

Education is clearly an important factor in women's (and indeed men's) labour force participation. However, dealing with female education, especially among marginalized and racialized groups such as Mizrahi and Palestinian women, requires a nuanced understanding of the context that has historically and contemporarily shaped their lived experiences in general and education in particular. Providing statistics on women's labour force participation without acknowledging their structural context is likely to be misleading. A proper contextualization of Palestinian and Mizrahi female education is provided in the next chapter. For the purpose of this discussion, we can observe that while education as a form of human capital is an important factor in developing women's social and gender position in the economic, social and political spheres, in itself it offers little or no guarantee of providing high-quality jobs, or even a safe place, for Palestinian women in the Israeli (Jewish) job market at large. The concept of 'human capital' is used here to refer to the individual who possesses education, knowledge and skills adequate to the needs of a given job market, whether through study or apprenticeship, factors that contribute to his or her development as well as to the productive process of society. The urban location of most Christian Palestinians, along with the role of colonial missionary schooling in Palestinian towns, has undoubtedly facilitated the higher participation of Christian women in the educational system. Moreover, the Zionist Orientalist view which, among other things, equated Arabs with Muslims has also indirectly resulted in Palestinian Christians having greater visibility as 'non-Arabs'. Their overwhelming concentration in the enclave or apartheid market denies Palestinian women (and men) the possibility of obtaining lucrative jobs in the Jewish labour market. In 2000, it was found that 45 per cent of all Palestinian women citizens in the Israeli labour force had over thirteen years' education, yet they were largely employed in the service sector within the 'local Arab market'. Of these, 21 per cent worked in education, primarily as schoolteachers; 16 per cent were employed in the health and welfare sectors, primarily as nurses and social workers; and 16 per cent were classified as working in industry, primarily in textiles. This last rate was found to be higher than that among comparable Jewish women, estimated at 11 per cent (Yaffe and Tal 2002: 10).

That higher education does not guarantee higher rewards or better-paying jobs was one of the conclusions of Dichter's report in 2002. This study found that unemployment was widespread among Palestinian citizens with higher degrees. For example, during January and February of 2001, 3,895 Arabs with higher degrees were registered at employment service offices for unemployed professional and academic job-seekers. They comprised 30 per cent of all Israelis looking for work at the professional level. In all, there were 131,071 people seeking work in Israel at the time, 31,730 of them Arabs. Arab citizens seeking employment constitute 24 per cent of all job-seekers in Israel. Arab academics looking for work constitute 30 per cent of all academic and professional job-seekers in Israel.[9] The numbers in Dichter's findings have hardly changed: eight years later, in a study conducted in 2010 by the Centre for Violence Against Women, it was found that more than 40 per cent of a total of 24,346 Arab women academics (hence around 10,000) were unemployed (Awwad 2010).

Based on 2000–2001 data, it was reported that Arab civil servants holding higher degrees totalled 975, representing 31.2 per cent of all Arab workers in the civil service (444 with a Bachelor's degree, 146 with a Master's degree, 385 with a doctoral degree). Among all civil servants, 19,125 had higher degrees (34 per cent). Arab civil servants with a university or other post-secondary education, totalled 1,903, or 60.8 per cent of all Arabs in the civil service (Dichter 2001: 7). In other words, for Palestinian citizens, academic qualifications – even the holding of a higher degree – are no guarantee of gainful employment.

To reiterate, although education has the potential to improve employment chances and provide better-paying jobs for both Jews and Palestinians, such an outcome is more applicable to Ashkenazi and Mizrahi Jewish women than to Palestinian women. The fact that education has more rewarding results in terms of labour force participation and attainment for Jewish women (and men) than for Arab women (and men) is corroborated by Haberfeld and Cohen's (2007) study, which found that, despite gradual convergence in educational attainment among Ashkenazi, Mizrahi and Arab males and females, earning differences were still polarized. Their analysis, which is based on the 1975, 1982, 1992 and 2001 income surveys, found that returns on human capital invested, such as a higher salary, did not equalize over time for all ethnic or religious groups. Rewards for education, they argue, 'have not grown as fast as educational attainment, and the latter continues to lag behind'. It is worth noting that although the authors suggest that direct discrimination against Arabs played 'a minor role', they were unable to answer the question as to why it is that the 'lag in return for human capital' affects Palestinians 'more than any other section of the Israeli society' (Haberfeld and Cohen 2007: 663).

The major problem of most economic studies, especially those applying quantitative approaches, is the lack of sufficient attention paid to the wider socio-economic and political environment within which Palestinian women (and men), as well as Ashkenazi women, find themselves. For a more comprehensive understanding of this problem for Palestinian women, the most marginalized group, an account will be given of the overall conditions within which these women have lived and received their education, including its quality, accessibility and availability. It is the circumstances of Palestinian women living under structural and institutional racism rather than their culture or education, it is argued here, which contribute most to their high unemployment rates. This conclusion is further corroborated by the OECD, which reports that 'low material living standards among the highly insular ultra-orthodox community stem more from choice than circumstance, as in the case of the Arabs' (OECD 2009: 8). But before we move into this discussion, some observations regarding Mizrahi and Ashkenazi women's access to and involvement in the Israeli labour market will be provided.

Mizrahi women in the 'bi-ethnic' or the Jewish market

Mizrahi women's position in the labour force is inferior to that of Ashkenazi women. This has been the case since their immigration/ importation and their settlement in Palestine/Israel. Haberfeld and Cohen write:

> [S]ince the early 1950s, a group-based hierarchy regarding the labour market was institutionalized in Israeli society, where

Ashkenazi men and women enjoyed the highest socio-economic status, followed by Mizrahi men and women, while Arab-Israelis have been occupying the lowest socio-economic status. (2007: 657)

Within each group, the authors also maintain, men are above women in respect of wage earnings. They conclude that, 'despite differences among studies on the gaps in occupational status and earnings, most studies confirm that the basic hierarchy in the Israeli labour market has not been significantly changed over the past 50 years' (2007: 657).

The inferior status of Arabs in terms of labour force participation has hardly changed despite mounting evidence that the educational disparities between Ashkenazis, Mizrahis and Arab men and women have somewhat narrowed (Haberfeld and Cohen 2006; Yonah and Saporta 2006; Cohen et al. 2007). In fact, even gainful employment by Arab women does not make them equal to their Jewish counterparts. According to a 2010 conference report, an 'Arab woman's average monthly wage is estimated at NIS 4,000 compared with that of a Jewish woman's estimated at NIS 6,000 (Baraka, 2010).[10]

Although a narrowing of the differences in educational achievement among the three categories of the population could potentially mean a simultaneous narrowing of economic inequalities among them, the reality is quite different. Referring to a study conducted over a period of twenty-six years, from 1975 to 2001, Haberfeld and Cohen (2007: 669) conclude that the transformation in the earnings structure – changes in returns to earnings determinants – that led to rising earnings inequality among Israeli workers is the single explanation for the rising mean earnings disparity between Ashkenazi men and Mizrahis (both men and women). Although Mizrahi women fare better than Palestinians in terms of labour force and economic participation, some studies suggest that Israel's racialized or ethnicized policies towards the Mizrahi community continue to be present in the economic sphere. For example, Ephraim Ya'ar suggests that the structural explanation does not alter the fact that the overlap between ethnicity and income levels has increased in recent decades, leading him to conclude that the 'worsening relative situation for Mizrahis on the economic level has contributed to strengthening the feelings of ethnic discrimination and relative deprivation among Mizrahis' (Ya'ar 2005: 107). Haberfeld and Cohen's study, while finding that Mizrahi women's wages have increased between 1975 and 2001 by 49 per cent, also confirmed that the structural and institutional marginalization and discrimination against Mizrahi women remains a major concern. Reflecting on the Ashkenazi hegemonic culture in Israel and its denigration of Mizrahi culture, Ya'ar writes: 'when at a young age Mizrahi boys and girls are told that their culture, ethnicity and family are inferior, their self-identity and experiences become largely delegitimized (2007: 561). Low self-esteem among Mizrahis, which became a structural factor, particularly for women, has contributed to their low aspirations regarding education and the possibility of finding a decent job.

Another barrier that inhibits improvement in Mizrahi women's socio-economic status, as it does that of Palestinians, is language. This applies particularly to first-generation Mizrahi women, for whom Israel's melting pot policy has had deleterious results, according to Ya'ar: 'the overwhelming triumph of Hebrew as a spoken language in everyday life ... has undoubtedly operated as an ideological tool of devaluation and de-legitimization for the Mizrahis' (2005: 96). But this is the reality not only for first-generation Mizrahi women and men but also for a large section of second-generation women who tend to spend more time in the domestic sphere than do their male counterparts. Living in homes where the culture is not Ashkenazi and the spoken language is largely Arabic makes it more difficult for these women to compete in the Hebrew-speaking Israeli market. The inability to use one's own language in the public sphere at large and in the market more specifically undoubtedly restricts one's options. Language is not just a means of communication; it is also a force of security and a symbol of cultural identity. Denial of this cultural identity enshrines feelings of inferiority and a lack of belonging within the dominated group.

Separate peoples, separate markets and separate economies

Studying marginalized women's labour force participation in general and among racially separated groups more specifically represents a major challenge for analysts of political economy. In order to comprehend Palestinian women's economic rights of citizenship compared to those of, say, Mizrahi and Ashkenazi women, and to provide a proper comparison, one should assume the presence of a generalized labour force that is one and the same (i.e. integrated) for all women. In such a situation, a comparison between the three groups of women citizens is possible. However, the situation in Israel is radically different. Here we have two separate markets and two separate economies: bi-ethnic and mono-ethnic or enclave. Khattab's notion of an 'enclave' market, which denotes an economy under siege, provides a step forward in defining the segregated Arab market and thus presents a more accurate picture than does the notion of 'mono-ethnic', which suggests normality, neutrality and objectivity. However, neither of these concepts, the bi-ethnic or the enclave market, I argue, is capable of describing adequately the actual dynamics and labour conditions of women participants.

While the notion of a bi-ethnic economy or market seems to suggest the presence of two ethnicities operating more or less equally in a given sector, the reality however is quite different. As will be seen shortly, the overwhelming majority of workers in this economy are Mizrahi and Ashkenazi Jews, with only a small proportion of Palestinians involved. Moreover, most Arab (Palestinian) workers in this economy are found in low-paid, semi-skilled jobs, and most are men. Characteristic of this market are policies and practices based on racialized inclusion. Arab workers are exploited on the basis of race and as well as class. Policies and practices in this economy mirror those of the state at large. This economy, therefore, will be identified in this chapter as the Jewish market.

Moreover, the overwhelming majority of Arab women's employment is confined to the so-called mono-ethnic or enclave market,

located within the spatially separate and structurally inferior Arab
sector of the economy (Khattab 2002; Lewin-Epstein and Semyonov
1992; Semyonov and Lewin-Epstein 1994). 'Spatial segregation', Semyonov and Lewin-Epstien rightly observe, 'dominates the employment
pattern of Arab ... women' (1994: 55). This market is not only
spatially and demographically separated but also highly racialized
at most levels. It is situated within a less developed – or, rather,
'de-developed' – infrastructure, with major consequences for the
quality and quantity of labour participation. In this chapter, the
characteristics of this sector are referred to as the apartheid market.

Women and labour force participation
in the Jewish market

As noted earlier, the notion of a 'bi-' or 'dual' ethnic labour market,
used almost universally (by officials and scholars of all political
strands) to characterize the Jewish economy, is highly problematic.
First, this ethnocentric designation, which assumes the presence of
two ethnicities, Palestinian Arab and Jewish, obfuscates Palestinian
identity as a national indigenous group. Second, by presenting Mizrahi
and Ashkenazi Jews as one and the same ethnicity – Jewish – such
a conception of the market obscures the historic and contemporary
racialization and ethnicization of Mizrahis. In order to highlight the
racialized position of Palestinian women, we use the designation
'Jewish market', though without losing sight of the inferior position
occupied by Mizrahi women in this economy.

Earlier in the chapter, we identified the problem of most economic
studies as the lumping together of Mizrahi and Ashkenazi Jews as
one, an action that also ethnicizes the Palestinian national group,
stratifying it into ethnic-religious subgroups of Muslims, Christians
and Druze. A prime example here is Levanon and Raviv's study (2007)
in which the authors use the latest Israeli census results to examine
income disparity between Jews and non-Jews in Israel. Whilst leaving
the Jewish sample non-stratified – that is, lumping Mizrahis and
Ashkenazis together – they nevertheless stratify the non-Jewish (Palestinian) sample into Muslims, Christians and Druze. These authors,

in common with others identified earlier, obscure more than clarify the complexity of labour force participation in the Jewish economy. Be this as it may, it is still possible to demonstrate the racialized and hierarchical structure of the Jewish economy by observing where the three categories of women are placed: Ashkenazi women occupy the upper levels; Palestinian women occupy the lowest position; Mizrahi women seem to be sandwiched in-between. This relationship of superiority/inferiority applies to all economic domains, including access to labour, income levels, education attainment, accessibility of government services, and access to proper and adequate health care, in addition to their public and political representation in the centres of state power. Thus, in their 'Equality Index of Jewish and Arab Citizens in Israel', Swirski and Konor-Attias found that Palestinian citizens of Israel had significantly lower labour force participation rates than Jews. The largest disparity was found among women, as 54 per cent of Jewish women were employed, compared to only 17.6 per cent of Palestinian women (Swirski and Konor-Attias 2007: 62).

A large proportion of the economic literature tends to be devoted to the correlation of ethnicity and class in examining income disparities between the groups. Using data based on the 1983 and 1995 population censuses, Khattab (2005) examines the role of ethnicity and class in earning disparities in Israel. Like Yaish (2001) before him, Khattab's study also includes women. As with Jews stratified into the Ashkenazi and Mizrahi categories, this study also stratifies Palestinian women into the religious subgroups Christian, Muslim and Druze. Khattab concludes that class more than ethnicity appears to be the factor that most affects women's income. Both Khattab (2005) and Yaish (2001) accept this assumption and conclude that Druze women, on average, earn much less than all other categories or subcategories of women.

Although most studies on income disparities within the context of ethnicity and class suggest that the direct impact of religion/ethnicity on income has gradually declined over time, they all also confirm that Jewish nationals continue to have an economic advantage over Palestinians (Dichter 2001; Haberfeld and Cohen 2007; Khattab 2005;

Levanon and Raviv 2007; Swirski and Konor-Attias 2005; Yaish 2001).
In other words, the role of ethnicity – or, more properly, racialized
policies, especially towards Palestinians – has not diminished; the
income gap between Ashkenazi, Mizrahi and Palestinian women
remains intact. As Yaish writes, 'Ashkenazi Jews continue to be the
dominant group within Israel. The Mizrahis, while better off than
Palestinians, continue to have poorer prospects in the economic
sphere than Ashkenazi Jews' (Yaish 2001: 420–21).

Although studies that apply the concept of ethnicity rather than
racialization as analytical category are somewhat problematic, their
integration of class as an important factor in income disparities makes
them a more credible source for understanding women's status in
the labour force. Nevertheless, the largely quantitative nature of the
approach taken in most such studies underestimates the role gender
differentiation plays. For example, how can such studies justify the
fact that within the same 'religio-ethnic' group of Druze, males are
found to do much better than male Muslim or Christian workers
while female Druze are found at the bottom of the income ladder?
Male Druze service in the Israeli military, as Levanon and Raviv
(2007) point out, is one contributing factor to higher income for
males, but what are the social, cultural and economic circumstances
that place Druze women in such a low position?[11]

Most progressive economic studies confirm the presence of significant income gaps in favour of Jews, especially Ashkenazi women. For
example, one study found that Arab citizens earned, on average, 75
per cent of the income earned by Mizrahi Jews, whereas Ashkenazi
Jews earned 135 per cent of the income obtained by Mizrahi women.
In other words, for every NIS 100 (new Israeli shekels) an Ashkenazi
worker earns, a Mizrahi Jew will earn NIS 74.1, and an Arab worker
will earn NIS 55.6 (Adva 2004). Such figures have not improved;
rather, the disparities have widened further since then. A 1999 Adva
study concluded that the average wage for all women in Israel was
NIS 4,917, whereas it was NIS 7,999 for all men (Adva 1999). Almost
all studies comparing women's and men's income corroborate these
findings, suggesting that women's income in Israel is, on average,

significantly lower than that of their male counterparts both within their own communities and across ethnic, racial and national bases (Haberfeld and Cohen 2006; Khattab 2005). Nonetheless, gender in studies in this vein is neither racialized nor ethnicized, especially within the category of Jewish women. As for the differentiation between Jewish and Palestinian women, most studies corroborate the fact that Arab women face triple exploitation on the basis of their gender, ethnicity/race and female role within their own patriarchal Arab society.

In terms of type of job and of job quality, studies have found that male and female Jews have higher representation in the more lucrative occupations, which explains in part why their incomes are generally higher. Jewish women are typically found in higher ranked jobs than Arab women. A large number of Jewish women (44 per cent) occupy managerial and clerical occupations, compared with only 23 per cent of Palestinian women; 29 per cent of Arab women are reported to be working in the skilled and unskilled work categories, while 14 per cent of Jewish women are represented there; Arab women are over-represented (25 per cent) in skilled manual labour, compared to only 6 per cent among Jewish women (Khattab 2002: Table 1). An earlier study conducted by Semyonov and Lewis-Epstein suggested that Arab women tend to be overly represented in semi-professional jobs, which includes teaching, nursing or social work. Some 63 per cent of Arab women work in these sectors. As mentioned earlier, such employment represents a type of work that mirrors that performed by Palestinian women in the domestic realm (Semyonov and Lewin-Epstein 1994: 58).

Palestinian women and men have poorer economic prospects than do Jewish Israelis. This is due in part to the general de-development of the Arab sector brought about by Israeli policies of land con-fiscation, and in part to the untenable competitive conditions and difficulties Palestinians encounter in the Jewish market. Palestinian women's poor economic prospects, combined with their low-level labour force participation, have a direct impact on family income and well-being. This reality is also a factor affecting the differences between Jewish and Arab workers' labour force drop-out rates. For example, studies which examined the impact of age, education, marital status and unemployment on the labour force participation of Jewish and Arab males found that such variables affect Jewish and Arab males differently (Sa'di and Lewin-Epstein 2001). Sa'di and Lewin-Epstein's findings also suggest that married Arab males are less likely than Jews to drop out of the labour market, as more Jewish than Arab females are employed; their husbands can therefore rely on them economically. The authors' study, which illustrates the precarious employment situation of Arabs in Israel, argues that 'Arab unemployment is usually the result of structural factors beyond their control, whereas Jewish unemployment is more frequently the result of an individual choice', and that Arab workers are 'often used during periods of high unemployment as shock absorbers for the Jewish workforce' (Sa'di and Lewin-Epstein 2001: 784). Moreover, longitudinal studies that examine mobility in terms of opportunity and access to resources have found that male Palestinian and Ashkenazi Jews have similar opportunity patterns, whereas Mizrahi Jews are most likely to experience downward mobility (Yaish 2001).

Discrimination against Arab workers does not necessarily benefit all Jews. In their 1990 study of income differentials between various groups in Israel, Semyonov and Cohen found that, starting from the fact that the Jews in Israel are a superordinate group and Palestinians the subordinate, not all Jews benefit from the exploitation of indigenous Palestinians. Discrimination against Arab workers, they believe, serves to intensify inequality among Jewish workers. In short, their study found that only those at the upper end of the economic spectrum among Jews (frequently Ashkenazis) benefit from discrimination against Arab workers, while other disadvantaged Jewish workers, including Mizrahis, are more negatively affected by this discriminatory process. Exploitation of Palestinian Arabs, which places them in a pool of cheap labour power, undoubtedly affects the wages paid to workers in the same pool, namely in the of construction trade as well as other forms of manual labour. This enables the employer to bargain for equally cheap or cheaper labour power from among other available Jews, for example Russians. It also opens the way to further exploitation of migrant labour, especially that from Asian countries (Semyonov and Cohen 1990: 109–10).

Authors using the Weberian notion of social status, which is largely confined to income and fails to take into consideration class and race, risk slipping into a simplistic analysis. For example, Khattab's conclusion that 'the most important predictor of income had become class and that ethnicity did not have a major effect on women's monthly income, as they were simply less likely to make a lot of money' (2005: 4) is only partially true. The author clearly shows that Mizrahi females made on average considerably less money than Ashkenazi females. However, although Mizrahi women's rate of labour force participation partially accounts for this, the fact is that their class position and their status as a racialized or ethnicized group play an important role in their overall economic performance. The same argument applies to Palestinian women's status in the labour force.

Again, all the studies cited agree that Jewish citizens have an economic advantage (through class location or otherwise) over Arab citizens. However, close scrutiny of the category 'Jewish' suggests that Ashkenazi Jews are the dominant group, followed by Mizrahis. To the latter category, one must also add the basically non-Jewish migrant labour that has become a major part of the cheap labour force, especially since the mid- to late 1990s, particularly among Asian migrants. Nevertheless, even though Mizrahi women citizens have the economic advantage over Palestinian citizens, they have poorer prospects than Ashkenazi women. Finally, sticking with the segmentation of the female population as given in the economic literature, the case is often made that, on the one hand, Mizrahi Jews are more likely to experience downward mobility than Arabs (Yaish 2001), while among Palestinians it is observed that female Christians occupy a better economic position than Muslims and Druze. Palestinian Christian women are perceived as possessing higher levels of capital, including human and cultural capital (e.g. Khattab 2005).

Nonetheless, almost all studies which account for women in their analysis corroborate the fact that, on average, women's wages are significantly lower than that of their male counterparts. In a recent study, Moore (2006) argues that the majority of women are employed in the public sphere, especially in the service industry, which limits their potential for growth in terms of development of their human and social capitals, as these are essentially dead-end jobs that provide no future. This fact has also resulted in 'women's lower earning capacity, estimated at 60 to 80 per cent of men's earning' (Moore 2006: 1924). Swirski and Konor-Attias's study (2007) confirms such findings. According to them,

> while approximately one quarter of Arab and Jewish workers are in the lowest wage level, significant differences are present among the top wage earners: 1.1 per cent of Jewish but only 0.3 per cent of Arab workers fall into the group of highest wage earners. Among Jews, 22.3 per cent of second generation Mizrahi Jews (that is, whose fathers were born in Asia or Africa) earn the lowest salaries, compared with 17.7 per cent of second generation Ashkenazi Jews, and 2.8 per cent of second generation Ashkenazi Jews earn the highest level of wages, compared with only 0.6 per cent of second generation Mizrahi Jews. (Swirski and Konor-Attias 2007: 22)

A gender perspective on the employment of women shows a much larger gap in terms of the proportion of women occupying low-wage positions vis-à-vis high-wage-earning brackets. Based on the income survey of 2005, Swirski and Konor-Attias report that more women (35.8 per cent) than men are in the low-wage category, while fewer women than men are found to be in the high-wage category. As for Arab men and women, more of both are found in the low-wage category than Jews, yet again with gender differentiation to the advantage of Arab men (2007: 23).

As shown in Table 3.1, Ashkenazi women are heavily represented in the high-wage occupations such as the academic, professional and managerial sectors, and are least engaged in the skilled and unskilled fields of agriculture, manufacture and construction. On the other hand, Palestinian women are more concentrated in the mid-level occupations, such as clerical work, sales and service jobs compared to Ashkenazi women, and over-represented in the skilled and unskilled

TABLE 3.1   Female occupation by ethnic group (%)

	Academic, professional and managerial	Clerical, sales and service	Skilled and unskilled workers in agriculture, manufacturing and construction
Other religions	34.2	40.6	24.7
Born in Israel			
Father born in Europe-America	53.5	41.9	4.2
Father born in Asia-Africa	31.6	59.6	8.2
Father born in Israel	44.3	51.0	3.6
All Jews	38.7	50.4	10.9

Note: This table is based on the 2003 Man Power Survey (ADVA 2007: 23). It should be noted here that category 'other religions' refers to Muslim Christian and Druze as well as non-Arab Christians (sic). Palestinians, in other words have turned into groups of religious sects gathered there accidentally!

jobs as compared to both Mizrahi and Ashkenazi women. The table also points to the important fact that among Mizrahis, second-generation women (those born to fathers born in Israel) fare much better than those of the first generation (born to fathers born in the Arab world). This is an indication of a change in the historical state of subordination experienced by this people.[12]

In terms of income and status, female Israeli citizens in general, as demonstrated here, occupy less important jobs than men and are less represented in lucrative jobs. However, most studies also confirm, directly or indirectly, that ethnicity and race are the major reasons for their exploitation. Palestinian women, most agree, are at the bottom of the ladder in all areas in terms of labour force participation: they fare much worse than their male counterparts (gender discrimination); they rank much lower in comparison to Ashkenazi and Mizrahi Jewish women (racial discrimination); and as workers in a developed capitalist economy they are often found at the bottom of the ladder (class discrimination) (Adva 1999; Swirski 2006; Haberfeld and Cohen 2007; Khattab 2005; Report 2006). Second to Palestinian women in terms of lower status are found Mizrahi women, who also fare worse than their male counterparts as well as in comparison to Ashkenazi women in general.

To solidify further the secondary data outlined above and to provide a better understanding of women's overall economic situation, I undertook a statistical analysis. This analysis presents women's labour force situation, taking into consideration a number of variables, such as level of education, ethnicity, nationality and age. The analysis is based on raw data collected by the International Social Survey Program (ISSP 1997), which gathers data on demographics, socio-economic conditions, employment status/position, and income. The sample was drawn from Israeli citizens aged 18 and over, both male and female. Altogether, 1,037 Jews and 496 Palestinians were selected for this survey. As with all official Israeli statistics, the ISSP also presents Palestinians as three separate religious groups.[13]

According to this survey (Table 3.2), Jewish Ashkenazis have, on average, the highest level of education; 36.8 per cent of respondents had a complete university education. In contrast, the figure for Mizrahi Jews is 9.2 per cent, and for Palestinians only 3.0 per cent. The ISSP data on Israel, largely based on Israeli official statistics, provides information on educational differences within Palestinian Arabs in Israel. An examination of this data suggests that Christian women were found to have the highest rate of education, at 5.7 per cent, while the Druze had the lowest at 0 per cent.

Unlike the studies cited above, data from the ISSP also indicate that more Jewish Ashkenazi women, 34.9 per cent, were employed full-time as compared to Mizrahi women, reported at 31 per cent, while Palestinian women were placed a distant third, at only 15.4 per cent. This analysis also found that the majority of Palestinian women, estimated at 52.3 per cent, were housewives and/or assisted family members. Not surprisingly, statistics here also corroborate

TABLE 3.2   Frequency distributions for dependent
and independent variables, by ethnicity (%)

	Jewish Ashkenazi	Jewish Mizrahi	Palestinian
	(n=135)	(n=89)	(n=199)
Age			
18–44 years	44.4	29.9	84.0
45–64 years	31.6	59.8	13.6
65 and older	24.1	10.3	1.5
Education			
Primary or less	7.5	32.2	27.6
Incomplete secondary	12.0	17.2	17.2
Secondary completed	36.8	37.9	40.7
Incomplete university	6.8	3.4	9.5
University completed	36.8	9.2	3.0
Occupation			
Armed forces/protective work	2.6	1.4	0
Senior official/management	5.2	5.6	2.0
Architect/engineer/sciences	6.1	1.4	0
Writer/artist	0	0	0
Health professional/nursing	13.8	2.8	2.0
Schoolteacher	5.2	5.6	13.9
Other teaching	4.3	4.2	1.0
Entertainment/sports	0	0	2.0
Electrical/mechanical/chemical	1.8	4.2	0
Secretary/government assistant	6.1	7.0	7.9
Numerical/office/client info clerk	16.3	12.6	10.9
Cashier/teller/sales	13.8	10.0	12.9
Textiles/garments	0.9	2.8	16.9
Travel attendant	1.7	0	0

	Jewish Ashkenazi (n=135)	Jewish Mizrahi (n=89)	Palestinian (n=199)
Domestic helper/personal care	19.0	38.0	20.8
Manufacture labourer	0.9	1.4	4.0
Employment status			
Full-time	34.9	29.8	15.4
Part-time	22.2	17.9	13.3
Unemployed	5.6	6	2.1
Student vocational training	1.6	0	15.9
Housewife/help family member	5.6	31.0	52.3
Permanently disabled	2.4	2.4	1.0
Earnings			
No income	7.1	0	5.5
Up to 2,000 NIS	21.4	28.2	47.3
2001–6000 NIS	65.8	61.5	47.3
6001–10,000 NIS	4.3	7.7	7.7
10,000 NIS or more	1.4	2.6	0

other figures putting Palestinian women's rate of participation in the educational sector above the other two population categories: 13.9 per cent for Palestinian women compared to 5.6 per cent among Mizrahi and 5.2 per cent among Ashkenazi Jewish women.

In the area of income and earnings, both Ashkenazi and Mizrahi Jewish women had, on average, higher incomes than Palestinian females. Palestinian women in general demonstrate a significant income disadvantage compared to other populations of women. For example, more Palestinian women were found in the low income bracket of up to NIS 2,000 per month (47.3 per cent), compared to Mizrahi Jewish women estimated at 28.2 per cent, while Ashkenazi Jewish women were at 21.4 per cent. In this same category, it was also found that Druze women had the lowest average income, with 100.0 per cent of respondents from this group reporting an income of NIS 2,000 or less, placing them at or under the poverty line.

In general, these statistics suggest that women across all ethnic/ religious groups, with the exception of the Druze, are mostly employed as domestic helpers/personal care workers. The most common occupation for Druze women was work in the textile/garment industry (50 per cent). The second most common occupation for Jewish Ashkenazi, Mizrahi and Arab Christian women was that of clerk, at 16.3 per cent, 12.6 per cent and 26.1 per cent respectively. For Druze women, the second most common occupation was found to be that of secretary/government assistant (25 per cent),[14] and for Muslim women it was schoolteacher (18.2 per cent). Moreover, Jewish women of both ethnicities (Mizrahi and Ashkenazi) tended to have higher representation in the professional occupations, such as health care, management, and science and technology, than did Palestinian Arab women. Nevertheless, the most glaring disparity between the three categories of women is found in terms of their respective representation in lower-level occupations. For example, in the textile industry, as seen in Table 3.2, we find a high representation rate of Palestinian women, at 19.6 per cent, followed by Mizrahi women at 2.8 per cent; Ashkenazi women come a distant third in this industry at only 0.9 per cent. This is another indication as to who avoids the most exploitative jobs and for whom such occupations are generally reserved.

Palestinian women in the 'apartheid' Arab economy

There is a new consensus that the enclave or mono-ethnic labour market is more advantageous to Palestinian women than is the 'bi-ethnic' (Jewish) labour market. The former market, some argue, provides women with equal treatment in terms of job opportunities, reduces or eliminates competition with Jews, and dispenses with the problem of commuting to Jewish towns (Semyonov and Lewin-Epstein 1994: 53). In fact, Khattab (2002) suggests that the enclave or racially segregated Arab economy is preferred by Palestinians over the bi-ethnic market because it reduces women's exploitation and discrimination and 'contributes to better human capital for women' (2002: 95). It is not clear how these authors arrive at such conclusions. On the one hand, and as already mentioned, female work in the racially segregated Arab market is not free of exploitation. On the other hand, the nature of women's employment, as described above, is an extension of their domestic experience and so is no guarantee of the development of women's human and social capital.

More importantly, such arguments seem to be more driven by culturalist concerns than properly contextualized in terms of time and place. Thus, when trying to explain what they mean by suggesting that the mono-ethnic market provides a 'safe place' for Palestinian women's human capital development, one author cites concepts such as 'traditions', 'culture' and 'family values' (Khattab 2002, 2005). Palestinian patriarchal culture and the family are often presented as the major hurdle for women's public labour participation. The mono-ethnic or enclave market, it is argued, provides employment for Arab women who wish to conform to their cultural norms (Semyonov and Lewin-Epstein 1994: 56; Khattab 2002, 2005).

Whilst the authors whose positions are described in the previous paragraph emphasize the 'social safety' that mono-ethnic market space provides for female workers, they are not oblivious of the fact that this racially segregated space is not free from political or government intervention. This intervention is often a negative one, resulting in more hardship and hurdles placed in the way of Arab employment, especially in so far as women are concerned. This is because a large proportion of the jobs provided within this economy are controlled by the government; this is particularly true of the education sector, which is still highly controlled by the government at almost every level, from the appointment of teachers to the kind of curriculum taught, the presence or lack of equipment, and so forth. Particularly significant in the area of job opportunities in this economy are the presence, quantity and quality of resources allocated by the state for the Arab sector.

One of the primary factors in this regard is government neglect and the almost total absence of state investment in the economic development of the Palestinian community (Raijman and Semyonov 1997). The racially segregated economy, most studies confirm, has very limited job opportunities and lacks high-tech jobs, being characterized by government under-resourcing relative to the Jewish sector (Khattab 2003). Comparing the Arab villages in the Galilee with the recently established Jewish settlement of Lavon on confiscated Arab land, Schechla notes that the Jewish settlement has only two families and yet enjoys all conceivable civic facilities courtesy of the Misgav Regional Council; the Arab village in the vicinity, with about 2,000 inhabitants, has no such facilities (Schechla 2001: 26). According to a 2005 report by the UN Economic and Social Council (ECOSOC):

> Instead of creating equal access to employment and increasing the participation of Palestinians in the work force, the Government has, inter alia, delayed planning processes; prevented designating budgets to establish industrial zones and new neighbourhoods and did not encourage accessibility to transportation. (ECOSOC 2005: 4)

The Orientalist, racist approach advocated by the state towards Palestinian women and their so-called 'backward families', as indicated in the government's Five Year Plan of 2000 (Dichter 2001), is paramount. This plan placed the blame for Palestinian women's low level of labour force participation on their own culture and families. In the preamble to the proposed plan, government officials expressed their 'concern' with the 'Arab sector' and especially 'Arab women' in the most racist, Orientalist fashion. The first draft of the Five Year Plan proposed improvement of the lot of Palestinian citizens, and in reference to Arab women the authors viewed their mission as one of 'civilization', aimed at supposedly redeeming women from their secluded, isolated and closeted families, considered plagued by 'omnipresent clan warfare'. Commenting on the draft plan, Dichter has the following to say: 'Tenets of the plan published in June 2000 relied on a superficial, stereotyped perception of Arab society, as if they'd been taken from books by [Zionist] Arabists of the 1940s' (Dichter 2001: 4). On the same theme, Dichter further notes:

It emerges that the basic assumptions on which the plan rests are taken from a conceptual world that doesn't reflect reality. According to the description in the booklet, Arab society keeps women closeted away from the outside world; the family-based social structure is completely pervasive with 'clan warfare'; the motivation of men who build their sons a home on the family plot of land is merely their own self-aggrandizement; and similar colourful descriptions. (Dichter 2001: 5)

Commenting on the conclusion to one chapter of the plan, he observes:

The plan puts at centre stage population groups that have hitherto been pushed to the sidelines: [Palestinian] women and children. The implication is that development plans involving a wealth of resources have, until very recently, been focused on the wellbeing of Arab men! Alas, it isn't so. (Dichter 2001: 8)

Dichter finds the racist tone of this plan particularly objectionable:

Would, for example, any decision-maker ever take it into his head to suggest making the budget for public housing or education for the ultra-Orthodox sector conditional on having Haredi women remove their head coverings, or on discontinuing the practice of arranged marriages? (Dichter 2001: 9)

While an increasing number of authors like Dichter have become more sensitive to the intentionally marginalized reality of the Palestinians, the majority of economic studies on Palestinian female force participation, as shown above, continue to perceive the traditional family and low educational achievement as major reasons for the scarcity of women's employment. Yet the lived experiences of Palestinians in the geographically and spatially, socially and economically, segregated area or 'sector' tell a more complex story with regard to why women are not active in the labour force.

Historically Palestinian women (and men) were actively involved in economic production as peasants and agricultural workers, but since the establishment of the state and the implementation of large-scale land confiscation, Palestinians have been left with less than 2.5

per cent of the land; through expropriation, most Palestinians were separated from their primary source of production and income and so proletarianized. But proletarianization, unlike in the English case of capitalist development where the creation of a wage-labour force was needed for the development of capitalist industry, Palestinian peasants lost their sources of income from agricultural land and were not necessarily absorbed in the Israeli industrial sector. In fact, the state showed little or no interest in developing the Arab sector; indeed, if anything this sector has been and continues to be largely de-developed. Thus, although over a million Palestinians live in the Arab sector, not a single large branch of any ministry has been built there. The fact that all ministries and most public offices are located within the Jewish sector further limits Palestinian women's access to government employment. Labour market figures provided for 2004 on the percentage of jobseekers in terms of localities in Israel place the overwhelming majority of Palestinian localities within the highest rates of unemployment, between 9.5 and 36.7 per cent, with the Bedouins at the higher end of the range. Jobseekers in Jewish localities are placed within the range of 11 per cent (almost the highest rate reached by Jewish localities) to 0.4 per cent (Swirski and Konor-Attias 2004: 20).

Discriminatory policies operating with respect to budget allocations to Arab local municipalities and village councils are another force that affects employment resources and impedes labour force participation, causing shortage in demand and also resulting in low salaries and wages paid to local Palestinian workers. Insufficient budgetary allotments for Arab towns and village councils, combined with an absence of city planning to demarcate town borders, serve to impede the development of infrastructure and roads, exacerbating the problem of labour accessibility. While it is true that, due to their spatial segregation, Palestinian women working in the apartheid market are seen as having the advantage of not competing with their fellow Jewish women, the structural conditions within which they work constitute major hurdles limiting their employment opportunities and lowering their income. A 2001 survey conducted in fifty

villages and towns with the lowest average monthly wages revealed
that forty-eight of these were Palestinian towns and villages, with
women earning a monthly average wage of NIS 3,191, far less than
the average monthly wage of women in Israel, estimated for the same
year at NIS 5,835 (Swirski and Konor-Attias 2004: 15).

The average wage of Arab women in Israel has not changed by
much in recent years; in 2008 it was estimated at 47 per cent lower
than that of Jewish women. More than half earn the minimum wage
or less, compared with one-third of Jewish women (Schwartz and
Agbarieh-Zahalka 2008:2).

The situation is not very different for Palestinians employed in
Israeli ministries. For example, a 2000 survey of the employees of
fifteen ministries in Israel reveals that the percentage of Palestinian
employees in such ministries ranges between 0 and 6.3 per cent.
Whereas the 0 per cent Palestinian employment figure refers to the
Ministry of Media and Communications, the maximal 6.3 per cent
figure refers to employees within the Ministry of Religion – and these
are civil servants, not employees of the Ministry proper. Palestinian
citizens' employment was distributed as follows: five ministries employed less than 1 per cent Palestinian Arab citizens; three employed
between 2 and 3 per cent; five employed between 2.4 to 2.8 per
cent, and one (the Ministry of Health, which includes employees
in all hospitals) employed 6.3 per cent Palestinian citizens.[15] Such
low representation of Palestinian citizens in the civil service has not
changed much over the years. *Targeted Citizen* (2010), a documentary
made by Adalah, suggests that Palestinian Arabs represent only 6
per cent of the civil servants in Israel, of which only 2 per cent are
women. Another finding on the dismal Palestinian representation in
high-quality jobs in the Jewish market reveals that Arabs employed
in government companies are 0.5 per cent of the total labour force.
In universities, there are 64 Arab lecturers, representing only 1.4
per cent of total faculty; while 6.7 per cent of the total number of
college lecturers are Arabs. Only 1.8 per cent of the total labour force
in the high-tech sector are Arabs, while in mobile phone industries
they make up 7.8 per cent of all employees.[16]

The absence of even a single Palestinian citizen employee in the Ministry of Media and Communication up to the year 2000 is particularly alarming, considering the fact that this is the ministry that frames public discourse on Israeli citizenship; the exclusion of Palestinian citizens from this arena for over half a century has left them excluded from public discourse. As already mentioned, Palestinians in the civil service generally fill professional positions involving the provision of health, welfare, education and religious services. A large concentration in the service sector not only explains their low wages but also speaks volumes about their absence from positions of power and decision-making. The absence of adequate professional government jobs or major industrial enterprises in the Arab sector means that women must commute to Jewish towns or settlements to find jobs. But even if they are willing to travel for jobs their chances of finding positions remain slim. The survey conducted on Arab academic women quoted earlier found that around 40 per cent of Arab female academics, most of whom are young, remain unemployed (Awwad 2007: 16).

The scarcity of government services such as affordable daycare and subsidized kindergartens in Arab towns, and their near non-existence in the villages makes travelling even harder for married women with children. The agricultural sector is a prime example here, where only deep poverty and lack of alternatives will bring a married, unskilled Palestinian woman to seek a job. Agriculture, which once provided jobs for Palestinian women without profes-sional skills, until after the foundation of the state, has changed drastically. Whereas in 1948, 90 per cent of Palestinians lived from farming, the figure today is 4 per cent. 'Of the 50,000 farm employ-ees in Israel today, about half are migrants, mostly from Thailand. Deep in debt on arrival and lacking organization, the Thais work for less than the legal minimum (a result of shady record-keeping), do not receive social benefits, and live on the job site' (Schwartz and Agbarieh-Zahalka 2008:3).

Work in agricultural Arab villages, as is the case in the textile industry, studied earlier, is largely done though 'local subcontractors, who transport the women to work and collect their wages, from which they skim around 40%. There is rarely a salary slip, not to mention benefits. The workers wind up with 80 to 100 shekels for an eight-hour day – that's about $20 to $25 – instead of the legal minimum of 160 shekels' (Schwartz and Agbarieh-Zahalka 2008: 4). Such working conditions are not suitable for unskilled women with children.

The depleted infrastructure in Palestinian towns, and especially in villages, and the lack of basic services such as daycare and kinder-gartens, are another reason for women's reluctance to look for a job away from home. Figures provided by the Ministry of Social Affairs for 2003 show that,

> of the 1,600 day care centres in Israel for children aged 0–3 who attend publically subsidized day care centres or house care programs, only 25 centres operate in Arab villages. Out of approxi-mately 80,000 children aged 0–3 who attend publically subsidized day care centres or house care programs, only 4,200 of them are Arab children. (cited in Espanyoli 1997: 34)

These figures must be seen in the light of the fact that Palestinian children constitute 26 per cent of all children in Israel, yet comprise only 5.25 per cent of those receiving daycare services (Adalah 2005: 29).

Women's public participation can be negatively affected by the family, a constraint especially for married women with young children. Children, however, are not the only impediment to Pal-estinian women's employment. Unemployment is also widespread among single women with university degrees, as the following discussion will show. The dire economic need in which most Palestinian citizens find themselves has tipped the scales at the educational level. Thus, in contrast to the traditional patriarchal family norms that prioritized the education of males over that of females – a choice based on economic considerations – recent sta-tistics suggest that almost half of all Palestinian university students are females.

Women, Poverty and the Family

As the above discussion has shown, Palestinian Arab women and Arab Jewish and Mizrahi women in theory share a great deal with other Arab or Middle Eastern women in terms of the roles of patriarchy, the family and religion, yet the former women's historically specific situations within the Zionist state make their citizenship experiences quite different from the others. To overemphasize familial relations as a major determinant of Palestinian and Mizrahi women's citizenship status, as do Swirski (2000) and Joseph (2000), does these women no justice. Although nation-states, including Israel, view the family as an important unit or institution for the survival and reproduction of the nation, as Yuval-Davis argues (1997), in the context of the Jewish state this applies to the Jewish family only (and basically to the preferred Ashkenazi family). Palestinian women citizens are not nationals in Israel. In the case of Palestinians, the main antagonism resides in the relationship between the state, on the one hand, and Palestinians (families and individuals), on the other, an antagonism characteristic of settler-colonial regimes – between the colonial state and the colonized subjects. Mizrahi women do not necessarily see themselves as belonging to the Zionist project or as part of Israeli 'Jewishness', any more than do Palestinian citizens, whose national identity is denied by the 'nation-state'. In fact, Palestinian citizens find themselves in a constant struggle with the state just to confirm and legitimate their national identity.

While Israel is concerned with women's reproductive activities and demographic growth, this concern only pertains to Jewish citizens. As for its Palestinian citizens, Israel has always systemically and systematically employed policies and practices aimed at curbing their demographic growth (Bannerji 2004). The processes that govern the relationship between the Palestinian family and the state are political and ideological within a colonial framework, wherein the state continuously tries to control and manage their demographic growth and geographical space. Thus, in addition to the various means used by the state, such as house demolition, land confiscation, denial of building permits and so on, other devices, such as citizenship entitlement, are also deployed to target this group. This is particularly true in terms of the relationship between Palestinian women's family, their labour force participation, the state and (primarily Jewish) employers. The following example, which relates to women employed in the textile industry, is presented in some detail to highlight the intricate and complex gendered relationship between the state and the Palestinian family.

Until the early 1990s and prior to the influx of Russian and other migrant labourers, the textile industry constituted a major source of work for thousands of Palestinian women. By the early 1990s, over 600 small textile plants and sweatshops had been built in Arab villages in the north, especially in Druze villages in Galilee. Work in the textile industry, which was established in the segregated Arab sector, constituted a special form of overexploitation and marginalization for Arab (especially Druze) women. To begin with, in all of the small textile plants and sweatshops, the managerial positions were largely held by Jewish men, while Palestinian men functioned basically as middlemen who were subcontracted by larger firms owned by either Jewish or Arab capitalists. By the early 1990s, Palestinian women working in the industry were estimated at about 33 per cent of the entire Israeli labour force in this sector (Espanyoli 1997: 36).

An ethnographic study of a number of these sewing plants in Galilee employing about 6,000 workers in the early 1990s classified as 'Arab' and 'Druze' women (as Arabs are largely seen by Israeli official accounts as Muslims) reveals the way in which labour relations were structured around what the author of the study refers to as the 'traditional Arab family and village' values (Drori 2000: 32). All workers and some floor supervisors in the plants were Palestinian women, while most owners, managers and some supervisors were Jewish men. Local Palestinian men, often members of the same family as female employees, were brought in as workforce recruiters; they also functioned as drivers for the female employees, ferrying them to and from work. In this system, male Arab family members (fathers, husbands, brothers) ensured total control over female workers' movements. This was coupled with constant supervision, as the women workers were placed under the 'protection' and surveillance of men of their own community who were often hired by the plant managers. As most female plant workers were not adequately represented by the Histadrut or by Na'amat, its women's affiliate, they had to complain directly to the Jewish plant manager when grievances arose. In one letter of complaint about working conditions, 90 workers in a plant employing 180 Palestinian women citizens had the following to say:

> We, the undersigned, work in a sewing plant owned by you. We are writing to you to bring to your attention the terrible working conditions we face. In our plant work 180 workers, most with seniority of over five years. We work in terrible conditions and feel we are being taken advantage of. We are made to work many overtime hours as well as Fridays, in spite of the fact that our working day is already nine hours long. Our production quotas are high compared to the rest of the industry and we work rapidly. Still we have high motivation and work ethic. Sir, what we get in return is not what we deserve. We do not receive the legal minimum wage, but much less, and we are not appropriately compensated for our overtime. We are forced to work on holidays, sometimes without adequate pay. We do not receive decent uniforms. What we get are reprimands and threats. Sir, we are still human, we cannot accept this situation. We demand action to repair this damage without delay. (cited in Drori 2000: 189–90)

Managers in these plants intervened in every aspect of women's lives, including in personal matters. They also prevented workers from taking sick leave by bribing the village doctor. Drori, the ethnographer, quotes one manager, who said: 'I visit the doctor occasionally and make sure to give him a nice package of underwear for him and his sons' (2000: 118). In reference to the 'phenomenon' of worker absences due to illness, which managers tried to prevent, Drori comments that the manager

> tries to curtail the phenomenon by speaking to the families or personally going to the sick woman and pleading with her to work. In one of the plants, for example, the manager attempted to

curtail his workers' frequent absences by coming to an agreement with the village doctor to strengthen his criteria for illness. (2000: 115)

Although most of the plants have been closed down and relocated to other countries with cheaper labour power, especially Jordan and Egypt – after the signing of the Oslo Accords – but also Romania and China, the fact of their existence and the way in which they were operated by primarily Jewish capitalists and employers with the assistance of Arab subcontractors, provides a vivid example of the manner in which the state, Jewish capitalists and employers, and the Palestinian male patriarchy utilize Palestinian traditional culture and patriarchal family values to control women both socially and economically. This example, in other words, confirms the collusion of capital and patriarchy in the exploitation of women and testifies to the overall racist structure of the Israeli state and institutions as they deal with indigenous Palestinians. The state in this example may have not been directly involved, but its silence and that of its institutions, expressed in the lack of concern in enforcing, for example, labour laws (e.g. involving the Histadrut and/or Na'amat services and regulations) makes both a party in the exploitation and oppression of Arab women. Such employment practices, rather than contributing to women's development, public visibility and market participation, which might lead to their emancipation, serve instead to reproduce women's marginality and inferiority, subjecting them to further control.

In the late 1990s, the structure of the Israeli economy changed drastically, and with it the status of Palestinian women workers. Whereas between the 1970s and the early 1990s most Arab women occupied unskilled jobs in the textile industry and in agriculture, subsequently both sectors became almost entirely closed off to them. Globalization and the further development of Israel's neoliberal economy resulted in Israel's increasing focus on the stock exchange and high tech, disposing in the meantime of the 'old economy' – and, with it, of jobs for Arab women. Globalization has not only seen transfer of textile plants to cheap-labour countries, as mentioned earlier, it has also seen the replacement of Palestinians in the service sector, especially in nursing care, by imported cheap Filipino and Filipina workers.

Global and local structural economic changes, discussed above, have affected the structure of the Palestinian labour force as well. As Schwartz and Agbarieh-Zahalqa (2008) found, 'of the minority with jobs, about 70% are independent professionals in education, health or social work, while most of the remaining 30% are non-professionals in industry, agriculture, cleaning and other services' (2008: 4).

Finally, it is worth noting that Histadrut and Na'amat (Histadrut's women's branch) were never involved in the manufacturing or agricultural sectors, which made it easier for employers to exploit their workers. The leaving out of account of this traditionally large sector of employed Arab women until the 1990s meant that the labour organizations and service providers needed to supply only a minimal level of services to them. For example, a study in the late 1990s found that Na'amat, which reportedly runs 828 early child-hood centres serving 22,224 children in Israel, established only 24 kindergartens in the Palestinian sector, serving just 468 Palestinian children. In Nazareth over 10,000 female workers are members of Na'amat, yet the organization runs only one kindergarten in the city, which has a population of over 60,000 Palestinians (Espanyoli 1997: 38). As Espanyoli notes, dues paid by Palestinian workers are often 'siphoned off to serve and develop the Jewish sector, leaving the Palestinian sector underdeveloped', adding that 'in an annual budget estimated at NIS 72,488,000 in 1992, Na'amat spent only NIS 920,000 on activities in the Palestinian sector, or just 6.66 per cent' (Espanyoli 1997: 38).

With Palestinian women's low level of participation in the labour force, their confinement to the less developed (often de-developed) apartheid market, and their high levels of unemployment, it is little surprise that poverty among this group of citizens is recorded as the highest among all sectors of the Israeli population. A report published in 2004 by the Israeli Central Bank on the Palestinian citizens of Israel shows that half of the families are poor. Poverty among Palestinian families in Israel reached 64.2 per cent in 2003 (in Swirski and Konor-Attias 2004: 20). While overall poverty among Palestinians (especially women) is explained in part by unemployment, underemployment, low wages and other factors related to the economic realm, it is also the product of political processes involving discriminatory policies in other areas, such as social security entitlements accorded to Palestinian citizens. Of these, payroll deductions and income tax (e.g. child allowances, disability allowance and supplementary income) are justified by the state as being measures aimed at reducing poverty. Yet, as Swirski and Konor-Attias (2007) show, the high poverty levels among Palestinians, often calculated before deductions are made, are not positively affected by these deductions as the money collected is not redistributed to Palestinians. If anything, as one study monitoring poverty levels between 2003 and 2005 has found, the level of poverty among Palestinians – before deductions – was calculated to be 1.86 times greater than among Jews; after deductions, poverty levels jumped to 3.31 times greater than among Jewish families (Swirski and Konor-Attias 2007: 65).[17] The authors also establish a relationship between payroll deductions and poverty levels, suggesting that 'after payroll deductions, half of the Jewish families are extricated from the poverty, 44 per cent of Jewish individuals and one third of Jewish children, compared to 18.5 per cent of Arab families, 18 per cent of Arab individuals, and 15 per cent of children' (Swirski and Konor-Attias 2007: 67). This continuing discrepancy in poverty levels between Palestinian and Jewish families is partly due to the high rate of unemployment among Arabs, which, on the one hand, deprives them of adequate pension and other government stipends, and, on the other, forces them to depend more on transfer payments (more than half of the Palestinians depend on national insurance allowances). On the other hand, Jewish families have access to income from state and other private Jewish funding sources, to which Palestinians have no claim. An earlier study by the same authors emphasized this point, indicating that the income of a Palestinian Arab family from employment – after entitlements – is estimated at NIS 5,277, compared to

NIS 9,275 for a Jewish family, while the total pre-tax family income for an Arab family reaches NIS 7,363, compared to that of a Jewish family at NIS 11,978 (Swirski and Konor-Attias 2004: 65).

Unlike in the case of Jewish citizens, economic entitlements for Palestinian citizens are politically and ideologically motivated. The stringent bureaucratic procedures for applying for and receiving un-employment insurance benefits are one of the factors that leads many Arab workers, especially women, to give up seeking this source of income. Abject poverty, characteristic of the Palestinian family in Israel, creates a particular dynamic in which the relationship between education and labour force participation becomes a dialectical one rather than the one-way route of influence, as argued in the various studies cited above. Poverty forces young children, primarily boys, to drop out of school and seek additional income to support their families. A study conducted in 2002 suggests that the Palestinian labour force is much younger than the Jewish, with 62 per cent falling within the age range of 15 to 34, compared to 40 per cent among Jews; among female Palestinian citizens, the highest rate of labour force participation is between the ages of 25 and 34 (Yaffe and Tal 2002: 10).

Widespread poverty, along with racially separated markets, economies and residential spaces, combined with a long history of structural and institutional discrimination and marginalization create an environment conducive to the maintenance of 'traditional' family values, patriarchal norms and the existing gender division of labour, which favour early marriage and define women's role as the keeper of the household and the primary carer of the children. This is also the context for prioritizing male higher education over female in the name of parental security in old age, notwithstanding the fact that half of all Arab Palestinian university and college) students are now female (see next chapter).

Neither the institution of the family nor that of religion can be viewed as free-floating notions: they are tied to the economic structure prevailing in the society or country under discussion. For example, in the village of Jisr al-Zarqa, the most poverty-stricken Palestinian rural community in Israel, dire economic need has reversed the meaning of the terms 'public' and 'private', as many more women than men in the village are found in the public sphere of employment. In this village, which is just a few metres from the elite town of Caesarea, whose inhabitants are prevented from seeing the misery of the Palestinians courtesy of a 6 foot wall, the women are the main breadwinners. Here, although 75 per cent of the men are unemployed, some 30 per cent of the women do have jobs, which constitutes the highest rate of employed females among Palestinian communities, the average rate being 18.6 per cent. Despite the fact that women are the main providers in the village, their jobs have nevertheless been described as the least skilled, lowest paid and most boring: they clean the streets of Tel-Aviv, the universities, the hospitals, care homes for the aged, and banquet halls. Most of them earn less than the minimum wage, some less than half that, working eight hours a day – income which doesn't cover even their basic sustenance. Of a total female population of 12,000 in this village, 9,000 women, married and single, mothers and not, climb every morning at 5:30 a.m. into vans, returning home at about 5:00 p.m. to carry out their domestic chores (Schwartz and Agbarieh-Zahalka 2008: 2–3).

The reversal of gender roles in this village, nonetheless, has not necessarily redefined family patriarchy. Dire economic conditions tend to place more pressure on existing patriarchal structures, perpetuating and even strengthening traditional norms such as early marriage – most women in this village marry at 17 or even younger – and families continue to be large (Schwartz and Agbarieh-Zahalka 2008: 2–3).

The dynamic relationship between the family, religion and culture, and their impact on gender and women, as mentioned above, cannot be abstracted from the general socio-economic and political structure. Schwartz and Agbarieh-Zahalka (2008) succinctly capture this in their observation that

> the rise of conservatism on the Arab street is less the *cause* than the *result* of low workforce participation. The cause is the discrimina-tion and exclusion practiced against Arabs in all walks of life. Since the mid-1990s, moreover, the problem has been aggravated by

neoliberal economics and globalization. The new Israeli economy, focused on the stock exchange and high-tech, has disposed of the 'old economy' – and, with this, of jobs for Arab women. Their traditional sectors, namely textiles, agriculture and nursing-care, have vanished beneath their feet. (Schwartz and Agbarieh-Zahalka 2008: 5; emphasis in the original)

In the Israeli racist state, where a sizeable proportion of the indigenous population are considered not to be nationals and treated as undesired citizens, the presence of civil society organizations and NGOs is important. In the early 1990s a number of NGOs set out to improve the lot of Palestinians in Israel. This commitment has grown and the number of organizations expanded, so that women's economic, social and political conditions are now the focus of an increasing number of NGOs actively engaged in promoting women's rights in all areas, especially economic rights in general and the right to employment in particular. Of particular import here are two women's organizations and their projects that have made their mark in the area of women and employment: the women's section of Sawt el-Amel (the Labourer's Voice) and the recently established project on women and employment run by the Nazareth-based Women Against Violence Organization (WAVO). The women's section of Sawt el-Amel has been heavily involved with female agricultural workers, who are among the most exploited group. They hold public meetings and raise consciousness about this sector of the working population, visit workers in their work sites and take their complaints to employers. The public profile of this organization was raised when the group took on the case of Palestinian women involved in the Wisconsin plan, who were found to be enduring humiliating working conditions; Sawt el-Amel took their case to the United Nations and initiated a great deal of debate within Israel.[18] A second project, Women and Employment, run in conjunction with Palestinian academics, was initiated in 2005. In 2007, WAVO published their first research on academic employment/unemployment trends and labour conditions, and in 2010 held a conference on the topic and designed the first website on employment resources and opportunities for female academics.[19]

Excluded Citizenship

This chapter has delineated the historically specific conditions of Mizrahi women citizens living in a state that has not fully included them. This exclusion on the basis of their cultural background, and despite their ascribed status as Jews, has left them in a lower socio-economic position as compared to Ashkenazi women. A particular focus was on indigenous Palestinian women, whose overall economic position grants them a rather different and perhaps unique citizenship status. The specificity of Palestinian citizens in Israel makes it difficult to lump them in with the notion of 'Middle Eastern' women in general. Although issues of family and religion might be a factor in structuring gender relations in general, Palestinian women citizens' nationalism is not part of their nation-state, but rather antagonistic to it. The status of these women would be more comprehensible if placed within the relationship that characterises settler-colonial regimes: that between colonizer and colonized.

Finally, in the absence of feminist studies comparing the citizenship status of Palestinian, Mizrahi and Ashkenazi women, this chapter, like the rest of the book, aims to contribute to the debate on women's citizenship in the Middle East.

FOUR

Women's Citizenship, Education and Human Capital

EDUCATION IS CONSIDERED a basic right in most countries, but its scope in most developed democracies goes far beyond literacy. Education geared towards the development of human capital is what is sought in most states concerned with the advancement of science, technology and industry, creating in the process an improved state of well-being for those in possession. Developmental states are therefore capable of facilitating the development of women's – and men's – social capacity as well as access to political and economic resources in the public and private spheres, regardless of whether or not a woman chooses to be in the labour force. The concept of human capital has been used by various international human development organizations and United Nations bodies as an indicator for measuring the status of women. The United Nations Development Programme (UNDP) employs the concept of human capital in its recent *Arab Human Development Report* (2005) as a broad category to identify the socially deficient and marginal status of women in the Arab world, particularly in so far as their educational attainments and labour force participation are concerned.

Women's education and human capital in the context of the Arab world, while undoubtedly linked to structures and institutions such as the family, religion and the general social-cultural fabric of

Arab Palestinian (as well as Arab Jewish) society, is in large part an attribute of social class and status as well as race and ethnicity. Women's (and men's) education is intimately linked to the structures and institutions of the state within which they find themselves. Access and availability constitute major elements in the process of human capital development. This is particularly true for women (and girls), as they constitute the weakest link in any traditional society, let alone if they are members of a nation/collectivity that has historically been subjected to different forms of colonial rule. As this chapter will demonstrate, human capital for Mizrahi Jews has largely been underdeveloped, at least in the first two or three decades after the establishment of the State of Israel. As for Palestinians in general and women in particular, while education, even in the form of elementary literacy, was woefully underdeveloped in towns and almost non-existent in the villages in pre-Israel Palestine, in the last sixty years under the Israeli state it has been, to say the least, of an inferior character compared to Jewish education.

As with economic or labour force participation, discussed in the previous chapter, education in Israel is divided into two separate systems: a superior Jewish sector and an Arab racialized and inferior one. Abu-Usbeh (2006) identifies within the Jewish sector two schooling systems: one for the secular Jews and another for the ultra-Orthodox. Abu-Rabia-Queder identifies four separate systems: state-secular, state-religious, ultra-Orthodox and independent. Each enjoys control over the curriculum, its own budget and a distinct approach to decision-making. The Israeli state's multilayered approach to education among the Jews is not adopted for its Palestinian citizens. Abu-Rabia-Queder considers this absence a prime reason for the low level of education among Palestinian Bedouins in the Naqab (Abu-Rabia-Queder 2004: 3). The distinction between the schooling systems in the Arab and the Jewish sectors, officially justified as being geared to 'accommodate Arab traditional culture', is in reality designed with the 'purpose of serving the interests of the dominant Jewish (Ashkenazi) ethnic group while maintaining the marginalization and subjugation of the Palestinian Arab community' (Abu

Saad 2006: 1088). Notwithstanding this multiplicity of schooling or education systems, this chapter focuses on the two largest, defined for our purpose here as Jewish (mostly secular) and Arab. It will be demonstrated that this arrangement, which oversees two distinct sets of policies, budgets and curricula, is an integral part of the racist nature of the Israeli settler-colonial regime. A similar system of segregation is found in Canada, where the indigenous population has been and continues to be governed through the Ministry of Indian and Northern Affairs.

One of the major consequences of this binary division between Jewish and Arab education is the creation of different skills and requirements for indigenous Palestinian teachers and students, on the one hand, and Jewish teachers and students, on the other.

Against the general thrust of the Israeli 'modernist' school system, which views Palestinians' – and until recently also Mizrahi women's – inferior status in education as mainly the result of Arab traditions, family and religion, especially in so far as Arab Bedouin are concerned, this chapter will build on existing critical studies to demonstrate the complexity of women's education within the context of a largely exclusivist and exclusionary state. The role of the educational system in othering and subjugating Palestinian and Mizrahi women citizens, on the one hand, while prioritizing white (European) Ashkenazi women, on the other, will be investigated through a comparative historical analysis.

Women, Education and Racism

Education in general and women's education more specifically is a central tool for achieving social and economic advancement. It is a key element in creating equality of opportunity and enabling social mobility. In contexts that are highly classed, gendered, racialized and ethnicized, as in Israel, inequality in education becomes one of the dominant factors influencing all other forms of inequality including income, health and social status, as well as participation in the political process (Sikkuy 2006: 53). Discrimination against the Arab Palestinian population in the education sector has significant implications for the ability of Palestinian women to participate in society, have a presence in the public sphere, and become culturally and politically active and economically productive. Before outlining the status of women in the Israeli educational system, it is important to look at some of the main reasons why women's status in the education system is depressed. The previous chapter discussed the debate in Israel on the relationship between Palestinian women's education and labour force participation, showing how the Zionist Orientalist perspective places the blame for Palestinian women's low status on their culture, traditional family system and religion. It also pointed to the discrepancy among Palestinian women in terms of educational achievements. To account for this discrepancy, an understanding of the historical context of Palestinian women's educational status is necessary.

The Zionist discourse on Arab Palestinian women did not just appear with the establishment of the State of Israel. The current process of denigration and denial of the presence and national identity of Palestinians continues and cements the historical process that began with the emergence of the Zionist settler movement and British colonial rule in the 1920s. The Zionist project, which aimed at creating an exclusively 'Jewish home' in Palestine with the aid of the British colonial regime, was developed in tandem with another process of denial of the existence and rights of the indigenous Palestinian population. The ideal way to promote the new Jewish generation in the nation-state project was seen to be through integration of Zionist ideology and values in the educational and cultural system, and specifically by means of the curriculum and school textbooks. The following brief account of the state of Palestinian women's education under British and Zionist colonialism illustrates this point.

Female education, British colonialism and the Zionist settler project

Except for Abdel Latif Tibawi's *Arab Education in Mandatory Palestine* (1956), literature on Palestinian education in general, and that of women in particular, prior to 1948 remains scant. This source has been used

by scholars (Katz 2003; Jad 2007; Abu Usbeh 2006) to confirm that
the British colonial government favoured urban over rural areas in
the provision of education in general, and particularly in the case of
females. It also favoured male education over female. In urban areas,
such as Nazareth, Beit Lahem, Beit Jala and Ramallah, missionary
schools were already in existence prior to the British Mandate period,
and the government built a few additional elementary schools in these
areas. The British favoured urban development basically for Jews.
Arabs (indigenous Palestinians) were to remain as they were, 'uncivilized', 'cattle herders', 'backward peasants' and 'underdeveloped'. This
was a romantic aristocratic ideology within the Mandate government
and administration: Jews should be in business; Arabs would farm
and work the land (Segev 1998; Shepard 2000; Abu Usbeh 2006). The
British policy, which was based on a racist colonial civilizing mission,
in fact contributed to the widening of the gap between urban and
rural women (the overwhelming majority of whom were Muslims).
Within the urban centres, Mandate government policies were largely
oriented towards the minority Christian population.

The British colonial system of education was built on a foundation
created by the Turkish imperial system, which provided a very limited
type of education, most of which was in the form of *kuttabs* (religious
schools). Academic education was considered a luxury enjoyed by the
upper classes, whose financial means enabled them to send their male
children to Europe for schooling. The only elementary schools for
Arabs found in Palestine during British rule were those established
by missionaries for both boys and girls, which were largely located
in Arab towns. Until the second half of the 1960s, these schools were
exclusively attended by the urban, and mostly Christian, minority.
Before World War I, it was reported that Christian women enjoyed
a literacy rate of 80 per cent compared to 90 per cent among men,
whereas 5 per cent of Muslim women and 10 per cent of Muslim
men could read (quoted in Katz 2003: 122). It is important to note
here that the term 'literacy' used in this context refers to the basic
ability to read and/or write. More specifically, the reference here is
to elementary education. One major reason for these rates is that,

until 1935, the total number of British colonial elementary schools established throughout rural Palestine (in the villages, which were overwhelming populated by Muslim Palestinians) did not exceed fourteen schools.

The gender bias in the government education system is indicated by the fact that the total number of Palestinian schools during the British colonial period was estimated at 514, with a population of 8,042 pupils; of these, only 50 schools existed for girls (Jad 2007: 338). The civilizing mission of the British was clearly evident in its educational goals for village women, who were looked upon as 'traditional' and 'conservative' and as having 'small brains'. In the colonial perspective, village women needed to be educated so as to be familiar with 'the value of a good home where cleanliness, sanitation and above all care of children are to be regarded as the aim of every woman' (cited in Katz 2003: 125). In other words, women's education was about women keeping in their 'right place', the home, and not about providing them with knowledge and skills for a potential job in the labour market or a space in the public sphere. It is no surprise that the only institute for teaching and train-ing rural women, established by the British in 1935 in Ramallah, was the Rural Women's Teacher Training Centre. By 1946, this institute had 34 pupils, the number the British believed to be the desired maximum of women in rural education (Katz 2003: 124). It has been noted that the British were critical of the academic orientation of education provided in towns by the missionary schools on the grounds that they were 'cultivating too much the literary side of education and ... neglecting almost entirely what may be termed the domestic side' (cited in Katz 2003: 125).

Palestinian education under British colonialism is best compre-hended by contrasting it to that enjoyed by the European Jewish settlers in Palestine during the same period. Here, unlike the case of Palestinians, whose education was fully controlled by the British colonial government, education for the minority Jewish settlers was under the full control of the Zionist movement through its various subsidiary organs. It has been reported that prior to the establishment of the State of Israel, European Jewish settlers in Palestine had established some 760 schools and educational institutions, staffed by 4,645 male and female teachers, teaching a cadre of around 93,000 male and female students, and with a developed teachers' union (Abu Usbeh 2006: 28).

This is the historical context of Palestinian female education under British colonialism which explains why more Christian women have more education than Muslims. This context, as discussed earlier, clearly demonstrates the racism and sexism embedded in the colonial system of rule: favouring urban over rural, men over women, European (Jewish) over indigenous (Palestinian), and Christianity over Islam. The power relation of superiority and inferiority between Ashkenazi women and Arab women was already established with the advent of the Zionist settler movement through the process of racial separation under British rule. While the British Mandate ruled over Jews and Arabs in Palestine, the experiences of each were quite different. Zionist settlers, including women, enjoyed human and financial resources and possessed the necessary human capital required for reproducing the new generation of settlers, while indigenous people were deprived of such capacities.

Zionist (Ashkenazi Jewish) curricula for Mizrahi and Arab Palestinian children

Although the educational system designed for Palestinian citizens has always been separate from the Jewish system, it has been and continues to be totally controlled by the state under a special 'Arab Branch' in the Ministry of Education (MOE). As various authors note (Abu Usbeh 2006; Al-Haj 1995; Abdo 2009), almost all subjects taught in Arab schools, including children's stories, depict Arabs in racist ways – as inferior beings lacking culture or values. Racism, whether individual (i.e. through officials and high-status men – and women – in education) or institutional, has been characteristic of the Israeli Zionist attitude towards and perception of Arab values. Referring to the view of Bedouin, Moshe Shohat (chair of the Committee for Arab Education in the Negev) was quoted as saying: 'The Bedouins are bloodthirsty; they live polygamous, immoral lives; they give birth to thirty children and continue to expand their illegal villages and control state land.' Responding to the question of why they lack running water and toilets in their schools, Shohat added: 'According to their culture, they execute their physical needs in the open; they are incapable of flushing the toilet' (cited in Abu Usbeh 2006: 81). Quoting Adir Cohen, Abu Usbeh points out that '80 per cent of children's literature books which deal with Arabs present them in stereotypical, racist and derogatory ways' (Cohen cited in Abu Usbeh 2006: 82).

The racist content of educational textbooks presented to Palestinian Arab citizens of Israel has been critically addressed by various Palestinian Arab and Israeli Jewish scholars.[1] What is important to note, however, is that central to these textbooks is the Zionist message of the 'Jewish' nature and character of the country and the total denial of Palestinian national identity and actual lived experience in the country. Consider the sociological textbook used in the Arab curriculum for twelfth grade. To pass in the field of sociology, students are required to take five units and pass them all. The textbook, written in Hebrew and translated into Arabic, contains five major sections: 'Culture', 'The group', 'The family', 'Socialization' and 'Scientific research methods'. The choice of these topics is not accidental; these concepts constitute the fundamentals of the Israeli school of functionalism, established by Shmuel Eisenstadt and still used as the primary approach in Israeli sociology at large. To begin with, the Arabic translation of the textbook is extremely poor and replete with mistakes and incomprehensible phrases. In the whole of the textbook there is no reference to Palestinians, to the Nakba, to Arab or Palestinian history; while the terms 'Jewish', 'Israel', 'Zionist', and 'Jewish history' are well covered. The textbook has no analysis, no why or how: it is heavily descriptive, with examples taken from all over the world, but never from Palestinian history. In short, Palestinian students studying sociology at high school complete the course with little or no understanding of what sociology is, why it is an important field of study, and how it is relevant to their lives and experiences in Israel. It is no surprise that Israel's educational policy towards Palestinians is known among Arab citizens as the policy of *tajheel* (enforcing ignorance) and not *taa'leem* (education) (Abdo 2009). The following discussion elaborates on these points.

The type of curriculum designed for Arab schools has been and continues to be of grave concern to an increasing number of scholars. Daphna Golan-Agnon's personal and professional experience in this regard is worth noting. Golan-Agnon was hired by the MOE to devise a plan that would address inequalities in the school system, with US$10 million budgeted by the state every year for a period of five years for this. Reflecting on her experience in the field, Golan-Agnon expressed the great dissatisfaction she felt while working on the project. She began by noting the disparities between Jewish and Arab education and the discrimination against the Arab sector of education at almost every level of the project. She took pains to explain the particular problems she had found in the design of the Arab curricula, which, she asserted, has been a major cause of discrimination against Palestinian Arabs.

The school system ignores all aspects of Palestinian national identity, yet is replete with emphasis on Jewish/Zionist values. The Arab education system, as Golan-Agnon observes, is 'used by the Israeli government to institutionalize fear among Palestinians' (Golan-Agnon 2006: 1082). The system, she adds, has also been a vehicle for disputing Palestinian history through textbooks and curricula. Quoting Ramzi Suliman, a Palestinian intellectual, the author asserts: 'the state and its various institutions, in particular the education system and state media, continue to play a key role in creating and perpetuating the marginal "Arab-Israeli" culture' (Golan-Agnon 2006: 1082).

Golan-Agnon's contention was reaffirmed in a recent report by Hesketh and Zaher (2009), who confirm that the MOE retains centralized control over the form and substance of the curriculum for Arab schools. They also assert that the State Education Law (1953), as amended in February 2000, sets educational objectives for state schools that emphasize Jewish history and culture. Article 2 of the amended law specifies that 'the primary objective of education is to preserve the Jewish nature of the state by teaching its history, culture, language, etc.', but it states that should also acknowledge the needs, culture and language of the Arab population in Israel' (Hesketh and Zaher 2009: 2). However, as Hesketh and Zaher (2009) as well as Abu Usbeh (2006: 100) maintain, this article remains on paper and was never implemented.

Students in Arab state-run schools 'receive very little instruction in Palestinian or Arab history, geography, literature, culture, and traditions and spend more time learning the Torah and other Jewish texts than they do on studying the Qur'an, Islamic texts or the New Testament' (Hesketh and Zaher 2009, 2).

The racist curricula devised for the Arab schooling system, which, as seen above, prevents pupils learning about their culture and history, and instils fear in them, has prevailed throughout the life of the state. In 2007, in an attempt to restore some balance, Yuli Tamir, then Labour minister of education, approved the use of a history textbook which mentions the Nakba as part of the experience of Palestinians. According to Minister Tamir, 'this textbook, which was evaluated by a professional viewing board and was sent to dozens of readers prior to being approved for distribution, offers the Arab pupils a balanced picture, so that they may put what they are exposed to in their home environment in the proper context.'[2]

This innovation, however, was short-lived. In 2009 under the Netanyahu and Lieberman government, the MOE issued a report entitled *The Government of Israel Believes in Education* that instructs that references to the Nakba be removed from new Arabic textbooks. Later the same year a slate of racist bills were introduced, aimed specifically at Palestinian citizens with the intention of reminding them of the 'Jewish' nature of the state and demanding their loyalty and allegiance. One such bill, which is commonly called 'the Nakba Law', proposes to forbid all bodies that receive state funding from spending money on an activity that, inter alia, 'commemorates Independence Day or the day of the establishment of the state as a day of mourning'. Since Arab schools, including teachers and students, are actively involved in commemorating the Nakba, they stand to be particularly targeted by this bill.[3]

Although Arab schools have their own separate curriculum, it is designed and supervised by the MOE, with little to no decision-making power in the hands of Arab educators or administrators. Comparing Arab schooling with that of religious Jews, Hesketh and Zaher write:

> Arabs account for only 6.2% of the total number of employees in the MOE, and are never found in the upper echelons of the MOE. The majority of these employees work in Arab towns and villages or mixed cities providing services directly to Arab communities. By contrast, state religious schools established only for religious Jewish students maintain autonomous control over their curricula. (Hesketh and Zaher 2009, 2–3)

This conclusion is not far from that arrived at by Golan-Agnon (2006). The Orientalist and racist policies and practices of the Israeli state have specific implications for indigenous Palestinian citizens, but they also target the East/Orient and Arab culture in general. Mizrahi Jews from Arab and Muslim countries have not escaped the racist Zionist discourse oriented towards them, especially the women. Official Israeli discourse on Mizrahi women is derogatory, based on the so-called cultural assets supposedly inherent to each group. Whereas Ashkenazi Jews are thought to be descendants of European, Western and modern culture, thus having acquired modern educational, human and cultural capital, Arab or Mizrahi Jews are perceived as backward and traditional, with women imagined as being concerned only with the domestic sphere. Zionism, in the person of Ashkenazi Jews, it is believed, has been the 'saviour' of Arab Jews, 'modernizing' them, pulling them out of their 'primitive state', 'poverty' and 'irrationality' and 'integrating' or absorbing them into Western society – which is characterized by 'democracy' and 'human virtues' (Abu Usbeh 2006: 75).

In the process of obtaining education, Golan-Agnon reports, Mizrahi women 'must navigate issues of gender, ethnicity, socio-economic status, as well as language. Within schools there is strong emphasis on Jewish Zionist values; there is no teaching of Mizrahi values or similarly of Palestinian values' (Golan-Agnon 2006: 1082).

Complete assimilation and acceptance of the status quo have been and continue to be expected of all students attending Israeli schools. This alienation and forced integration are designed to destroy feelings of cultural and national identity among Mizrahi Jews. The process is also an attempt to remind female Mizrahis of their subordinate position in society, their status on the next-to-bottom rung of the social hierarchy. The Israeli school system, in other words, serves as a method of disseminating institutionalized racism and cementing the subjugation of Arab (Mizrahi and Palestinian) children from an early age.

In 'You're so Pretty – You Don't Look Moroccan', Dahan-Kalev (2003) describes her childhood and education as a Mizrahi Jew. She narrates how in elementary school she and her classmates were forced to read texts on Israeli literature and history which completely ignored and excluded any non-European Jewish history. As she describes, this created a sense of exclusion, devaluation, inequality and non-existence for Mizrahi Jews. Non-Western Jews were portrayed as 'dirty, poor, riddled with contagious or infectious diseases, spiritually impotent, lacking in moral capacity, ignorant, violent and lazy' (Dahan-Kalev 2003: 171). The feeling of non-existence is one that Mizrahi women carry throughout their lives if they do not also have positive cultural experiences to help them understand and define themselves. The negative effect of the devaluation of Mizrahi Jews passes into their adult years, when women seek to enter the labour market.

The wide disparity between the educational status of Ashkenazi and Palestinian Arab women in many ways resembles that constructed between Ashkenazi and Mizrahi Jews, with the accent on denial of nationality. Saporta and Yonah (2004) argue that the gulf between Mizrahi and Ashkenazi Jewish education is the result of systematic and institutionalized discrimination directed against Mizrahi Jews. This discrimination, they write: 'has been stemming from a complex economic and cultural system employed by the founding generations of modern Israel, who were of East European origin'. It is a system 'that answers a capitalist and colonial logic embedded in Zionist Israel' (Saporta and Yonah 2004: 252).

More poignantly, state and institutional racism in education is not confined to the level of discursive or abstract theory, but has been deliberately implemented as an educational policy inserted into the curricula and content of teaching and education delivered to the Palestinians and the Mizrahi Jews. For example, the official Israeli *Third Periodic Report*, sent to the United Nations Committee for the Elimination of All Forms of Discrimination Against Women (CEDAW), by state feminists, instead of highlighting the racialized separation of the Palestinians, had the following to say: 'the number of Palestinian female students in Israel is inversely related to the level of education, and that more Muslim men receive higher education than Muslim women in general' (Adalah 2005: 34). The report, which aims, as it were, to stroke the state's ego, suggests that 'non-Jewish' women's entry into higher education has undergone a significant increase, participation among non-Jewish students in general growing from 8.9 per cent in 1970–71 to 41 per cent in 1992–93 (Adalah 2005: 34). Leaving aside the official report's essentially racist language, which denies the very existence and identity of Palestinians, referring to them, like the Israeli establishment, as shown in the first chapter, as non-Jews, the official perspective of the report obliterates the historical context of Palestinian education, including the treatment of this section of the population by this very state. More importantly, this official account also fails to ask why, after several decades of being citizens of Israel, Palestinian women have continued to show low levels of educational achievement in general and especially so in higher education.

Another major problem in Israeli official discourse and reports is the tendency to abstract a group, an ethnicity or a national collectivity such as Palestinian women and then attempt to present them in isolation from their counterparts – for example, from Mizrahi women, whose record and experiences suggest they did not fare much better. Such reports and discourses, in other words, mask systemic and systematic Israeli discrimination against Palestinian women and veil the fact that some citizens, especially Palestinians, are citizens nominally only and are excluded from the Israeli (Jewish) national project.

Racial and gender subjugation of certain sectors of citizens – Mizrahi and, especially, Palestinian women – is manifest at all levels of education: pre-school, elementary, secondary and university. Whereas the racialized separation of Palestinian schools from government-run Jewish schools represents a continuous trend in Mizrahis' colonial status, the ethnicization of Mizrahis in general and Mizrahi women in particular, most literature suggests, is a product of the establishment of the State of Israel under the hegemonic rule of white Ashkenazi (European) Jews (Dahan-Kalev 2003; Moore 2004; Haberfeld and Cohen 2006; Resnik 2006; Cohen et al. 2007).

During the first couple of decades after the establishment of Israel, the state attempted to assimilate, though not grant equal status to, Mizrahi Jews, relegating them instead to second-class citizenship. Mizrahi women's experiences, we have seen, varied radically from those of Ashkenazi women, as the former experienced a double oppression at the level of both gender and ethnicity. This status is clearly evident in the way in which the Israeli state has historically treated Mizrahi women's education. Literature detailing Mizrahi women's experiences in the educational sector is relatively scarce, and what is available is largely anecdotal. In fact, the main critical voices in this field are Mizrahi women (and men), some of whom articulate educational concerns through their own personal stories and experiences (Dahan-Kalev 2001, 2003; Shohat 2002) or through specific examples, as in the case of Saporta and Yonah (2004) and Yonah and Saporta (2006). Almost all Israeli official data and studies on Israeli education address Jewish education as a unified category without disaggregating the ethnic composition of the Jewish population.

In their study, Yonah and Saporta (2006) reaffirm the colonial Orientalist and racist perception of the Zionist state towards Mizrahi Arab women. Echoing the rationale behind British colonial discouragement of women's academic endeavour in favour of technical education, Israel in the first two decades adopted a similar system for Mizrahi women. Thus, in 1955 the Israeli MOE began implementing a pre-vocational training programme to encourage children to attend vocational schools after completing elementary schooling. For Mizrahi women, Yonah and Saporta write, pre-vocational training meant an introduction to a type of learning aimed at pushing girls into the 'private patriarchal order' – that is, to be future housewives (Yonah and Saporta 2006: 89). The goal of pre-vocational education for Mizrahi females, to reiterate, was designed to train them for 'domestic' work – how to manage their kitchen, their children and their families in ways deemed appropriate by Ashkenazi Jewish standards. This policy, it should be observed, reflects the colonial attitude in general. French colonialism in Algeria, as Marnia Lazreg reminds us, also adopted similar methods in dealing with the supposedly 'inferior' and colonized Algerian women (Lazreg 1994, 1988).

It is important to note, with Yonah and Saporta, however, that the result of the 'pre-vocational' education introduced during the 1950s turned out to run counter to the system's intentions. After completing their pre-vocational training, most girls, the authors found, went on to pursue high school and post-secondary education instead of staying at home. However, this does not alter the reality of Israel's racist system of education and its othering intentions. Even in cases where Ashkenazi and Mizrahi Jewish ethnicities settled in the same locality after the establishment of the state, Ashkenazis were almost fully integrated into the educational and occupational sphere whereas Mizrahis lagged behind. By 1975, it has been noted, 'Ashkenazis' schooling, occupations and earnings were no different from those of native-born Israelis or of veteran immigrants who arrived in Israel during the pre-state period' (Cohen et al. 2007: 898). Mizrahi Jews, by contrast, had not achieved the same levels of equality with the native populations, particularly in terms of educational attainment. When other factors, such as the physically and geographically isolated and dilapidated areas in which Mizrahis were initially placed and settled by the state, are taken into consideration, it is little surprise that their overall lived experiences have been such a shambles. The initial inferior status accorded to Mizrahis in general and to women more specifically, despite some improvements in their socio-economic conditions, has also affected the educational status of the second generation. The Israeli educational system has continued to demonstrate favourable treatment and attitudes towards Ashkenazi women as compared to Mizrahis, as the former can claim the highest qualifications and credentials in the country.

As for the educational status of Palestinian citizens in general and women in particular, it is worth noting that the effects of the inferior system of education of Palestinians, which was first shaped by racist British policies, then by Israeli colonial rule, especially in the two decades following the state's establishment, continued to linger on. Confined to military rule between 1948 and 1966, while the state was primarily focused on building its Jewish nation and military capability as a measure of security against the so-called Arab threat, Palestinian citizens were considered to be a security threat and treated as such. During this period the Arab Palestinian educational infrastructure was not so much left underdeveloped as actively 'de-developed'.

Adalah's report (2005), referred to above, regarding the low level of education among Palestinian women up until the early 1970s fails to mention that these citizens were subjugated under Israeli military rule. Until the late 1970s and early 1980s, the only Arab urban area which remained populated exclusively by Palestinians was Nazareth. And, despite its dilapidated infrastructure and the underdevelopment of its schools, Nazareth has in fact catered for the whole of the Galilee region, where the overwhelming majority of Arabs continue to live. Until the late 1970s most classrooms were overcrowded, with over forty pupils jammed into a small room, often rented. These classrooms were extremely hot in the summer and very cold in the winter. Such conditions characterized all government schools in Nazareth during that period.[4]

The disparity between Jewish and Palestinian education has narrowed only slightly over the years. In 2006, the average class size in Arab schools was estimated at 30 pupils per room, compared to 26 pupils in Jewish schools (Sikkuy 2006: 54), figures that had not changed by 2009 (Hesketh and Zaher 2009: 4). This meant that for some schools, especially in the Naqab region, and in some villages, one would find classes of around 40 pupils. The differentiated and separated systems of Jewish and Arab education have been and continue to be characterized as racialized, classed and gendered. The system also favours urban over rural dwellers, males over females,[5] the middle class over the poor, and Christians over Muslims and Druze. Arab Bedouin, it will be further argued, have been most isolated and disadvantaged in the system.

The lifting of the state of emergency, of military rule, by the Israelis in 1966 did not see the democratizing of the Israeli system of education; nor did it herald equity of status between Palestinian citizens and their Jewish, especially Ashkenazi, counterparts. Quite to the contrary, the state continued to practise systematic legal and institutional discrimination against Palestinian citizens in almost all fields of education. This included a chronic budgetary shortfall, which led to the further deterioration of physical infrastructure and equipment; a reduction in the number of teaching staff and teaching hours; and a worsening of classroom overcrowding. An example of the stark discrimination practised in education in the Palestinian sector can be gleaned from the 2001 figures provided on the number of teaching hours in Palestinian schools compared to those in the Jewish sector. Distribution of the total number of teaching hours for the school year 1999–2000 in percentage terms was estimated at 17.6 per cent in Palestinian schools compared with 82.4 per cent within the Jewish sector. These teaching hours break down as follows: official kindergartens, 11.5 per cent for Arabs compared with 88.5 per cent for Jews; primary schools, 21 per cent for Arabs, 79 per cent for Jews; intermediary schools, 17.4 per cent for Arabs, 82.6 per cent for Jews; secondary schools 14.4 per cent for Arabs, 86.6 per cent for Jews (Central Bureau of Statistics 2001: Table 8.26). More recent data also demonstrate major shortcomings in this area. Thus, although the Compulsory Education Law (1949), as amended in 1984, lowered the age of compulsory education from 5 to 3 years old, today 'state funding for kindergarten education for three and four-year-old Arab children', report Hesketh and Zaher, 'remains minimal'. Few state-funded preschools, they argue, 'operate in Arab towns or villages in Israel, as compared with Jewish communities.

As a result, in 2006/7 about 32% of Arab 2–5 year-olds were not enrolled in kindergartens, compared to just 15.6% of Jewish children of the same age group' (Hesketh and Zaher 2009: 3)

Although such figures might appear at first glance compatible with the demographic weight of Palestinians in the state, the historical and existing injustices that have afflicted them since its establishment demand that special measures be taken to rectify their overall low socio-economic status. This logic has been adopted by most socio-economic reports and human rights organizations concerned with the Palestinians in Israel, both locally and internationally (Dichter in Sikkuy 2003-2004 and 2006; B'Tselem 1999; Adalah 2005; UNDP 2004), the argument being that Palestinian students have unique needs due to their situation, and that an affirmative action plan must be implemented if these needs are to be met. A similar conclusion was arrived at by the Or Commission Report, which stated:

> The State must initiate, develop and implement programs to eliminate the disparities [between Arab and Jewish citizens], notably in funding for all aspects of education, housing, industrial development, employment and services.... The State, through its most senior echelons, must act to eliminate these disparities promptly and unequivocally by setting clear and tangible targets with well-defined timetables. (Or Commission, cited in Sikkuy 2002: 3)

These findings and recommendations for affirmative action were reiterated in 2003 by Ronit Tirosh, director general of the MOE, who argued at a Knesset Education and Cultural Committee meeting:

> Within 5 years we will be going to an egalitarian, open reserve supply [of hours], and there will then be an increment of 100,000 hours, of which 70,000 hours will go to the Arab sector... I emphasize that although that sector is only 20 per cent of the population it is entitled to more due to affirmative action, and in fact receives more. Overall, if I look at the increment in the context of the total hours given to that sector compared with the total hours given to the Jewish sector, there will be an increment

of 30 per cent for the [Arab] sector as compared to 5 per cent for the Jewish sector. This is certainly affirmative action, which I very much commend. (Tirosh 2004: 28).

The figure of 100,000 hours, it should be noted, was provided by the Shoshani Commission, appointed in late 2001 to report on education in Israel with a view to the implementation of affirmative action in the education sector. However, official reporting is one thing and actual implementation another. The Israeli Bureau of Statistics for the 2006 reported that about a third of the Arab population completed only eight years of schooling or less, and is thus likely to find itself in the lower socio-economic stratum within the state; it also found that about 20 per cent of the Jewish population, compared to only 8 per cent of the Arab population, completed sixteen years or more in education (Sikkuy 2006: 45–55).

Unlike the situation within Jewish schools, where since the 1970s students have enjoyed extracurricular programmes such as psychological counselling services, tutoring provision, and computer services aimed at 'improving skills, raising grades, and preventing drop out', in the Palestinian educational sector such programmes were introduced only in the late 1980s. In 2000, for example, only 15.3 per cent of the counsellors specializing in preventing students dropping out (a service recommended by the MOE) were in fact operating in Palestinian schools, compared to 43.4 per cent working in Jewish schools (Adalah 2005: 24).

The context of Arab education has been described succinctly as follows:

The Arab sector suffers from many shortages, including: teachers without motivation who lack trust in the educational system and lack faith in education as such; the alienation of teachers and students from the material studied, beginning with the emphasis on Jewish history and the justification for Zionism while the question of the students' own identity and their link with the Palestinian people is glossed over; violence on the part of teachers toward students; a family-based communication network within the schools, which obscures the educational considerations that should be driving day-to-day functioning. (Sikkuy 2006: 55).

All these, the report concludes, have one thing in common: 'A sense of perpetual detachment, alienation from the state and, most especially, no expectations, prospects, hopes, or anticipation of the future – these are the fuel that drives education ... without which, learning is hollow and all its light extinguished' (Sikkuy 2006).

Under such conditions, it is little surprise that cultural and human capital among Palestinian citizens is relatively underdeveloped. Obstacles and restrictions in the educational system encountered at an early age are undoubtedly carried forward to the secondary level and then on into university. Using the governmental educational system as a means for the 'Israelification' of Palestinian citizens – albeit with little to no success, especially in the last couple of decades – was and continues to be the driving force in the Israeli Arab educational system.

Although the state budget for education is structured in such a way as to prevent analysis of exactly how much funding Arab education receives, one item, namely the Pedagogy Administration, is known: in 2006 the Pedagogy Administration of the MOE allocated 4 per cent of its budget to Arab education; in 2007 the proportion was 3 per cent (Hesketh and Zaher 2009: 5).

In the absence of political will on the part of Israeli officials and institutions, all legal amendments and recommendations for affirmative action remain of little relevance. Outside of academic education one could also envision other practical education and training programmes, the implementation of which in the Palestinian (Arab) sector could ameliorate the current situation – for example, vocational training. But such education is largely concentrated in the Jewish sectors across the country, benefiting Jewish students for the most part. For example, Israel's Science and Technology Schools Network (also known as ORT) provides technical and various other practical skills to high-school students more interested in professions and career-building than in academia; these could be encouraged more within the Arab sector as well. Such programmes receive large sums of money donated by European and North American Jewish and Zionist organizations.[6]

Also, a more interactive or participatory approach, in which Palestinian Arab parents are involved, could potentially improve education in the Arab sector. Addi-Raccah and Mazawi have rightly observed that 'Greater local sharing in decision-making may reduce drop-out rates, within defined parameters, by granting local authorities a greater role in determining the organizational context of schooling' (Addi-Raccah and Mazawi 2004: 156). Finally, allowing Palestinian scholars and educational experts to take an active role in the process of taking decisions at the institutional level, a practice that is still not an option, would undoubtedly contribute to changing Palestinian education in Israel.

Elementary Education for Palestinian Female Citizens

Despite the fact that elementary education was mandated by the Israeli legal system, very few Palestinians, especially females, benefited from this in the first two decades. This was especially true for village residents, who lacked sufficient schools, proper infrastructure and educational facilities. Citizens in the unrecognized villages were largely isolated and cut off from the rest of their people and could not afford to send their children, especially females, to school in urban areas – not that Arab urban areas, which existed prior to the founding of the state, remained intact after its establishment.

Education at all levels, including elementary, requires an environment that is minimally capable of guaranteeing a level of democracy, freedom of expression and critical thinking on the part of both educator and educated. Israel's educational policy of 'subjugated separateness' – to use Majed Al-Haj's (1995) phrase for the racializing of Arabs – lacks this minimal condition. Whilst it is necessary to acknowledge the presence of some traditional cultural factors that constrain female Arab education (including socialization and traditional family belief in gendered roles, wherein the woman's place is in the home as mother and wife), objective conditions (including socio-economic status and policy constraints) have the greater determining force. Among the major policy constraints, as indicated above, is inadequate funding of the Arab education sector. Thus the state's five-year plan to close the gap between Jewish and Arab education failed because the MOE did not set aside enough money for Arab education. The issue is stated clearly by Golan-Agnon, who notes that 'Arab education receives inferior allocations for training, supervision, nature and art lessons ... in general the physical infrastructure of the school is more dilapidated ... lower funding means lack of good or special programming for Arab schools' (Golan-Agnon 2006: 1077).

One study on school funding based on data from the Israel Central Bureau of Statistics (ICBS) found that on average schools spent US$1,097 per Jewish student, but only $191 per Palestinian student (Golan-Agnon 2006: 1078). Palestinian parents and the Arab community at large are excluded from taking part in the education of their children. Arab education is controlled: determined from above and handed down to Arab students. Material generated during discussions around affirmative education were not translated into Arabic, thereby excluding many Palestinian Arab citizens from taking part. 'The head of the Arab education system', Golan-Agnon observes, 'does not possess any authority over budgets and never says anything in meetings.' Concluding her observations as a scholar involved in developing affirmative action for Israeli education in the Arab sector, Golan-Agnon has the following to say:

> Here were less than 10 Arabs working at the Ministry's administrative headquarters among thousands of Jewish workers; the school system completely ignores all aspects of the Palestinian national identity yet there is a huge emphasis on Jewish Zionist values; education is a way for the Israeli government to institutionalize fear. It is also a vehicle to dispute Palestinian history through textbooks and curriculum. (2006: 1079)

Most significantly, she asserts, 'the very system which is expected to teach students democracy is undemocratic' (2006: 1080). The

exclusion and resulting absence of Palestinian representation in all
official decision-making processes is emblematic of Israeli state policies and practices. Golan-Agnon's observations and conclusions have
been corroborated by various other Israeli and Palestinian scholars
of education. For example, Ismael Abu Saad, in his 'State-controlled
Education and Identity Formation among the Palestinian Arab Minority in Israel' (2006), makes a similar argument when he suggests
that Palestinians are marginalized in all aspects social, cultural and
economic life, including their entitlements to state services in the
areas of language education and religion. Education for the Arabs is
just another form of control to keep them inferior and marginalized.
Arab education, he asserts, 'serves the state's objectives and continues
to ignore historical and cultural aspects that pertain to Palestinians'
(Abu Saad 2006: 1091).

Writing on the discrimination against Palestinian citizens' education status, Shalom Dichter, in the Sikkuy Report, has gone even further
in his criticism of Israel's plan to spend 4 billion shekels to improve
education:

> Well-intentioned but cosmetic; a narrowly conceived, hastily
> planned attempt to boost matriculation scores without a thorough
> reform of the system; lacking in a meaningful participation by
> Arab stakeholder constituencies (Arab educators and academics,
> parents, teachers, principals) ... in 2001–02, actual allocations fell
> short – by NIS 21 million – of amounts budgeted in the plan, and
> 40% of this funding is really for special education programs that
> should be budgeted separately. (Dichter 2004: 1090)

Citing hatred, rejection and racism towards Arab citizens from
Israeli politicians and the Israeli establishment, Dichter warns against
'more frequent, more blatant and more public expressions of hatred,
rejection, and racism – from the Knesset plenum to an elementary
school party for second-graders' (Dichter 2004: 45). Arab education
as a system of fear is best expressed in the character of staff and
teachers hired into the Arab educational system. Historically and
contemporarily, appointments have been guided more by teachers' political orientation or even loyalty to the state than by their

professional qualifications. Palestinian teaching staff are regularly subjected to extensive background security checks and approval by Shin Bet (Sherut ha-Bitahon, domestic security service). This body, subsequently called Shabak (Sherut ha-Bitahon ha-Klali, general security service), which includes both internal security service and counterintelligence, has played and continues to play – especially after September 11 – an important role in screening Palestinian men and women to ensure their political suitability as educators and government employees.

Once admitted by the MOE, Palestinian teachers face other forms of marginalization as they are denied any discretionary power or control over how or what they teach. To further institute the depoliticization and denationalization of Palestinian teachers and students, the Shin Bet/Shabak have retained the upper hand in terms of hiring: promotion is based on political criteria rather than merit, qualified candidates can be rejected, and teachers may be dismissed on account of their political views – all of which powers are specifically intended to apply to Palestinian citizens.[7] In fact, since September 11 the state's security checks on its Palestinian Arab citizens have been increased, causing more harm to Arabs, as they were 'marked as threatening to the social order, the dominant identity, and or/national security' (Hertzog 2004: 60). It is no surprise, therefore, that in this environment of fear, lack of democracy and no respect for Palestinian citizens' basic rights, female Arab students exhibit higher rates of illiteracy and drop-out than do their female Jewish counterparts. Depoliticization, denationalization and de-Palestinianization are used by the Israeli state as means of 'assimilation', similar to the processes of 'de-Arabization' of Mizrahis in general and Mizrahi women in particular, as shown earlier. These practices have in fact constituted Israel's official ideology of education in the Arab sector. In an article entitled 'Who's Afraid of Educated Arabs?' (Ha'aretz, 24 July 2009), Yousef T. Jabareen, founder and director of the Arab Centre for Law and Policy, has confirmed the continuous presence of such disparities in the curricula of the Jewish and Arab systems of education. He also stresses the fact of unequal budget allocations, arguing that the state invests roughly $200 per Arab pupil annually, against $1,000 per Jewish pupil.[8]

Illiteracy and dropping out of school among Palestinian females

It comes as no surprise to realize that the state's education system ignores the rights, the needs and the priorities of Arab students, and thus denies them the opportunity to develop a positive cultural and national identity. Hesketh and Zaher (2009) have identified three primary sources of inequality in the Arab educational sector: 'the right to determine educational goals and objectives; the discriminatory allocation of state resources to Arab schools and students; and the inadequate representation of Arab citizens in decision-making positions in the MOE.

Within these overall racist structural conditions, it is clear that Palestinian Arab females are more likely to be negatively affected by the existing educational system than their male counterparts. The patriarchal structure of the Palestinian family and traditional culture, which historically has favoured, and to a large degree still favours, male children's education over that of females, constitutes another obstacle to female educational achievement. The Palestinian family, especially but not exclusively among the poor, perceives male education as a financial investment with rewards accruing to the parents and family in their old age. Females, who are often expected to leave the agnatic family and move to the husband's home, are not seen in the same light. The relatively high rates of fertility in Palestinian families, combined with the widespread poverty in the Arab sector (especially in rural areas) and the heavily de-developed areas such as the Naqab, constitute further obstacles to female education, especially beyond elementary schooling. When combined with existing dilapidated infrastructural conditions, there is no doubt that the impact on females of gender/cultural constraints, along with structural forms of racism practised by the state, is much greater than that on males; hence the higher rates of illiteracy and school drop-out among Palestinian female citizens.

In 1993, it was reported that 39.1 per cent of female Palestinian citizens had fewer than nine years of education, compared to 15.4 per cent of Jewish women; and 15 per cent of Palestinian women had post-secondary education, compared to 38 per cent of Jewish women (Al-Haj 1995: 96). While such figures have improved in absolute terms, women citizens continue to lag far behind Jewish women in terms of educational provision. Statistics for 2003, for example, show that female Palestinian citizens have the lowest median educational level, estimated at 10.9 years, compared to 11.2 years among Palestinian men and 12.6 years among Jewish men. The disparity is also evident in the data on school drop-out rates: for pupils in grades 9–12 for the years 2006–08, the estimate for Palestinians is 7.2 per cent, almost double the figure for Jews, at 3.7 per cent per year.

Illiteracy and drop-out rate are particularly alarming among the Arab Bedouin in the Naqab, data showing that the numbers leaving school early are as high as 70 per cent overall (Hesketh and Zaher 2009: 5). Until 2009 there existed not a single high school for the Bedouin living in 'unrecognized villages'. Consider the region of Abu-Tulul–El-Shihabi, which has approximately 12,000 Arab Bedouin citizens, with around 750 female and male students of high-school age, of whom only around 170 attend school. According to Hesketh and Zaher (2009):

> The nearest high school [in this region] is located 12–15 kilometers away; no public transportation is provided for the students and many parents will not allow their daughters to travel unaccompanied outside the vicinity of this area. The remainder – around 77% of the total – drop out of the system permanently as a direct consequence of the lack of a local high school. (Hesketh and Zaher 2009: 5).

As for the general Arab population, the cohort of grades 9–11 – considered as the transition between junior high school and high school – constitute the most alarming evidence in terms of drop-out rate, as the figure is double that of the drop-out rate among Jewish pupils. For the school year 1999–2000, drop-out rates were recorded as follows: by age 14, 7.2 per cent for Palestinian students compared to 0 per cent for Jewish students; by age 15, 19.1 per cent for Palestinian students compared to 1.7 per cent for Jewish students; by age 17, 29.3 per cent for Palestinian students compared to 11.8 per cent for Jewish students (Israel Central Bureau of Statistics 2001: Table 8.11). Notwithstanding the fact that the official drop-out rate has declined significantly within Arab education, the Arab school drop-out rate between 2006 and 2008 nevertheless remained at twice that in the Jewish sector (Sikkuy 2006: 59; Hesketh and Zaher 2009: 6). Similarly with the case of illiteracy rates among Palestinian female citizens: figures for 2003 suggest that they have the highest illiteracy rate in the country, estimated at 14.7 per cent, compared to 4.5 per cent for Jewish females. Palestinian females also registered the highest drop-out rate, at 9.9 per cent, compared to 3.3 per cent for Jewish women (Adalah 2005: 21).

Using statistics based on ICBS/Statistical Abstract of Israel 2006 the Sikkuy Report demonstrates that the rate for Palestinian pupils who completed sixteen or more years of schooling was 8 per cent, compared with 19.6 for Jews; the respective rates for those who completed between thirteen and fifteen years are 10 per cent and 23.3 per cent. The rate for elementary schooling (grades 1–8) is recorded at 30.3 per cent within the Arab sector, compared to 10.8 per cent within the Jewish sector. These latter figures are accounted for largely by the fact that, compared to the Jewish population, the Arab population contains a high proportion of youth (Sikkuy 2006: 56).

The deplorable state of education among Palestinian female citizens has generated and continues to generate national and international criticism of the State of Israel. It was one of the concerns of the UN CEDAW report addressed to Israel. Education also figured prominently in a report prepared in 2005 by five major human rights, civil rights and women's rights NGOs that was sent to the Pre-sessional Working Group on the Status of Women (see Adalah 2005: 17). According to the Human Development Report of 2004 (UNDP 2004) illiteracy among Palestinian females is ranked high as a problem even at the international level. Israel, which is ranked 22 in terms of overall performance, according to the report, lags behind all developed and developing and some underdeveloped countries in the area of female youth literacy; it stands alongside countries like Myanmar, which has an overall ranking of 132 (UNDP 2004: Index 26, 239–40). Data for the years 2000, 2002 and 2003 suggest that female Palestinian citizens continue to be at the bottom of the scale in terms of educational achievement. For example, a labour market survey conducted in 2000 on women citizens – divided by religion – indicates that of a total number of 115,992 Muslim women surveyed, 6.6 per cent had no education at all; 41.2 per cent had primary or junior high education (grades 1–9); 40.5 per cent had senior high education (grades 10–12); 7.1 per cent had community college education; and 4.6 per cent had post-secondary academic (B.A. or higher) education (Sikkuy 2003: 21).

The 'social-cultural' context of the gendered dimension of education among Palestinian citizens remains seriously underdeveloped as a research area. However, and despite their marginal status, female Palestinian citizens, when given the opportunity and access, are able to assume responsibility and take the development of their education and human capital seriously. It has been observed that Palestinian Arab girls on a national scale are less likely than boys to drop out of school. Between the 1998/99 and 1999/2000 school years, 53.1 per cent of Palestinian Arab twelfth graders were girls. And in grades 9–12, Palestinian Arab boys dropped out at a higher rate than girls. However, during this period only 47.7 per cent of Palestinian Arab ninth graders were girls, suggesting that while girls are less likely to make the transition to high school, those who do are more likely than boys to remain in school. This holds for Bedouin girls as well as the rest of the female Palestinian Arab population (Human Rights Watch 2001).

The trend of greater numbers of Palestinian females beginning and completing higher education as compared to males was recently corroborated by a study conducted by the Centre for Research and Information of the Knesset. According to the study, presented by

M.K. Jamal Zahalka, until 2005 the proportion of Palestinians passing the Bagrut (matriculation) exams[9] favoured males over females. But since then the trend has been reversed: in 2006, the rate was 55.8 per cent among females compared to 36.5 among males, while in the Jewish sector the rate for females was 64 per cent and 55.3 per cent for males. In 2007, the proportion of Palestinian females passing these exams was 51 per cent; for males the figure was was 34 per cent. The study also revealed that more Palestinian females achieved the requisite Bagrut scores for university acceptance than did males during the same period. There was a similar pattern in the rates of university and college enrolment: for the year 2008, 63 per cent of the cohort was female, 36 per cent male. While praising women's high achievements, Zahalka nevertheless found this data alarming, as one of the main factors informing these trends seems to be economic. Zahalka demanded that the Knesset take this study seriously, analyse it and find solutions for the low educational attainment among Palestinian males (Zahalka 2009).

A combination of economic and cultural measures could provide an answer to the problem indicated by this trend. Notwithstanding the fact, noted earlier, that some 40 per cent of academics are unemployed, Palestinian women still believe in the virtues of education, considering it a necessary asset for their future employability and perhaps a means to improving their social status before marriage. As for many males, family economic pressure drives them to drop out of secondary school or higher education in order to look for a job. With the grave restrictions on and discrimination against Palestinians in the labour force, it is also probable that some have lost faith in the educational system as a vehicle for obtaining decent jobs.

There is no doubt that the MOE should extend special assistance to students in communities that are socio-economically disadvantaged by categorizing these communities as a 'national priority'; however, Arab communities are not included in this category even though most of them meet the criteria of deprivation (Sikkuy 2006: 27; Abu Usbeh 2006). Another study conducted in 2009 by Sorel Cahan of the Hebrew University (Cahan 2009) has further corroborated this contention, providing qualitative and quantitative analysis of a recent plan by the MOE to rectify the failing objectives of the five-year plan with regard to poor families, including the Arab sector. The main argument made by Cahan is that the plan severely discriminates against Palestinian students, who are most in need of such assistance. According to the study, the 'average per-student allocation [of resources in general] in Arab junior high schools amounts to only 20 percent of the average in Jewish junior high' (Cahan 2009: 380). Cahan criticizes the plan, first, for being too modest to account for the actual needs of poor students, and, second, for the way financial resources are distributed between Jewish and Arab students – as the outcome has been that most of it goes to Jewish and not Arab students. According to Cahan, because the Arab sector has more students who meet the MOE's criteria for assistance but fewer students overall within the education system, 'educationally needy' Jewish students receive anywhere from 3.8 to 6.9 times as much funding as more or equally needy Arab students. Institutionalized budgetary discrimination against Arab citizens, he concludes, defeats the whole point of the special assistance budget (Cahan 2009: 390).

Secondary and post-secondary education

Women's agency, along with factors such as national pride and the commitment to surviving and prevailing in difficult circumstances, subjectively empowers them while they remain objectively (structurally and institutionally) held back. Among the obstacles facing Palestinian students is difficulty in obtaining the credentials necessary for university admission: that is, passing the matriculation exams, the Bagrut. These exams are designed largely with Jewish (Ashkenazi) students in mind; they can therefore stand in the way of other students who want to attend university. For example, in 1996 only 23 per cent of all Palestinian students passed the Bagrut, compared to 45 per cent of Jewish students. In the Naqab (Negev) only 5.9 per cent of Palestinian students passed. Figures for the academic year 1999–2000 show that of Israel's 17-year-olds who passed the Bagrut 27.5 per cent were Palestinian students and 45.6 per cent Jewish students; of these, the proportions who also qualified for university admission were 66.9 per cent and 88.6 per cent respectively. For the same year, the qualifying rate for university admission among all 17-year-olds was 18.4 per cent for Palestinian citizen students and 40.4 per cent for Jewish students (Ministry of Education in Israel, cited in Adalah 2005: 45). The situation seems not to have improved since then. In 2009, the town-by-town data published by the MOE on the percentage of high-school students who passed their matriculation exams show that most Arab towns appeared once again in the bottom half of the list. Although female Palestinian secondary school students on average outperform boys in the matriculation exams, this does not necessarily translate into an advantage in terms of their university entrance rates, especially if compared to Jewish females. In 2002 it was reported that only 32.7 per cent of Palestinian females met university entrance requirements, compared with 52.5 per cent of Jewish females (Adalah 2005: 21).

There is a need for specific research outlining the differences between Mizrahi and Ashkenazi Jews in terms of educational provision and attainment. Nevertheless, scholars have corroborated the fact that the relationship between the quality of education and educational attainment are heavily linked to such factors as race, class and ethnicity. For example, Arab local councils and 'development towns' that are overwhelmingly populated by Mizrahi Jews receive less state funding, infrastructural support and attention than municipalities that are overwhelmingly populated by Ashkenazi Jews (Motzafi-Haller 2001: 703; Addi-Raccah and Mazawi 2004; Adeeb 2003). The former localities are also characterized by having fewer job opportunities, higher unemployment, larger and poorer families, as well as underdeveloped infrastructure in general, especially in terms of education budgets. It comes as no surprise that graduating from poorly equipped schools which lack, for instance, adequate counselling and ancillary staff, labs, computers – amenities available in Jewish schools – constitutes a great disadvantage to Arab students (Addi-Raccah and Mazawi 2004: 152).

Higher education for Palestinian Arab students is a struggle; it is part of the national struggle. This struggle against racial, ethnic and class discrimination is further complicated by the patriarchal structure of the state and Arab society (both Palestinian and Mizrahi) alike. Despite the relative lack of information on Mizrahi women's education, it has been observed that there is still a disparity between the number of Mizrahi women obtaining post-elementary education and the number going on to post-secondary education as compared to Jewish women in their cohort (Yonah and Saporta 2006). It is likely that the matriculation exams are an obstacle to Mizrahi students. In their study, Addi-Raccah and Mazawi found that 'Arab pupils who remain in the system and pursue their high school studies have a significantly higher chance of obtaining a matriculation certificate compared to their Jewish counterparts of Middle Eastern and African origin' (Addi Raccah and Andre Mazawi 2004: 147). The class, gender and ethnic marginalization of Mizrahi women in Israel undoubtedly constitutes a primary reason for their weak academic performance (and that of men). However, the official lumping together of all Jews makes such a disaggregated analysis difficult to achieve.

Women's university education cannot be isolated from the overall context of their education. The Bagrut is in fact only one route to obtaining a university place. Applying to Israeli universities requires the taking of a Psychometric Entrance Test (PET). This test covers three areas: quantitative reasoning, verbal reasoning and the English language. Administered by the Israeli National Institute for Testing and Evaluation (NITE), this exam, again informed by Ashkenazi cultural norms and expectations, has also proven to be an obstacle to Palestinian Arab and Mizrahi Jewish students. For example, in 2001, 44.7 per cent of non-Jewish (Palestinian citizen) students who applied to university were rejected, compared with only 16.7 per cent of Jewish applicants; acceptance rates were 41.2 per cent and 65.1 per cent respectively.[10] For the academic year 2003–04, Palestinian Arab students comprised 10 per cent of the total student population studying for a Bachelor's degree in Israel, 5 per cent of those taking for a Master's degree, and only about 3 per cent of those engaged in doctoral research. In the final analysis, the disparities in scholarly achievement at all stages are reflected in the smaller proportion of Arab students who go on to higher education (Dichter 2004). NITE administers the PET test for undergraduate entry to all Israeli universities. Data for 2006 suggests that a matriculation certificate was earned by 46.3 per cent of Arabs and 54.9 per cent of Jews who sat the test; those who met university requirements numbered 34.4 per cent among Arab applicants compared with 48.3 per cent among Jews; overall, Arab students account for just 11.2 per cent of all first-degree students (Hesketh and Zaher 2009: 6).

At the level of higher education, especially in the university sector, the gender gap among the Mizrahis continues to be relatively wide. Although the gender gap between female and male Mizrahi school students, especially at the primary and secondary levels, has narrowed, that between Mizrahi and Ashkenazi Jews is still considerable (Adeeb 2003: 30). In this regard, Ya'ar, for example, observes that 'the more modern the Israeli economic and occupational systems become, the greater the influence of academic education on the structure of opportunities in the labour market' (Ya'ar 2005: 107). Nonetheless, the patriarchal, dominating, elitist and exclusionist Zionist structures of the State of Israel shift benefits and opportunities towards Ashkenazi Jews and away from Palestinian citizens, and limit Mizrahis' access to benefits and opportunities.

Insisting on the conceptual framework of exclusion and marginalization as the historical and contemporary context for Mizrahi lives in Israel, Ella Shohat observes that

> during the 1980s, published documents proved that discrimination was a calculated policy that knowingly privileged the Ashkenazi Jews, at times creating irregular situations in which educated Mizrahis became unskilled labourers, while much less educated Ashkenazim came to occupy high administrative positions. (Shohat 1997: 12)

The segregated and unequal educational system has served to perpetuate further the ethnic division of labour by, on the one hand, orienting Ashkenazi students toward prestigious, high-status and well-paying jobs, and, on the other, directing Mizrahis towards low-status blue-collar jobs. Israeli racist policies which historically disregarded and silenced Mizrahis, and Mizrahi women specifically, have undoubtedly led to their lower socio-economic and educational status. Such status, as Shohat observes, has not changed much (Shohat 1997: 12).

As with Israel's racialized policies towards Palestinian Arab citizens, the ethnicization of Mizrahi Jews is widely responsible for the latter's low educational status, even in terms of subsequent generations. With regard to second-generation Ashkenazi and Mizrahi Jews, Ashkenazis are about three times as likely as Mizrahis to be university graduates. Cohen et al. note that 32 per cent of Ashkenazi men and 40 per cent of Ashkenazi women are university graduates, compared to 10 and 13 per cent among Mizrahi men and women, respectively. Of third-generation Jews, 33 per cent of Ashkenazis and 9 per cent of Mizrahis are graduates; although for women the proportions have increased noticeably: 50 per cent of Ashkenazis and 18 per cent of Mizrahis (Cohen et al. 2007: 904). These statistics, while suggesting an increase in the number of Mizrahi women achieving higher education, do not actually point to an equalizing shift; in other words, the percentage may have increased, but compared to Ashkenazi women, approximately half of whom receive a university education, Mizrahi women still proportionately lag behind.

Moreover, comparing matriculation rates among Mizrahi and Ashkenazi Jews, Cohen et al. report that in the older birth cohort (born 1950–54) of second-generation men 61 per cent of Ashkenazis and 25 per cent of Mizrahis were successful, whereas in the younger birth cohort of the same generation (born 1965–69) the corresponding rates were 65 per cent and 40 per cent. A more considerable reduction in the disparity, according to their findings, occurred among the women of the same birth cohort and generation: Ashkenazi women, 68 per cent and 77 per cent; Mizrahi women, 30 per cent and 51 per cent. A similar trend is observed in terms of the those studying in universities. For example, among males of the same birth cohort of the second generation of Asian-African and European-American Israelis studying in universities in the mid-1990s, the rates were 37 per cent and 14 per cent, respectively, while for the third generation they were 37 per cent and 32 per cent. A sharper reduction in disparity at the same educational level occurred among the women: in the second generation the corresponding rates were 35 per cent and 9 per cent, and in the third generation they were 38 per cent and 33 per cent (Cohen et al. 2007: 902).

Golan-Agnon has rightly observed that 'Israeli schools are methods of disseminating institutionalized racism, and they begin the process of subjugation at an early age' (Golan-Agnon 2006: 1082). Whereas Israel's racist policies have kept the Palestinian Arab educational sector separate and largely underdeveloped, with curricula aimed at denationalizing them, the type of education provided to Mizrahis, historically and until recently, has been aimed at humiliating them and masking their cultural and national identities.

As in the case of data presented on Palestinian women's higher education, the above statistics do not tell the whole story. Although all forms of higher education have the potential to enhance women's human capital, the overall context of education for Palestinian and Mizrahi women seems to create – even if unconsciously – a hierarchical system based on gender: women are largely concentrated in the social sciences and humanities, potentially destined for occupations in the educational sector, in social work or in the extension of women's domestic domain. It is in this context that Cohen et al. observe that 'a disproportionate share of Mizrahi women graduated from teachers' college while Ashkenazi men and women graduated from Israel's major universities' (Cohen et al. 2007: 907). This observation holds for Palestinian women's higher education.

Discrimination against Palestinian citizens who want to attend Israeli universities is also age-based, a condition which is not applicable to the Jewish population at large. For example, Palestinian students below the age of 20 (the majority of high-school graduates) are denied entry to Israeli universities in fields such as nursing, occupational and physical therapy, and communication disorders. Such fields provide relatively stable and secure employment in the labour market. While the official reason for this exclusion is that these and similar programmes require more maturity in students, the real reason relates largely to the fact that at this age Jewish youth are in the military and so cannot enrol in such programmes (Ilani 2009).[11] Discrimination against Palestinian citizens in the Israeli academy, combined with access to universities in neighbouring Arab countries (primarily Jordan), which became possible after the Oslo Accords in 1994, has led to a large number of students enrolling in universities outside of Israel. Indeed the increase in the number of Palestinian students studying in Jordanian universities in the past decade or so has been phenomenal: from fewer than 100 in the late 1990s to around 5,000 in 1999 (Ilani 2009).

Ethnic and racial discrimination against female Mizrahi and Palestinian citizens undoubtedly has major consequences for their labour force participation, especially in terms of the types of job they do and salary rates they earn. Mizrahi feminists have rightly suggested that Ashkenazi women's socio-economic advantage allows them more access and freedom to pursue full-time academic positions and other elite posts. Smadar Lavie has gone further, suggesting that 'work for Ashkenazi women is more of a luxury than a necessity, but that for Mizrahi women it is the opposite' (Lavie 2005:13). While I accept the fact that for most Mizrahi women work is necessary, I would add that lower-class and poor Ashkenazi women are in the same boat.

In this chapter, as throughout the book, an emphasis has been placed on the importance of acknowledging the historical and contemporary experiences of Mizrahi women as the condition for understanding women's citizenship status in Israel. However, it is argued here that of the three major categories of women – Ashkenazi, Mizrahi and Palestinian – it is Palestinians who have been at the receiving end of the largest share of racial segregation and institutional prejudice. Discrimination within this group, due largely to historical circumstances, was also differentially distributed, to the advantage of Christian females over Muslim and Druze women and placing Palestinian Bedouin women at the bottom. The complex yet particularly oppressive lived reality experienced by Bedouin women, both historically and contemporarily, has placed them in extremely difficult circumstances, with their education and human capital development suffering the most. In this case, socio-economic and political marginalization and discriminatory state policies, in terms of land confiscation – leaving about 60,000 living in unrecognized villages with no running water, electricity, paved roads, proper transportation and state services in general, combined with traditional patriarchal norms governing gender relations – have rendered women's position more precarious (Abu-Rabia-Queder 2004, 2006; Nimni 2003a; Hesketh and Zaher 2009).

The particular discrimination practised against Bedouin women, whose human capital is already deficient, along with their suffering ongoing land confiscations in favour of Jewish immigrants and their efforts at resisting Israel's modernizing approach to their education, is discussed by Sarab Abu-Rabia-Queder in her 'Women, Education, and Control' (2004). She criticizes Israel's educational system, which she argues is pluralistic in its application to the Jewish population – taking into consideration degrees of religiosity and cultural differences – but 'modernist' or 'modernizationalist' within the Bedouin community. She advocates the need for the state to recognize Arab Bedouin traditional cultural values and create schools that are sex-segregated, as they are in the religious system of education employed in ultra-Orthodox Jewish schools. For Abu-Rabia-Queder, 'the state's approach to modernization in the area of education creates control, leads to the segregation of Arab Bedouin women, and makes them dependent' (Abu-Rabia-Queder 2004: 3).

Using a cultural relativist approach, Abu-Rabia-Queder criticizes what she calls the state monolithic approach to education among the Arab Bedouin and calls for implementation of the pluralistic approach employed in the Jewish sector, which she contends is gender-based and most desired by the Arab Bedouin in the Naqa (2004, 2006). 'Boys and girls', she states, 'study together in all the Arab schools in the permanent towns, which conflicts with the culture of the local society that separates the genders. This failure to segregate the sexes primarily harms female Arab Bedouin students, among whom the drop-out rate increases with age' (Abu-Rabia Queder, in Adalah, 2004).

A 1999 survey by the Arab Human Rights Association in Israel conducted among 55 Palestinian Bedouin women in the Negev aged 15 to 65, which included unrecognized and recognized villages, revealed that 43 per cent of the women interviewed were illiterate. According to the survey, only 16 per cent of the women had completed high school; only 4.5 per cent had passed their Bagrut matriculation exams; and only one person had begun some form of higher education. And when asked what they felt was the most important need for themselves and their community, 65 per cent responded that their most essential needs were educational: the provision of schools and kindergartens, as well as adult education and literacy classes (B'Tselem 1999).[12]

To reiterate, human capital is a commodity in short supply among Bedouin women. For the first two decades following the state's establishment, the Bedouin were left totally isolated from the rest of the Palestinian population, with no infrastructure or possibility of education, let alone economic activity. During this period and ever since, the same state has busied itself confiscating Palestinian lands in the Naqab, building settlements and towns for Jewish immigrants and developing infrastructure and educational systems to absorb immigrant children. The Jewish immigrants placed in these areas, as noted elsewhere in this book, were largely Mizrahi Jews. Even after the period of military rule (1948–66), when the state opened more schools in the Palestinian Arab sector, the Bedouin, especially in the Naqab, remained heavily marginalized. A later study by Abu Rabia-Queder (2006), which adopts the same cultural relativist approach to modernization, reaffirms the low educational status of Bedouin women, many of whom drop out of the school system at a relatively early stage of their education. Drop-out rates among the Bedouin are the highest in Israel, especially for girls. Reports from the late 1990s give drop-out rates of 10 per cent in the Jewish sector, 40 per cent in the entire Arab sector and in excess of 67 per cent among the Bedouin. In Rahat, the first Bedouin city in Israel, the overall drop-out rate among 17-year-olds reached 40 per cent in 2002, while several of the city's neighbourhoods showed a 100 per cent drop-out rate for girls (Abu Rabia-Queder 2006: 5).

Abu Rabia-Queder's expanded study of Bedouin women's education (2006) deserves special attention, as it is the first ethnographic study carried out by a Bedouin female academic on Bedouin women. The study is important for its discussion of the structural and systematic oppression of the Bedouin, and of their initial exclusion and marginalization, especially in the area of female education. Its critical stance on Israel's 'modernizing' approach to education among the Bedouin, a system that is basically racist and racializing, is also worthy of note. The author criticizes much of the literature, which places the blame for the high drop-out rate on Bedouin traditional culture, and argues instead that state policies of modernization in the Western sense have failed to take into consideration the traditional life of the Bedouin.

However, at the point of analysing her data, Abu-Rabia-Queder unfortunately drops this critical political approach, adopting instead a cultural relativist perspective. Issues such as 'fear of rumour of romantic contact with boys', raised especially by uneducated parents, were taken at face value and accepted uncritically as a rationale for the high drop-out rate for females. Given that most educated families in Abu-Rabia-Queder's study believed in the importance of education for their daughters (2006: 10–13), one wonders why the focus of analysis is on the responses of the uneducated rather than the educated. In fact, for the latter sector the issue of 'female honour' was not a concern that would prevent them securing education for their female kin. This begs the question of what happened to the structural forces, state racist policies and other oppressive measures mentioned by the author at the beginning of the article. Why emphasize gender and patriarchy as the most disabling forces for Bedouin women, brought about by Bedouin cultural tradition, while de-emphasizing or even dropping the wider structural forces that govern their lives?

That said, it is important to remember that Bedouin women are not victims or passive recipients of oppression. They also have a voice and agency and the potential to change their own situation. A strong voice for change, like that of Abu-Rabia-Queder herself, could undoubtedly serve as a role model in the Bedouin community: a voice that could point to a brighter future for the new generation of Bedouin females instead of focusing on their victimization.[13]

In conclusion, this chapter has demonstrated the complexity of the educational status of women in Israel. It has detailed the differential treatment received by Ashkenazi, Mizrahi and Palestinian women. While in some cases it appears that the rate of Palestinian female education exceeds that of Mizrahi women, overall racialization and discrimination against Palestinian education, especially women's education, remains overwhelming. The chapter has also delineated the differential institutional racialization of Muslim and Bedouin women and Palestinian Christians, with the last historically enjoying greater opportunities than the other groups.

The Israeli educational system, it has been shown, is not just gendered but also racialized and ethnicized. Finally, as the case of extreme oppression of and discrimination against the Bedouin population demonstrates, the Israeli educational system serves little more than a means to ensure the superiority of Ashkenazi or Zionist policies and practices in Palestine. That is, Jewish security, the Judaization of land, geography, economy, the educational system, the market and the public sphere take precedence over all 'non-Jewish', namely Palestinian, citizens' rights and needs.

Conclusion

THIS STUDY'S PREMISS is that understanding women's citizenship status within the Israeli state requires a proper appreciation and analysis of the nature and character of the state within which women find themselves. But in order to achieve this one must acknowledge the historical moments that have shaped their lives and continue to inform their existence. It has been argued that attending to the history of Palestine, which witnessed the emergence of the Zionist settler colonial movement, means recognizing the fundamental role of that movement in the development of the power relations between Jews and Arabs and between Jewish Mizrahi and Ashkenazi women. As we have seen, most of the literature, including progressive and critical studies, has approached citizenship in Israel from an ethnocentric perspective. Some approaches – such as that of Oren Yiftachel, who uses the framework of ethnocracy – provide a more advanced and critical definition of the state, its policies and its institutions. But, as argued here, situating the debate around ethnicity remains problematic as it assumes the presence of multiple ethnicities within the state and the latter's privileging of one – superior – ethnicity. While the Jewish/non-Jewish schism is an official marker of the Israeli state's policies and practices, around which the whole system of racialization, discrimination and exploitation is established, the reality is much more complex.

The history and lived reality of Mizrahi Jews, and especially Mizrahi women, point to Zionism's mythological construction of Jewishness as a unified and undifferentiated notion. The dilapidated spaces in which Mizrahi Jews were settled, such as the *ma'abarout* (transit camps) and the *ayarot pituah* (so-called development towns), combined with the overall inferior socio-economic and political status that Mizrahi women have been assigned within the Israeli polity, provide strong evidence of their Jewish otherness rather than their affiliation with Zionism, the philosophy upon which the Israeli state was established. The conception of Mizrahi women adopted in this study, in common with the other categories of women, Palestinians and Ashkenazis, recognizes the diversity within the group and does not treat them as homogeneous or monolithic. However, the aim of the study is to analyse the dynamics of the relationship between the three largest groups of women who make up the demography of the State of Israel, and to whom the Israeli state is responsible.

Zionism, it has been argued, was and has continued to be more than a national movement for ingathering Jews, lifting them up from oppression in their European homelands and equalizing them socio-economically within a Jewish state. Zionism has been and continues to be a settler-colonial and fundamentally racist movement most interested in the white European Jewish domination of indigenous non-Jews as well as non-European Jews.

Centring the debate on Israel as an ethnic state or ethnocracy, it was argued, cannot but logically position Palestinian citizens as another ethnicity, stripping them of their national indigenous identity, and ignoring the racist character of Zionism and the Israeli settler-colonial state. The reality, however, is different. Palestinian citizens, who formed their national identity prior to the establishment of the state, as they engaged in a national movement resistant to British colonialism and the Zionist settler project, continue to struggle against Israeli state efforts to de-indigenize and denationalize them. The forceful cleansing and expulsion of Palestinians from their homes and land, their places of origin, their confinement for almost twenty years under military rule, and their continued treatment as nonentities (non-Jews), have without a doubt placed them in a category somewhat distinct from a straightforwardly 'ethnic' group one. Hence the rejection from the outset of the term 'ethnicity' as an identifier for the Palestinians, and the need for an alternative theorization of Zionism and of Israel in order to contextualize women's citizenship appropriately. This necessitated the deployment of the concepts of racism and racialization in the study: concepts that more accurately describe the institutionalization of Zionism within the body of the Israeli state.

Critics of the ethnic democracy paradigm, some of whom also adopt the more sophisticated notion of ethnocracy, accept the conceptualization of Zionism and Israel as a settler-colonial regime. However, the majority of authors argue that such a description is accurate only for certain historical periods and not for others. As seen in the case of Peled and Shafir, the settler-colonialism concept has been used to describe Zionism before the establishment of the state or to explain Israel's regime after 1967 with regard to the occupation of the West Bank and Gaza. As to the nature of the state in terms of its policies towards Palestinian citizens since 1948, the concept of settler colonialism is dropped from the analysis. Instead, Israel is defined in ethnic terms as a Jewish state stratified by ethnicities.

The Zionist settler-colonial and fundamentally exclusionary and exclusivist policies in historical Palestine must be seen as a continuum, and not as belonging to discrete historical periods. Even if one opts to exclude from the account the phenomenon of Israel's elastic geographical borders and the citizens of Jerusalem (and the Golan Heights), and deals only with the state's indigenous Palestinian citizens – namely those in Galilee, the Triangle and the Naqab – it is not possible to ignore the settler-colonial character of the state, not least in terms of its racialized policies and practices towards this group of citizens.

How otherwise can one explain Israel's constant and consistent policies of land expropriation and alienation of its indigenous Palestinian citizens? How can one account for the fact that some 20 per cent of Israel's indigenous Palestinians have been left to live on less than 3 per cent of their historical land? How is one to comprehend the systematic denial of Palestinians' essential citizenship rights, especially the right to own and live on the land? Defining the State of Israel as a settler-colonial regime has furnished an appropriate framework for contextualizing the inherent and embedded racism characteristic of the system. This understanding of racism explains Israel's policies and practices towards not only its indigenous population but also its immigrant population of Arab Jews, the Mizrahis.

Feminist conceptualization of citizenship in the Middle East, it has been argued, has largely adopted a culturalist approach, focusing its analyses on the relationship between familialism, religion and nationalism. These three frameworks have been presented as the primary constituents of the structures of women's oppression. In other words, Palestinian women, as well as other Arab women (Mizrahis from Arab countries) have been and continue to be seen primarily as victims of their own culture and patriarchy, and not of the very state within which they live. Within the context of Palestinian and Mizrahi women citizens of Israel, it has been argued, there is a need for a different feminist approach, one that allows a wider space to account for the vital role played by the settler-colonial state in shaping these 'cultural institutions'. The debate on feminism and nationalism acquires a distinct character in the context of Israel. For example, Ashkenazi nationalist identification as Zionists and Jews has been debated and contested among Mizrahi women, who do not consider themselves to be part of the Zionist movement or as citizens treated on an equal basis with Ashkenazis. If anything, anti-racist feminist and other Mizrahi critics have argued against collapsing Mizrahis and Ashkenazis into a common Jewish nationalism. For Mizrahi women, it is not their culture or patriarchy but rather the Zionist project which constitutes their major oppression. Theorizing citizenship within the confines of familialism, nationalism and religion is limiting, especially if these are discussed within the context of the Israeli state. For Palestinians, the state has played a vital role in shaping and reshaping the family, in suppressing and denying their national and cultural identity, and in controlling religious laws and institutions. The type of study that locates, or centres, analysis of citizenship within the framework of the state condemns itself to replicating and thereby supporting its values and function.

Defining Israel as an exclusivist and exclusionary settler-colonial state has enabled a better understanding of the status and position of the various sectors of women within the state. The focus here has enabled us to highlight what otherwise is clearly missing from most feminist analyses, namely the role of economic rights, especially the right to landed property and to education, in the shaping of citizenship. A political economy approach to Israeli citizenship, it has been demonstrated, complements and further advances existing critical feminist studies on citizenship in the Middle East. Replacing ethnic-centred paradigms with a political economy approach conscious of the role of racism and racialization in settler-colonial states has made it possible for this study to provide a deeper understanding of women citizens in their differentiated statuses and actual lived experiences.

Among the areas of stark racialization of Palestinian women citizens, and ethnicization and discrimination against Mizrahi female citizens, the focus here has been on the fields of education and economy, and specifically labour force participation. The study has demonstrated the vast disparity and differentiation that exist among the three groups: among Jews, between Ashkenazi and Mizrahi women, and between Jews in general and Palestinian Arabs as a separate group, more specifically. While this study rejects the ethnicization or segmentation of the Palestinians and their division into ethno-religious groups as an analytical strategy, it nevertheless recognizes that the existing differentiation and marginalization of some over others is a historical and actually existing reality, with Christian Arabs being more advantaged than Muslims, Druze and Bedouin Palestinians. Important in this respect has been the study's insistence on the significance of the historical moments that have led to the emergence of such differentiation, while accounting simultaneously for Israel's role in producing and reproducing ethnic and racial differentiation.

The historically specific case of Israel, it has been argued, constitutes the primary reason for the need to advance a particular set of concepts in order to understand and articulate women's citizenship status. It is true that in certain aspects of state policy and women's citizenship status vis-à-vis the state, one can find commonalities between the Israeli state and other Middle Eastern and even non-Middle East states. However, this does not license a lumping together of this case with other studies on women and citizenship in the Middle East. The presence of common cultural or religious practices or beliefs among Arabs, in other words, is not a legitimate or logical reason for treating Israel as just any state.

Investigating culture, tradition and familialism in a manner which refuses to see them as independent, immutable or ahistorical categories, but which instead understands them as institutions affecting, and affected by, state policies and practices, has served to further clarify the political economic context of social phenomena and substantiate the understanding that all social and cultural concepts and categories are historical and specific. Hence the importance of one of the main premises of this study, namely restoring the economic – especially in the form of land and landed property rights – to the political system and the material reality to the historical record: an analysis which has opened up a wider space for challenging Israel's present regime while simultaneously envisioning a future without existing forms of oppression. This analysis has facilitated a clearer theorization of women and citizenship by highlighting not only cultural, social and political citizenship, but also economic citizenship. This analysis, it is argued, has further contributed to the growing debate among Jewish, Palestinian and other scholars who advocate equal citizenship rights within Israel, as they call for the establishment of a single secular democratic state for all its citizens: Jews and Palestinian Arabs in Palestine–Israel. It is for all of the above reasons that this study has adopted a multilayered conceptual approach, with anti-racist and anti-colonial feminism embedded in the wider Marxist understanding of political economy. It is also for the purpose of advancing a clearer vision of a just society that I have employed various elements of Juris's 'militant ethnography'.

Notes

INTRODUCTION

1. The debate on the naming of the Mizrahi group (i.e. whether Mizrahi, Sephardi, Oriental or primarily Arab) is addressed throughout the book.

ONE

1. The term 'knowledge/power' and the idea that knowledge equals power are used by Dorothy Smith in her *Institutional Ethnography: A Sociology for People* (2005), especially ch. 9. The notion is borrowed from Foucault.
2. For more on the dismal state of writing by and on Mizrahi Jewish women, see Motzafi-Haller 2001.
3. In addition to the work of a number of Palestinian women NGOs that have been in existence since the 1990s, which produce various documents and reports (e.g. Organization of Violence Against Women, Al-Siwar; another is Al-Fanar, which no longer exists), over the past five years or so Mada Al-Carmel has developed a women's studies programme, which has begun to produce important reports and writings contributing further to feminist literature.
4. Examples of studies at national and regional levels, see Rouhana 1997; Rouhana and Ghanem 1998; Rouhana and Sultany 2003; Peled 1992; Shafir and Peled 2002.
5. Shmuel Noah Eisenstadt is a well-known Israeli sociologist; for many he is the father of Israeli sociology. Eisenstadt adopted Talcott Parsons's functionalist theory. He considered the Western (liberal capitalist) model of development as the best for Israel. In doing so, he also justified the existence and policies of the State of Israel and deemed these necessary for the country's growth and development.

191

6. According to Oren Yiftachel: 'Ethnocratic regimes promote the expansion of the dominant groups in contested territory and its domination of power structures while maintaining a democratic facade. Ethnocracy manifests in the Israeli case with the long-term Zionist strategy of Judaizing the homeland – constructed during the last century as the Land of Israel' (2006: 3).

7. The notion of 'ethnic democracy' used to define Israel was preferred by both Peled and Shafir until the late 1990s (see, e.g., Peled 1992; Peled and Shafir 1996). In this paradigm they divide the Israeli system of rule into two tiers: first-class citizens (Jews) and second-class citizens (Palestinian Arabs). In a later book (Peled and Shafir 2002), they developed a more nuanced approach to citizenship based on a three-tier system of rule, recognizing a multiplicity of citizenship rights associated with three basic 'ethnic' groups: Ashkenazis, Palestinians and Mizrahis. Their new approach, which replaces the concept of ethnic democracy with that of 'ethnocracy', also recognizes gender as an important component of citizenship – albeit that they are concerned with Ashkenazi women only.

8. For more on the grim future of Israeli policies of land confiscation, demographic racism and treatment of its citizens, see Nadim and Sultany 2003.

9. Nils Butenschon uses the term 'singularism' or 'singularist ethnocracy' to define the State of Israel. Singularism refers to the 'idea that the state community is organized by a single and specific collective identity, that the state is the embodiment of that identity, and where citizenship is allocated according to specific ethnic criteria' (Butenschon et al. 2000: 16–27).

10. 'Such complacency', Yuval-Davis argues, 'helped to foster the illusion during the so-called "Oslo Process" that the Israeli–Palestinian conflict is basically a conflict on borders between two neighbouring nations, each with its own distinct homeland, rather than a conflict between an ethno-settler project and a resisting indigenous population: or, rather, that the difference between these two analytical models is not crucial' (Yuval-Davis 2003: 193).

11. Said's concept of the 'exilic intellectual' is particularly pertinent to this study. In his definition of the concept, Said says that the intellectual is 'neither a pacifier nor a consensus-builder, but someone whose whole being is staked on a critical sense, a sense of being unwilling to accept easy formulas, or ready-made clichés, or the smooth, ever-so-accommodating confirmations of what the powerful or conventional have to say, and what they do. Not just passively unwilling, but actively willing to say so in public' (1994: 9). The intellectual, in short, engages in the act of 'speaking truth to power'.

12. See 'The Future Vision for the Arabs in Israel', a document prepared by the National Committee of the Heads of Local Arab Counsels in Israel 2007 (in Nakhleh 2008).

13. Badal marriage refers to the form of marriage where a sister and her brother are married to a brother and his sister from another family. It is often the case that such marriages occur between first cousins on the agnatic (father's)

line and primarily for economic reasons, especially inheritance in landed property.

14. Yom al-Ard or Land Day is a day of national demonstrations for Palestinian citizens, dating from 30 March 1976. It is now an annual event that sees demonstrations against Israel's land policies, which have resulted in the confiscation and Judaization of most of the land owned by Palestinian natives.

15. The JNF is known in Hebrew as the Keren Kayemet L'Yisrael (KKL) (literally, 'the Perpetual Fund for Israel'). In some states, JNF affiliate organizations use this name instead of JNF. Today, the JNF controls vast numbers of properties belonging to millions of Palestinians, developing them exclusively for persons of 'Jewish nationality', a concept established and promoted in the JNF's charter to exclude all others. The JNF was created in 1901 to acquire land and property rights in Palestine and beyond for exclusive Jewish settlement. While indigenous Palestinians are barred from leasing, building on, managing or working their own land, the JNF holds the land in trust for 'those of Jewish race or descendency' living anywhere in the world. In 1953, the Israeli Knesset legislated special status for the JNF, enabling it to carry out governmental functions as a Zionist institution ('for Jews only'). The JNF continues to operate as a state-chartered organization under Israeli law, with direct control over some 13 per cent of the land in pre-1967 Israel. Further, the JNF appoints six out of thirteen members of the governing board of the Israel Lands Authority (ILA), which manages the JNF's 13 per cent, in addition to a further 80 per cent of all land in Israel. It is through this relationship with the JNF that Israel, while portraying itself as the only democracy in the Middle East, in fact outsources the land-management functions of the state to this discriminatory state-chartered organization. For more on this, see http://bdsmovement.net/?q=node/749.

16. For more details on this case, see *Adalah's Newsletter*, volume 42, November 2007, www.adalah.org/newsletter/eng/nov07/8.php.

17. The issue of 'land swaps' has emerged several times in the recent 'peace negotiations' between the Israelis and the Palestinian Authority. This places Palestinian citizens currently living in the Triangle in danger of being 'transferred' to the Palestinian Authority, thereby losing their current citizenship status in their own homeland.

18. In his letter, Bush announced: 'The United States is strongly committed to Israel's security and well-being as a Jewish state.' Gordon Brown, in his speech, said: 'I think of David Ben Gurion – who from humble beginnings in Poland built up the Jewish National Institutions – and in 1948 said it was not enough for the Jewish state simply to be Jewish, it had to be fully democratic.' He spends a great deal of time on reaffirming the Zionist myth of 'Palestine as the only homeland for the Jewish people' ('Address of UK Prime Minister, Gordon Brown to the Knesset, July 21, 2008', www. knesset.gov.il/description/eng/doc/speech_brown_2008_eng.htm.

19. For a detailed description of women's rights in the Middle East, see Freedom House 2005.
20. Souad Joseph uses the term 'relationality' to indicate the connectedness or relationship a concept has with larger socio-political and ideological structures.
21. The 'millet' system was the term adopted by the Ottomans to refer to the different religious sects in the empire. The millet system stipulated the relationship between the different religions and the land, in terms of control, ownership and use.
22. Kumari Jayawardena's seminal work *Feminism and Nationalism in the Third World* (1986), in which she establishes an intimate link between women's liberation and national liberation, has become a classic for Middle Eastern feminists concerned with women's status.
23. Elsewhere it has been argued that the constructions of Israeli citizenship have incorporated major exclusionary and inclusionary policies and practices. For more on this, see Abdo and Yuval-Davis 1995. The relationship between women and nationalism was first discussed by Kumari Jayawardena (1986). Regarding the Israeli declaration of independence, Abdo and Yuval-Davis maintain that 'the country was never meant to be a political expression of its civil society, of the people who reside in its territory, or even of all its citizens. The country was never meant to be a democracy, but the state of the Jewish people, wherever they are' (1995: 306).
24. Israel does not have a constitution; the reference here is to its Basic Law.
25. The phrase 'to some extent' is used here to account for the changes accrued to Mizrahi women's lives in terms of economic participation and other entitlements they gain by default for being Jews. The chapters on women and the economy and women and education elaborate further on this change.
26. The 'Against House Demolitions' event was scheduled for 5 April 2008 in Nazareth, to be followed by a demonstration. Among the participating organizations were the Women's Council: Kufur Qarea'; Women's Coalition for Peace; Progressive Women's Union; Woman to Woman; Democratic Women's Movement; Women Against Violence; and many more.
27. The Wisconsin Plan, named after the plan applied in the state of Wisconsin in the United States in the early 1990s, was initiated in Israel in August 2005. It is known in Hebrew as the Plan Mehalev (Hebrew for 'From the Heart'). This programme of 'workfare' sets out to put people on employment benefit back to work, but in a labour market context which suffers high rates of unemployment and is undergoing a great deal of privatization and the importing of cheap labour. Between 2005 and 2007 the implementation of the plan was at an experimental stage and aimed at including 17,000 of the 160,000 who were receiving income maintenance. The plan targeted areas such as East and West Jerusalem, Nazareth and Nazareth Ilit, Hadera and the villages of Wadi Ara and Ashkelon – in other words, overwhelmingly Arab, Mizrahi and other poor communities. The crux of the programme

is this: '[E]very participating welfare recipient will be required to remain in the Wisconsin centre between 30 and 40 hours per week, receiving counselling, training, and job referrals. If he does not succeed in finding salaried employment, the counsellor may assign him to full-time non-paid work in a community institution such as a hospital or charity. Only by doing this work will he continue to receive a welfare check (NIS 2200 per family = $488 monthly)' (Assaf 2005). For more on the plan, see Sawt el-Amel/The Laborers' Voice, www.laborers-voice.org/home-e.aspx.

28. The Three Documents are public political statements by major Palestinian civil society organizations expressing their resentment of Israel as a self-defined 'Jewish' state and suggesting an alternative future in which all citizens will be equal. The documents are: 'Future Vision', prepared by Lajnat al-Mutaba'a al-Ulya (The Higher Committee for Arabs in Israel); 'The Democratic Constitution', prepared by Adalah; and 'Haifa Document', prepared by Mada Al-Carmel. For more on these documents, see Nakhleh 1997.

29. Commenting on this bill, Adalah's general director, Attorney Hassan Jabareen, stated that 'while many democratic states around the world have loyalty oaths, this bill differs in that it forces Arab citizens of Israel to accept their inferiority, inequality and exclusion, as it deems the state as one for Jews only, and serving the Jewish people alone.' He warned that 'the approval of this loyalty oath may serve as a slippery slope, as declarations of allegiance to a Jewish and democratic state may soon be required from all newly elected ministers, members of Knesset, workers in the Israeli civil service and/or required when trying to obtain an Israeli identity card or passport, etc.' See Adalah, 'The New Loyalty Oath Bill Aims to Force Arab Citizens of Israel to Accept their Inferiority, Inequality and Exclusion', Press Release 11 October 2010, www.adalah. org/eng/pressreleases/pr.php?file=11_10_10.

30. This information was released by Knesset member Jamal Zahalqa at a conference (Zahalqa 2008).

TWO

1. Recognition should be given to the two-volume collection of oral history recording Palestinian women's lived experiences and struggles during the 1930s and 1940s (Abdel-Hadi 2007, 2008). Despite the absence of analysis in these collections, the information provided is vital for a proper understanding of Palestinian women's experiences during this period.

2. The author is well aware of the development in the past two decades of attempts at joint meetings, workshops and small group discussions between established feminist NGOs representing Palestinians and Jewish Ashkenazi Jews. But these have been few and far between, and in the overwhelming majority of cases have taken place in Jewish centres or towns. The Zionist

racist image of Palestinians is replicated among the overwhelming majority of Ashkenazi feminists who are Zionists.

3. For a critique of identity politics as a white middle-class feminist paradigm, see Nira Yuval-Davis 2006: 277.

4. *Amiri*, unlike *miri*, was not state land but rather the land on which usufruct rights were inherited generationally by the fallaheen. The term *miri* was often used by Israeli officials to justify state control over land that belonged to the peasants. For more on this distinction, see Warriner 1936.

5. For a detailed account of Palestinian socio-economic and political living conditions under British and Zionist colonialism, see Abdo 1989, 1987.

6. The assessment of the tax, which was made by British officials, was based on the average amount of tithe that had been paid by the village during the four years immediately preceding the application of the ordinance, ignoring the difference between tenants, small land holders or even renters, and not taking into account such natural factors as low rain or locust plagues that may have disastrously reduced yields.

7. The means by which such vast tracts of cultivated land were acquired by the European-Jewish settlers varied; they included the purchase of land which became available as indigenous peasants were rendered impoverished and unable to pay state taxes and dues, which resulted in their lands being publicly auctioned and sold to the highest bidder. Research in this historical epoch also suggests that there was direct transfer of land considered to be 'state land' from the British to the Zionist settlers.

8. The term 'absentee landlord' here refers basically to merchant capitalists from Lebanon (e.g. the Sursock family, the Twaynee and the Khouri). These merchants also invested money in land ownership in Palestine when the latter was part of Greater Syria (until its division after World War I).

9. For a detailed analysis of the 'Tower and Stockade' policy, see Abdo 1992.

10. For more detail on the importation of Yemeni Jews to Palestine, see Kimmerling 1983: 34.

11. Both Chaim Weismann and David Ben-Gurion, the guardians of the Zionist movement, who at the time represented the Jewish Agency, recommended the stocking of settlements on the borders of Palestine. According to Ben-Gurion, 'settlements on the frontier will reinforce our rights on the upper Galilee' (cited in Rayman 1981: 33). Concerning this, Tabenkin, the 'socialist Zionist' philosopher of the movement at the time, added: 'We were the pioneers to work on the sea. None of our members were born sailors or fishermen. Yet the very fact that we were a colonizing movement made us realize that Jews do not require only the land but the sea as well. We have to conquer the sea with our fishing boats and our merchant ships. Only thus can the country be protected from the sea' (Tabenkin 1985: 61–2).

12. A full account of Palestinian economic transformation from a basically agrarian social structure into colonial capitalism can be found in Abdo 1989.

13. This film was premiered at the Toronto Palestinian Film Festival 2010. For
    more on the film, see http://tpff.ca/?page_id=331.
14. The agricultural festivities loom especially large in the collective memory
    of the Lebanese, as expressed in the music of the Rahbani family. The
    cultural–gender value of the agricultural seasons is emphatically highlighted
    in the musical *Mays Al-Reem*, produced by the Rahbani brothers and featuring
    Fairouz, among others.
15. For more on this, see Office of Statistics [Palestine] 1939: 97, Table 107.
16. This and the following citation referring to Smadar Lavie are taken from
    Encyclopaedia of Women in the Muslim World, vol. 6, pp. 6–15.
17. The concept of 'de-development' was originally coined by Sara Roy (1995)
    to describe the situation of the Gaza Strip under Israeli colonialism. 'De-
    development' refers to a state whereby the occupied or colonized economy
    and especially infrastructure, including education and other forms of
    social reality, are actually rendered 'backward' from above. The context
    of de-development is used to describe the effects of Israeli colonialism on
    the Gaza Strip, which Roy considers to have been more developed before
    occupation. This concept can be used aptly to describe the destructive
    policies of the Israeli state towards its indigenous citizens and in order to
    highlight the de-educational role played by the Israeli legal, institutional and
    administrative policies and regulations in dealing with the Arab educational
    system.
18. See note 1, above.
19. Katznelson-Rubashov's book was written in Hebrew and published in 1932
    by Nicholas L. Brown, New York. In 2002 it was translated into English by
    Maurice Samuel, edited by M. Raider and M. Raider-Roth, under the title
    The Plough Woman: Records of the Pioneer Women of Palestine (Katznelson-Rubashov
    2002).
20. The massacre at the Arab village of Tantura (population 500) on the
    Mediterranean shore, documented by Theodore (Teddy) Katz, is another
    case. Katz's M.A. thesis (2000), which was based on extensive interviews he
    conducted among a hundred Arab and Jewish people, including members of
    the Alexandroni brigade veterans who took part in the massacre, is a study of
    this particular massacre. In his thesis, Katz accuses the soldiers of butchering
    between 270 and 280 residents of Tantura immediately after its conquest in
    May 1948. In a 22-minute video, Katz tells the story of how the massacre
    happened: 'all the men in the village were taken to a cemetery of the
    village; they put them in line and ordered them to begin digging. Everyone
    in the line that had just finished digging was shot and fell into the hole.'
    Although the thesis scored the highest grade ever given to a Master's degree
    at Haifa University – 97 per cent – it generated a huge controversy both in
    Israel and worldwide. The university, despite the high recommendations
    of the supervision committee, rejected the thesis. Following this, Dr Ilan
    Pappé, who supervised Katz, was immediately targeted by a campaign of

denigration, which led him to leave the country and reside in the UK. The video is on YouTube: www.youtube.com/watch?v=N4CBj_fQ678.

21. The Hebrew term *Sabra*, borrowed from the Arabic *Sabr*, which means cactus, is used to refer to Jewish men and women of the first and second *aliyah* or European Jewish immigration. These, especially the men, are described as the cactus fruit: tough on the outside and sweet on the inside. It is worth noting that the Sabr or cactus tree was one of Palestine's traditional wild trees, growing all over the hills and mountains of the country.

22. It should be noted here that the names Tzfadia and Yiftachel are found on the latter's website; their names as they appear in Arabic literature are transliterated as Safadiyya and Yiftahel, changing the Ashkenazi terminology into a Mizrahi or Arab one.

23. In the Hebrew literature, this author appears as Udi Adeeb. The reference here is to his article in Arabic; his name appears this form in the article

24. The term *aliyah*, which refers to the major waves of Jewish immigration to Palestine and later Israel, was coined by the Zionist movement to signify ascendance to a more proper life for Jews. The three major *aliyout* (the plural form), as officially recognized, are: first, the period of the early Ashkenazi settlers' immigration (882–1903); second, the immigration wave of 1904–14; and third, the immigration wave of 1919–23. The fact is that since then, many other *aliyout* followed, including the *aliyah* from the Arab countries, Iran, Iraq, France, Argentina and North America to name just a few. In contrast, the term *yeridah* is used to refer to Jews who leave Israel to return to their homes, especially Ashkenazim hailing from Europe and North America. This term also has a nationalistic connotation, as it means Jews are leaving the Holy Land or the 'good life' behind them.

25. It is worth noting here that the term 'Mizrachi' is used exclusively by Ashkenazi and Ashkenazified writers who do not have or have lost the Arabic letter 'h' found in the term 'Mizrahi'.

26. In an essay entitled 'Epistemology of Mizrahiyout in Israel, produced by the Forum on Social and Cultural Studies at the Van Leer Institute, it is stated that identity is not defined by the test of 'reality' or 'imagination', but rather is a product that is real and imagined at the same time. Mizrahiyout in this definition is seen not as a stable phenomenon but as a fluid one. It is, they argue, a product of systems of discourse that work in socially and economically unequal practices. Mizrahi identity refers to a politicized perspective on historicized ethnic relations in Israeli society (Hever et al. 2002: 16–17).

27. For more detail on women's resistance in the OPT, see for example Kuttab and Abu Awwad 2004; Labadi 2003; Abdo 1991, 1994; Dajani 1994.

THREE

1. See Chapter 1, note 6, on Yiftachel's notion of 'Ethnocratic Regimes'.
2. For example, 'discouraged' workers – those who, after becoming unemployed,

have given up looking for work – are not included; nor are women working in agriculture, domestic services and small-scale manufacturing.

3. The reference here is especially to economic studies that use statistics as evidence for cultural impediments to participation in the labour market. For example, in his 'Ethnicity and Female Labour Market Participation: A New Look at the Palestinian Enclave in Israel', Nabil Khattab argues that traditional cultural constraints are a major impediment to women, especially married women, participating in the labour force. The evidence he presents is that 'married women … are three times less likely to be in the labour force than unmarried women' (Khattab 2002: 102). Although his reference is to participation in the Jewish market, the author fails to explain why this is the case. What specific obstacles do married women face that impede their labour force participation in the Jewish centre of the economy? And, by the same token, the author fails to explain why the overwhelming majority of working women in the racialized Arab sector are married!

4. The term 'social capital' was first coined by Pierre Bourdieu (1988) to refer to the knowledge, experience and/or connections some people accrue during the course of their lives that enable them to achieve greater success than someone from a less advantaged background.

5. Disparities between Palestinian women in terms of education are discussed in the next chapter.

6. Israeli literature argues that the presence of two labour markets, especially the 'enclave' market, is beneficial to Arab women because it ensures that women conform to the cultural norms of working within their community. Further, it is claimed that this 'enclave' or mono-ethnic labour market 'protects women from discrimination present in the Jewish dominated labour markets' (Semyonov and Lewin-Epstein 1994: 58). This culturalist approach is also shared, albeit to a lesser extent, by Nabil Khattab, who suggests that 'the ethno-religious identity is one of the basic factors for the dismal participation of women in the Israeli labour market as it determines the social, demographic, economic and cultural mobility of ethnic Arabs' (Khattab 2005: 103). A major problem in this approach is the assumption that the enclave economy is free of exploitation, while the opposite has been shown. While Khattab accepts the fact the enclave economy does not receive proper government resources and supports, he still views it as a positive place which provides women the opportunity to develop social capital (Khattab 2005: 94). This is another problematic area, as this chapter shows.

7. This information is based on a long discussion with a group of women researchers who were investigating the conditions of female retail work in Nazareth. This research, part of the larger project 'Women and Labour' undertaken by the Nazareth-based Women Against Violence organization, was in its initial stages during my visit to Nazareth in the summer of 2009.

8. It is noteworthy that, unlike in various Arab countries where human rights in general and labour rights more specifically are not protected, Israel has developed certain social welfare laws – for example, maternity benefits, social insurance, health and medical coverage and other entitlements for workers; however, these laws have proven to be of little benefit for the majority of Palestinian women, who are outside the labour market.

9. These figures, incidentally, represent 'registered unemployed' people only and not the actual numbers, which includes those who have given up on finding a job. See Dichter 2001: Table 9).

10. Figures presented here were included in the speech given by M.K. Muhammad Baraka at a conference of all the major Palestinian civil society organizations held in March 2010. This conference, which included the Data-Bank Research Centre (RAKAZ), an organization that produces its own economic reports based on Israeli statistics, estimated poverty among Palestinians for the year 2009 at 55 per cent (*Hadeeth Annas*, 5 March 2010: 3).

11. A proper understanding of the role of gender and of male culture is necessary, but unfortunately does not come within the purview of this study.

12. Table 3.1 is based on the 2003 Manpower Survey compiled by Adva Center (Information on Equality and Social Justice in Israel), edited by Shlomo Swirski and Etty Konor-Attias, entitled *Workers, Employers and the Distribution of Israel's National Income* (2007: 23). It should be noted here that the category 'other religions' refers to Muslim, Christian and Druze as well as non-Arab Christians – in other words, Palestinians have been turned into groups of religious sects gathered in Palestine by accident.

13. The IPSS was formed in 1983. It evolved from a bilateral coalition between the Allgemeinen Bevolkerungsumfragen der Socialwissenschaften of the Zentrum für Umfragen, Methoden, und Analysen (General Popular Questions of the Social History of the Centre for Surveys, Methods, and Analyses) in Mannheim, Germany and the General Social Survey of the National Opinion Research Centre, University of Chicago (ISSP). Since then it has grown to include forty-three nations, including Israel and Canada. According to the ISSP website, 'The aim of this program is to bring together pre-existing social science projects and coordinate research goals, thereby adding a cross-national, cross-cultural perspective to the individual national studies.' Surveys are conducted in a one-year collection cycle, which means simply that each year a general, all-encompassing survey on a specific topic is conducted. Every five to ten years the same topic is revisited. For example, the survey 'Work Orientations II', which is used in this book, was first administered in 1989; it was administered again, to a different but still representative sample, in 1997.

14. Recent local, regional and global changes have effected changes to the status of Druze women. In a recent visit by this author, it was observed that Druze females, especially the young women, had a greater public visibility. Some

were managing stores; others were employed as sales women in family enterprises, while others owned and operated their own enterprises. This development merits further study.

15. These figures were calculated from Dichter 2001, in which thirty-five cases of 'structural discrimination against Arab citizens' are detailed.

16. See M.K. Ahmad Tibi, paper delivered at the 2009 Herzlia Conference, published in *Hadeeth Annas*, 5 February 2009: 5.

17. Swirski and Konor-Attias are the authors of the Adva report of 2006 (Swirski and Konor-Attias 2007).

18. Further details on Sowt el-Amel and its women's affiliate organization can be found on www.laborers-voice.org.

19. WAVO (Women against Violence Org) is one of the major Palestinian NGOs in Israel that is focused on fighting all forms of violence against women. Its early focus was domestic violence, which led it to establish the first shelter for women in the Arab sector. More recently WAVO has expanded its research and activism to include violence in the labour force, in education and in various other areas where women are involved. The most recent research project WAVO conducted focuses on female academics and labour force participation. See www.wavo.org/?LanguageId=1.

FOUR

1. For a critical literature review of the education system in Israel, see Abu Usbeh 2006; see also Barghouti 2003.

2. For more on this textbook and the position of the then Ministry of Education, see Moran Zelikovich, 'Education Ministry okays new textbook featuring Nakba', 22 July 2007, *Israel News*, www.ynetnews.com/articles/0,7340,L-3428223,00.html.

3. See Adalah (the Legal Center for Arab Minority Rights in Israel), *Inequality Report: The Palestinian Arab Minority in Israel*, December 2010, www.old-adalah.org/eng/Christian%20Aid%20Report%20December%202010%20final.pdf.

4. Author's personal experience.

5. Most government schools at this time adopted gender separation: one set of schools for girls and another for boys. However, the distance of such schools from surrounding villages led many villagers to opt for sending their boys (usually not girls) to the city.

6. See http://israel-scitech-schools.org.

7. The personal experience of the author confirms the humiliation and oppression under which teaching and learning took place, especially in the late 1970s. As a Palestinian educator in Israel for more than seven years, I felt the humiliation of having to use the curriculum imposed by the Board of Education. Most humiliating of all, however, was the fact that every year, around the anniversary of the establishment of the State of Israel, we were forced to celebrate 'their independence' with our students. Recognizing that this very day was the anniversary of the Nakba – of the dispersion, killing,

rape and expulsion of Palestinians – this demand was very difficult to implement. It is true that by the late 1970s, and more specifically after the 1976 Day of the Land and the strengthening of Palestinian national identity, many Palestinian teachers discontinued the farce and began instead to instil Palestinian national pride through their teaching. This did not last long. Under the Netanyahu government, the affirmation of Israeli Jewish identity was expressed by imposing the Israeli flag on all institutions, including Palestinian ones. This was later reaffirmed through a law proposed by Communication Minister Limor Livnat and passed by the Knesset.

8. For more information on this issue, see Yousef T. Jabareen, 'Who's Afraid of Educated Arabs?', Ha'aretz, 24 July 2009, www.haaretz. com/print-edition/opinion/who-s-afraid-of-educated-arabs-1.280663.

9. The Bagrut exam results represent the final grade of students completing high school or grade 12.

10. 'Non-Jewish citizens' is an Israeli classification referring to Arab citizens, but it excludes East Jerusalemites. Figures here are taken from a comprehensive report on Palestinian Arab children's education in Israel prepared by Human Rights Watch (2001). Further details on the overall system of education in Israel can be found in Abu-Usbeh 2006.

11. In his 'Increasing Numbers of Israeli Arabs Studying at Jordanian Universities', Ofri Ilani (2009) narrates the story of one Arab women from Nazareth who wanted to study occupational therapy and communication disorders. The student tried to gain a place at the University of Haifa and was invited for an interview. But the University subsequently discovered that she was under 20, which disqualified her. This woman and the 'thousands of young high school graduates who want to study nursing or occupational or physical therapy have to wait until their 20th birthdays because of limitations [set] by universities', a policy described by the author as 'de facto discrimination against Israeli Arabs' (Ilani 2009).

12. For more on the situation of Bedouin, especially in relation to education, see Arab Human Rights Association Reports: www.arabhra.org/HRA/SecondaryArticles/SecondaryArticlePage.aspx?SecondaryArticle=1416b.

13. As I was writing this section in April of 2010, Al-Jazeera (Arabic) broadcast a documentary on Palestinian Bedouin, confirming their historical and contemporary racialization by the Israeli state. Among the issues discussed was the concentration of industrial and chemical waste, as well as the presence of high-voltage electricity poles, which are apparently causing cancer among villagers. Also important were the interviews with Bedouin academics, including both Sarab Abu-Rabia-Queder and her sister Safa Abu-Rabia. The latter narrated her own experience of the hate and anger levelled at her by her Jewish colleagues, as she in very strong terms defined herself a feminist Palestinian, proud of her nationality.

References

Abdel-Hadi, F. (2007) *Women's Political Role in the Thirties*, Ramallah, Palestine: Palestinian Women's Research and Documentation Centre (in Arabic).

——— (2008) *Women's Political Role in the Forties*, Ramallah, Palestine: Palestinian Women's Research and Documentation Centre (in Arabic).

Abdo, N. (1987), *Family, Women and Social Change in the Middle East: The Palestinian Case*, Toronto: Canadian Scholars Press.

——— (1989) 'Colonial Capitalism and Agrarian Social Structure: Socio-economic Transformation in Palestine, 1920–47', Ph.D. thesis, Department of Sociology, University of Toronto.

——— (1991) 'Women of the Intifada: Gender, Class and National Liberation', *Race and Class*, 32(4): 19–35.

——— (1992) 'Racism, Zionism and the Palestinian Working Class, 1920–1947', *Studies in Political Economy*, 37, Spring: 59–93.

——— (1993) 'Middle East Politics through Feminist Lenses: Negotiating the Terms of Solidarity', *Alternatives*, 18(1): 29–41.

——— (1994) 'Nationalism and Feminism in the Palestinian Women's Movement', in V. Moghadam (ed.), *Gender and National Identity: Women and Politics in Muslim Societies*, London: Zed Books.

——— (2009) 'Teaching Sociology in Arab Schools in Israel: A Policy of Education or Ignnorance', *al-Ittihadd*, 22 May (in Arabic), www.aljabha.org/index. asp?i=42322.

Abdo, N., and R. Lentin (2002a) 'Writing Dis-location, Writing the Self: Bringing (Back) the Political into Gendered Israeli Palestinian Dialoguing', in N. Abdo and R. Lentin (eds), *Women and the Politics of Military Confrontation: Palestinian and Israeli Gendered Narratives of Dislocation*, London and New York: Berghahn.

Abdo, N., and R. Lentin (eds) (2002b) *Women and the Politics of Military Confrontation: Palestinian and Israeli Gendered Narratives of Dislocation*, New York: Berghahn.

Abdo, N., and N. Yuval-Davis (1995) 'Palestine, Israel and the Zionist Settler Project', in D. Stasiulis and N. Yuval-Davis (eds), *Unsettling Settler Societies: Articulations of Gender, Race, Ethnicity and Class*, London: Sage.

Abu Baker, K. (2002) '"Career Women" or "Working Women"'? Change Versus Stability for Young Palestinian Women in Israel', *Journal of Israeli History*, 21(1–2): 85–109.

Abu-Rabia-Queder, S. (2004) 'Women, Education, and Control', in *Adalah Newsletter*, vol. 8, December 2004, www.adalah.org/newsletter/eng/dec04/ar3.pdf

——— (2006) 'Between Tradition and Modernization: Understanding the Problem of Female Bedouin Dropouts', *British Journal of Sociology of Education*, 27(1): 3–17.

Abu Saad, I. (2006) 'State-controlled Education and Identity Formation among the Palestinian Arab Minority in Israel', *American Behavioural Scientist*, 49(8): 1085–1101.

Abu Usbeh, K. (2006) *The Educational System in Israel: Structure, Contents, Streams and Mechanisms*, Ramallah, Palestine: Palestinian Forum for Israeli Studies (MADAR) (in Arabic).

Adalah (1997) *The Working Group on the Status of Palestinian Women in Israel NGO Report: The Status of Palestinian Women Citizens of Israel*, Nazareth: Adalah.

——— (2005a) *NGO Alternative Pre-Sessional Report on Israel's Implementation of the United Nations Convention on CEDAW*, Working Group on the Status of Palestinian Women Citizens of Israel, 21 January, Adalah: Haifa.

——— (2005b), 'UN CEDAW Issues Concluding Observations on Israel, Emphasizing 14 Areas of Concern Regarding Israeli Violations of Rights of Palestinian Women', 8 August, www.adalah.org/eng/pressreleases/pr.php?file=05_08_08.

——— (2007) *Adalah's Newsletter*, vol. 42, November, www.adalah.org/newsletter/eng/nov07/8.php.

——— (2010), *Annual Report of Activities*, Haifa, Israel, www.adalah.org/newsletter/eng/feb10/docs/adalah_annual_report_of_activities_2009_final%20pdf.pdf.

Addi-Raccah, A., and A.E. Mazawi (2004) 'Dependence on State Funding, Local Educational Opportunities, and Access to High School Credentials in Israel', *Educational Studies*, 30(2): 145–58.

Adeeb, U. (2003) 'Mizrahi Jews in Israel: Present and Future Possibilities', *Journal of Arab Unity Studies*, 16(2): 17–62 (in Arabic).

Adva (1999) 'Income of Women and Men', *Information on Equality and Social Justice in Israel*, www.adva.org/pages.asp?lang=en&navigate=9.

——— (2004) 'Income of Ashkenazim, Mizrahim, and Arabs', *Information on Equality and Social Justice in Israel*, www.adva.org/pages.asp?lang=en&navigate=9.

——— (2007) *The Right to Higher Education in Israel: A Legal and Fiscal Perspective*, Annual Report, Tel-Aviv: Israel, www.adva.org/uploaded/Educationfull1.pdf.

Al Haj, M. (1986) 'Adjustment Patterns of the Arab Internal Refugees in Israel', *International Migration/Migrations Internationales/Migraciones Internacionales*, 24(3): 651–74.

———— (1987) *Social Change and Family Processes: Arab Communities in Shefaram*, Boulder, CO: Westview Press.

———— (1995) *Education, Empowerment, and Control: The Case of the Arabs in Israel*, Albany, NY: State University of New York Press.

———— (2004) *Immigration and Ethnic Formation in a Deeply Divided Society: The Case of the 1990s Immigrants from the Former Soviet Union in Israel*, Leiden: Brill.

Aminov, E. (2005) 'Why Secular Democracy', *Race Traitor: Treason to Whiteness is Loyalty to Humanity* (special issue), 16 (Winter): 72–89.

Amir, D., and O. Benjamin (1997) 'Defining Encounters: Who Are the Women Entitled to Join the Israeli Collective?' *Women's Studies International Forum*, 20(5–6): 639–50.

Anderson, B. (1991) *Imagined Communities: Reflections on the Origin and Spread of Nationalism*, London and New York: Verso.

Assaf, A. (2005) 'The Wisconsin Plan in Israel: Punishing the Poor', *Challenge*, 93 (September–October), www.workersadvicecentre.org/Sept_05/Wisconsin.htm.

Awwad, Y. (2007) *Arab Women Academics in the Labour Market*, Nazareth: WAVO (Women Against Violence Org) (in Arabic).

———— (2010) *Academic Women and Employment*, Nazareth: WAVO.

Bannerji, H. (2004) 'Demography and Democracy: Reflections on Violence against Women in Genocide or Ethnic Cleansing', *Resources for Feminist Research*, 30(3–4): 121–32.

Baraka, M. (2010) 'Arab Women in Israel', conference paper, *Hadeeth Annass*, 5 March (in Arabic).

Barghouti, S. (2003) *Ideology, Education and Multiculturalism: A Study of Jewish Education in Israel*, Ph.D. thesis, University of Liverpool.

Ben Rafael, E. (1998) 'Arab Citizenship in Israel' [review of Nadim Rouhana, *Palestinian Citizens in an Ethnic Jewish State*], *Ethnic and Racial Studies*, 21(3): 579–85.

Benjamin, O., and T. Barash (2004) '"He Thought I Would Be Like My Mother": The Silencing of Mizrachi Women in Israeli Inter- and Intra-marriages', *Ethnic and Racial Studies*, 27(2): 266–89.

Berkovitz, N. (1997) 'Motherhood as a National Mission: The Construction of Womanhood in the Legal Discourse in Israel', *Women's Studies International Forum*, 20(5–6): 605–19.

Bernstein, D. (1991) 'Oriental and Ashkenazi Jewish Women in the Labor Market', *Calling the Equality Bluff: Women in Israel*, New York: Pergamon Press.

———— (1992) (ed.), *Pioneers and Homemakers: Jewish Women in Pre-State Israel*, Albany: NY: State University of New York Press.

———— (1998) 'Between the Public and Private Spheres in Pre-State Israel', in Judith R. Baskin, *Women in a Historical Perspective*, Detroit, MI: Wayne State University Press.

Bernstein, D., and S. Swirski (1982) 'The Rapid Economic Development of Israel and the Emergence of the Ethnic Division of Labour', *British Journal of Sociology*, 3(1): 64–85.

Blanden, J., P. Gregg and S. Machin (2003) 'Changes in Educational Inequality', *CMPO Working Paper Series*, No. 03/079.

Bourdieu, P. (1988) *Homo Academicus*, Stanford, CA: Stanford University Press.

Branovsky, Y. (2007) 'Report: Poverty among Arab Population Growing', Ynetnews, 16 December, www.ynet.co.il/english/articles/0,7340,L-3483377,00.html.

Brayer, L. (1996) *Report on the Status of Jahaline Bedouins*, Jerusalem, Society of St. Yves.

B'Tselem (Israeli Information Center for Human Rights in the Occupied Territories) (1999) 'Cooperating against Justice: Human Rights Violations by Israel and the Palestinian National Authority Following the Murders in Wadi Qelt', Joint Report with Law – Palestinian Society for the Protection of Human Rights and the Environment, www.btselem.org/download/199907_Cooperating_Against_Justice_Eng.doc.

Budeiri, M. (1979) *Tatawwur al-Haraka al-Ummaliyyah fi-Falasteen* [The Development of the Arab Labour Movement in Palestine], Jerusalem (in Arabic).

Butenschon, N.A., U. Davis and M. Hassassian (eds) (2000) *Citizenship and the State in the Middle East: Approaches and Applications*, Syracuse, NY: Syracuse University Press.

Cahan, S. (2009) 'Discrimination in the Budget Allocated to Children in Need: Implications for its Cancellation', *Megamot*, 3: 380–97.

Cohen, Y., Y. Haberfeld and T. Kristal (2007) 'Ethnicity and Mixed Ethnicity: Educational Gaps among Israeli-born Jews', *Ethnic and Racial Studies*, 30(5): 896–917.

Dahan-Kalev, H. (2001) 'Tensions in Israeli Feminism: The Mizrahi Ashkenazi Rift', *Women's Studies International Forum*, 24(6): 669–84.

——— (2003) 'You're So Pretty – You Don't Look Moroccan', in E. Nimni (ed.), *The Challenge of Post-Zionism: Alternatives to Israeli Fundamentalist Politics*, London: Zed Books.

Dajani, S. (1994) 'Between National and Social Liberation: The Palestinian Women's Movement in the Israeli Occupied West Bank and Gaza Strip', in T. Mayer (ed.), *Women and the Israeli Occupation: The Politics of Change*, London: Routledge.

Davis, U. (2003) *Apartheid Israel: Possibilities for the Struggle Within*, London: Zed Books.

Dichter, S. (ed.) (2001) *Sikkuy Report, 1999–2000*, Jerusalem: Sikkuy (Association for the Advancement of Civic Equality in Israel), www.sikkuy.org.il/english/reports.html.

——— (ed.) (2004) 'Monitoring Civic Equality between Arab and Jewish Citizens of Israel', *Sikkuy Report 2003–2004*, Jerusalem: Sikkuy (Association for the Advancement of Civic Equality in Israel), www.sikkuy.org.il/english/2004/report%202003-4_cover.pdf.

——— (ed.) (2005) '*Sikkuy Report, 2003–2004: Health*', Jerusalem: Sikkuy (Association for the Advancement of Civic Equality in Israel), www.sikkuy.org.il/english//2004/report_2003-4_health.pdf.

Drori, I. (2000) *The Seam Line: Arab Workers and Jewish Managers in the Israeli Textile Industry*, Stanford, CA: Stanford University Press.

ECOSOC (Economic and Social Council of the United Nations) (2005) domino. un.org/unispal.nsf/9a798adbf322aff38525617b006d88d7/69a5b517c57cc06e85 256fbf00571d34!.

Edreich, L. (2006) 'Marriage Talk: Palestinian Women, Intimacy, and the Liberal Nation-state', *Ethnography*, 7(4): 493–523.

Ehrlich, A. (2003) 'Zionism, Anti-Zionism, Post-Zionism', in E. Nimni (ed.), *The Challenge of Post-Zionism: Alternatives to Israeli Fundamentalist Politics*, London: Zed Books.

Erdreich, L., and T. Rapoport (2002) 'Elaborating Ethnonational Awareness via Academic Literacy: Palestinian Israeli Women at the University', *Anthropology and Education Quarterly*, 33(4): 492–515.

Espanyoli, N. (1997) 'Women and Labour in Israel', in *The Status of Palestinian Women Citizens in Israel – NGO Alternative Report* submitted by the Working Group to CEDAW, Nazareth.

Farsakh, L. (2006) 'From South Africa to Israel: The Road to Bantustanisation in the West Bank and Gaza Strip', *Palestinian Society and History Review*, 1 (Spring): 31–55 (in Arabic).

Farsoun, S., and Aruri, N. (2006) *Palestine and the Palestinians: A Social and Political History*, Boulder, CO: Westview Press.

Freedom House (2005) *Women's Rights in the Middle East and North Africa: Citizenship and Justice*, New York: Freedom House.

Frenkel, S., and B. Shimshon (1984) *Hamushhateem: Ha-aristocratia ha-caspit bi-Yisrael* [The Desperate: The Moneyed Aristocracy in Israel], Tel Aviv: Kadima.

Gerber, H. (2003) 'Zionism, Orientalism, and the Palestinians', *Journal of Palestine Studies*, 33(1): 23–41.

Ghanem, A. (1998) 'State and Minority in Israel: The Case of Ethnic State and the Predicament of its Minority', *Ethnic and Racial Studies*, 21(3): 428–48.

—— (2001) *The Palestinian-Arab Minority in Israel, 1948–2000: A Political Study*, Albany, NY: State University of New York Press.

—— (2005) 'The Binational Solution for the Israeli/Palestinian Crisis: A Realistic Option', *Race Traitor*, 16: 90–106.

—— (ed.) (2003) *Ten Years of Transformations: Elections and Politics in Israel 1992–2002*, MADAR: Ramalla (in Arabic).

Ghanem, A., N. Rouhana and O. Yiftachel (1998) 'Questioning "Ethnic Democracy": A Response to Sammy Smooha', *Israel Studies*, 3(2): 253–67.

Gilad, L. (1989) *Ginger and Salt*, Boulder, CO: Westview Press.

Giladi, N.(1988) 'The Jews of Iraq', *The Link*, 31(2), April–May: 32–56.

Golan, G. (1997) 'Militarization and Gender: The Israeli Experience', *Women's Studies International Forum*, 20(5–6): 581–6.

Golan-Agnon, D. (2006) 'Separate but Not Equal: Discrimination against Palestinian Arab Students in Israel', *American Behavioural Scientist*, 49(8): 1075–84.

Haberfeld, Y., and Y. Cohen (2007) 'Gender, Ethnic and National Earning Gaps in Israel: The Role of Rising Inequality', *Social Science Research*, 36(20): 654–72.

Hadawi, S. (1970), *Village Statistics of 1945: A Classification of Land and Area Ownership in Palestine*, Beirut: Palestine Liberation Organization Research Center.

Halperin-Kadari, R. (2004) *Women in Israel: A State of Their Own*, Philadelphia: University of Pennsylvania Press.

Hertzog, H. (2003) 'Post-Zionist Discourse in Alternative Voices', in E. Nimni (ed.), *The Challenge of Post-Zionism: Alternatives to Israeli Fundamentalist Politics*, London: Zed Books.

—— (2004) 'Both an Arab and a Woman: Gendered, Racialized Experiences of Female Palestinian Citizens of Israel', *Social Identities*, 10(1): 53–82.

Hesketh, K., and S. Zaher (2009) 'New Data on Educational Access/Attainment of Arab Students in Israel', in *Adalah's Newsletter*, 63 (August), www.adalah. org/features/education/New_Data_on_Education_August_2009.pdf.

Hever, H., Y. Shenhav and P. Motzafi-Haller (eds) (2002) *Mizrahim in Israel: A Critical Observation on Israel's Ethnicity*, Tel Aviv: Van Leer Jerusalem Institute and HaKibbutz HaMeuchad (in Hebrew).

hooks, b. (1989) *Talking Back: Thinking Feminist, Thinking Black*, Boston, MA: South End Press.

—— (1992) *Black Looks: Race and Representation*, Boston, MA: South End Press.

Hope Simpson, J. (1930) *Palestine: Report on Immigration, Land Settlement, and Development*, Cmd. 3686, London: HMSO.

Human Rights Watch (2001) *Israeli Schools Separate, Not Equal: Palestinian Arab Citizens Face Discrimination in Access to Education*, New York: Human Rights Watch, www. hrw.org/en/news/2001/12/04/israeli-schools-separate-not-equal.

ICBS (Israel Central Bureau of Statistics) (selected years).

Ilani, O (2009) 'Increasing Numbers of Israeli Arabs Studying at Jordanian Universities', *Ha'aretz*, 1 November, www.haaretz.com/hasen/spages/1124913. html.

ISSP (International Social Survey Program) (1997) *Work Orientations II*, Inter-university Consortium for Political and Social Research (ICPSR), Ann Arbor, MI: Institute for Social Research, University of Michigan, www.icpsr.umich. edu/icpsrweb/ICPSR/studies.

Izraeli, D. (1999) 'The Women's Workers Movement: First Wave Feminism in Pre State Israel', in Deborah Bernstein (ed.), *Pioneers and Homemakers: Jewish Women in Pre-State Israel*, Albany, NY: State University of New York Press.

Izraeli, N.D. (2001) 'Paradoxes of Women's Service in the Israeli Defence Forces', in D. Maman, E. Ben-Ari and Z. Rosenchek, *Military, State, and Society in Israel: Theoretical and Comparative Perspectives*, New Brunswick, NJ: Transaction.

Jabareen, Y. (2009) 'Who's Afraid of Educated Arabs?', *Ha'aretz*, 24 July, www.haaretz. com/print-edition/opinion/who-s-afraid-of-educated-arabs-1.280663.

Jad, I. (2004) 'Feminist Narratives: Women and Gender in Early Jewish and Palestinian Nationalism', *Journal of Palestine Studies*, 33(4): 108–9.

Jad, I. (2007) 'Rereading the British Mandate in Palestine: Gender and the Urban Rural Divide in Education', *International Journal of Middle East Studies*, 3, (August): 338–42.

Jad, I., P. Johnson and R. Giacaman (2000). 'Gender and Citizenship under the Palestinian Authority', in S. Joseph (ed.), *Gender and Citizenship in the Middle East*, Syracuse, NY: Syracuse University Press, pp. 137–57.

Jamal, A. (2005) 'On the Morality of Arab Collective Rights in Israel', *Adalah Newsletter*, 12 (April), www.adalah.org/newsletter/eng/apr05/ar2.pdf.

——— (2007) 'Strategies of Minority Struggle for Equality in Ethnic States: Arab Politics in Israel', *Citizenship Studies*, 11(3): 263–82.

Jasarat, I. (2001) 'Zionism: Let the Facts Speak for Themselves', *Media Review Net*, 31 August, www.themodernreligion.com/jihad/facts.html.

Jayawardena, K. (1986) *Nationalism in the Third World*, London: Zed Books.

Jenson, J. (2000) 'Supra-national Citizenship? A Comparison of NAFTA and the European Union', 2000 Annual Conference – Citizenship 2020, 20–21 October, Montreal: Institute of Canadian Studies, McGill University.

——— (2001) 'Social Citizenship in 21st Century Canada: Challenges and Options', 2001 Timlin Lecture, University of Saskatchewan, 5 February.

Joppke, C. (2002) 'Multicultural Citizenship: A Critique', in E. Isin and B. Turner (eds), *The Citizenship Reader*, London: Sage.

Jorgensen, C. (1994) 'Women, Revolutions and Israel', in M. Tertreault (ed.), *Women and Revolution in Africa, Asia and the New World*, Columbia: University of South Carolina Press, pp. 272–96.

Joseph, S. (ed.) (2000) *Gender and Citizenship in the Middle East*, Syracuse, NY: Syracuse University Press.

Joseph, S., and S. Slyomovics (2000) *Women and Power in the Middle East*, Philadelphia: University of Pennsylvania Press.

Juris, S.J. (2008) *Networking Futures: The Movements against Corporate Globalization*, Durham, NC and London: Duke University Press.

Kana'aneh, R. (2002) *Birthing the Nation: Strategies of Palestinian Women in Israel*, Berkeley and Los Angeles: University of California Press.

Kandiyoti, D. (2003) 'Segregation, Ethnic Labour Market and the Occupational Expectations of Palestinian Students in Israel', *British Journal of Sociology*, 54(2): 259–85.

Kandiyoti, D. (ed.) (1996) *Gendering the Middle East: Emerging Perspectives*, New York: Syracuse University Press.

Kark, R., and M. Oren-Nordheim (2001), *Jerusalem and Its Environs: Quarters, Neighborhoods, Villages, 1800–1948*, Detroit: Wayne State University Press.

Kashti, O. (2009) 'Israel Aids Its Needy Jewish Students more than Arab Counterparts', *Ha'aretz*, 12 August, www.haaretz.com/hasen/spages/1106955.html.

Katz, S. (2003) *Women and Gender in Early Jewish and Palestinian Nationalism*, Gainesville: University Press of Florida.

Katz, T. (2000) 'The Founding Myths of Zionist Israel', M.A. thesis, Haifa University.

Katznelson-Rubashov, R. [R. Katznelson-Shazar] (2002) *The Plough Woman: Records of the Pioneer Women of Palestine – A Critical Edition*, ed. M. Raider, Tauber Institute Series for the Study of European Jewry, Waltham, MA: Brandeis University Press.

Kemp, A. (2004) 'Labour Migration and Racialisation: Labour Market Mechanisms and Labour Migration Control Policies in Israel', *Social Identities*, 10(26): 267–92.

Kemp, A., U. Ram, D. Newman and O. Yiftachel (eds) (2004) *Israelis in Conflict: Hegemonies, Identities and Challengers*, Brighton: Sussex Academic Press.

Khalidi, W. (1992), *All That Remains: The Palestinian Villages Occupied and Depopulated by Israel in 1948*, Washington DC: Institute for Palestine Studies.

Khattab, N. (2002) 'Ethnicity and Female Labour Market Participation: A New Look at the Palestinian Enclave in Israel', *Work, Employment and Society*, 16(1): 91–110.

——— (2005) 'Ethnicity, Class and the Earning Inequality in Israel, 1983–1995', *Sociological Research Online*, 10(3), www.socresonline.org.uk/10/3/khattab.html.

Khazzoom, A. (2005) 'Did the Israeli State Engineer Segregation? On the Placement of Jewish Immigrants in Development Towns in the 1950s', *Social Forces*, 84(1): 115–27.

Kimmerling, B. (1983) *Zionism and Territory: The Socio-territorial Dimensions of Zionist Politics*, Berkeley and Los Angeles: University of California Press.

——— (1994) *Palestinians: The Making of a People*, New York, Free Press.

Kovel, J. (2007) *Overcoming Zionism: Creating a Single Democratic State in Israel/Palestine*, London: Pluto.

Kretzmer, D. (1990) *The Legal Status of the Arabs in Israel*, Westview Special Studies on the Middle East in cooperation with the International Centre for Peace in the Middle East, Tel Aviv and Boulder, CO: Westview Press.

Kuttab, E., and N. Abu Awwad (2004) 'Developments in the Palestinian Women's Movement', *News from Within*, 20(2): 10–14.

Labadi, F. (2003) 'Palestinian Women's Emancipation and the Uprising for Independence', *Resources for Feminist Research*, 30(3–4): 121–36.

Lavie, S. (2002) 'Academic Apartheid in Israel and the Lilly-white Feminism of the Upper Middle Class', *Women in Judaism: A Multidisciplinary Approach*, www.utoronto.ca/wjudaism/journal/spring2002/documents/lavie.pdf. (Also in *Ha-keshet ha Democratit ha Mizrahi*, www.ha-keshet.org.il/english/lilly_pdf.pdf.)

——— (2005) 'Israeli Anthropology and American Anthropology', *Anthropology Newsletter*, January: 9–10.

——— (2007) 'Colonialism and Imperialism', *Encyclopedia of Women and Islamic Cultures*, 6: 6–15.

Lazreg, M. (1988) 'Feminism and Difference: The Perils of Writing as a Woman in Algeria', *Feminist Studies*, 14(1): 81–107.

——— (1994) *The Eloquence of Silence: Algerian Women in Question*, New York: Routledge.

Lentin, R. (2002) '"If I Forget Thee…:" Terms of Diasporicity', in N. Abdo and R. Lentin (eds), *Women and the Politics of Military Confrontation: Palestinian and Israeli Gendered Narratives of Dislocation*, London and New York: Berghahn.

—— (2005) 'Why Secular Democracy', *Race Traitor: Treason to Whiteness is Loyalty to Humanity* (special issue), 16 (Winter): 14–23.

—— (2008) *Thinking Palestine*, London: Zed Books.

Levanon, G., and Y. Raviv (2007) 'Decomposing Wage Gaps between Ethnic Groups: The Case of Israel', *Southern Economic Journal*, 73(4): 1038–65.

Lewin-Epstein, N., and M. Semyonov (1992) 'Local Labour Markets, Ethnic Segregation, and Income Inequality', *Social Forces*, 70(4): 1101–19.

—— (1993) *The Arab Minority in Israel's Economy: Patterns of Ethnic Inequality*, Boulder, CO: Westview Press.

Lister, R. (2004) 'Citizenship and Gender', in K. Nash and A. Scott (eds), *The Blackwell Companion to Political Sociology*, Oxford: Blackwell.

Lorde, A. (1984) 'Age, Race, Class and Sex: Women Redefining Difference', in *Sister Outside: Essays and Speeches*, Sydney: Crossing Press.

Mamdani, M. (2007) 'Good Muslim, Bad Muslim: A Political Perspective on Culture and Terrorism', *American Anthropologist*, 104(3): 766–75.

Manor, D. (2005) 'The Zionist Return to the West and the Mizrahi Jewish Perspective', in I. Kalmar Davidson and D. Penslar (eds), *Orientalism and the Jews*, Waltham, MA: Brandeis University Press.

Marshall, M. (1995) 'Rethinking the Palestine Question: The Apartheid Paradigm', *Journal of Palestine Studies*, 25(1): 15–22.

Marshall, T.H. (1950) *Citizenship and Social Class*, Cambridge: Cambridge University Press.

Martin, W. (2004) 'We Created Terror among the Arabs: The Deir Yassin Massacre', *Counterpunch*, http://counterpunch.org/martin05132004.html.

Mayer, T. (1994) *Women and the Israeli Occupation: The Politics of Change*, London: Routledge.

Mazawi, A. (1994) 'Palestinians in Israel: Educational Expansion, Social Mobility and Political Control', *Compare: A Journal of Comparative Education*, 24(3): 277–84.

—— (1998) 'Region, Locality Characteristics, High School Tacking and Access to Educational Credentials: The Case of Palestinian Arab Communities in Israel', *Educational Studies*, 24(2): 223–40.

—— (1999) 'Concentrated Disadvantage and Access to Educational Credentials in Arab and Jewish Localities in Israel', *British Educational Research Journal*, 25(3): 355–70.

Mazawi, A., and A. Yogev (1999) 'Elite Formation under Occupation: The Internal Stratification of Palestinian Elites in the West Bank and Gaza Strip', *British Journal of Sociology*, 50(3): 397–418.

Meir, Y. (2001) 'Class Structure in a Deeply Divided Society: Class and Ethnic Inequality in Israel', *British Journal of Sociology*, 52(3): 409–39.

Merchant, C. (1989) *Ecological Revolutions: Nature, Gender, and Science in New England*, Chapel Hill: University of North Carolina Press.

Mohanty, C. (1987) 'Feminist Encounters: Locating the Politics of Experience', *Copyright*, 1 (Fall): 30–44.

———— (1988) 'Under Western Eyes: Feminist Scholarship and Colonial Discourses', *Feminist Review*, 30 (Autumn): 61–88.

Mojab, S., and N. Abdo (ed.) (2004) *Violence in the Name of Honour: Theoretical and Political Challenges*, Istanbul: Istanbul Bilgi University Press.

Moore, D. (2004) 'Gender Identities and Social Action: Arab and Jewish Women in Israel', *Journal of Applied Behavioral Science*, 40(2): 182–207.

———— (2006) 'Why Don't Women Demand More? Entitlement and Work Values of Religious and Secular Women and Men in Israel', *Journal of Applied Social Psychology*, 36(8): 1924–60.

Moors, A. (1996) *Women, Property and Islam: Palestinian Experiences 1920–1990*, Cambridge: Cambridge University Press.

Morris, B. (2001) *Righteous Victims: A History of the Zionist–Arab Conflict, 1881–2001*, New York: Vintage.

———— (2004) *The Birth of the Palestinian Refugee Problem Revisited*, Cambridge: Cambridge University Press.

Motzafi-Haller, P. (1997) 'Writing Birthright: On Native Anthropologists and the Politics of Representation', in D. Reed-Danahay, (ed.), *Autoethnography: Rewriting the Self and the Social*, Oxford: Berg.

———— (2001) 'Scholarship, Identity, and Power: Mizrahi Women in Israel', *Signs: Journal of Women in Culture and Society*, 26(3): 697–734.

Nakhleh, K. (1977) 'Anthropological and Sociological Studies of the Arabs in Israel: A Critique', *Journal of Palestine Studies*, 6(4): 38–53.

Nakhleh, K. (ed.) (2008) *The Future of the Palestinian Minority in Israel*, Ramallah: MADAR (Palestinian Centre for Israeli Studies) (in Arabic).

National Committee for the Heads of the Arab Local Authorities in Israel (2006) 'The Future Vision of the Palestinian Arabs in Israel', Al Woroud, Nazareth.

Nimni, E. (2003a) *The Challenge of Post-Zionism: Alternatives to Israeli Fundamentalist Politics*, London: Zed Books.

Nimni, E. (ed.) (2003b) 'Introduction', in E. Nimni (ed.), *The Challenge of Post-Zionism: Alternatives to Israeli Fundamentalist Politics*, London: Zed Books.

OECD (Organisation for Economic and Co-operative Development) (2009) 'Economic Survey of Israel, 2009', OECD Policy Brief, December, www.oecd. org/dataoecd/41/30/44383721.pdf.

———— (2010a) *Israel*, OECD Economic Surveys, Vol. 2009/21 – January, Supplement 3, Paris: OECD.

———— (2010b) *Labour Market and Social Policy Review of Israel*, Paris: OECD.

Pappé, I. (2003) 'The Square Circle: The Struggle for Survival of Traditional Zionism', in E. Nimni (ed.), *The Challenge of Post-Zionism: Alternatives to Israeli Fundamentalist Politics*, London: Zed Books.

———— (1994) *The Making of the Arab–Israeli Conflict 1947–51*, London: I.B. Tauris.

————— (2004) *A History of Modern Palestine: One Land, Two Peoples*, Cambridge: Cambridge University Press.

————— (2005) 'The One-State Solution in Historical Perspective', *Race Traitor: Treason to Whiteness is Loyalty to Humanity* (special issue), 16 (Winter): 49–60.

Pateman, C. (1989) *The Disorder of Women: Democracy, Feminism, and Political Theory.* Stanford, CA: Stanford University Press.

Pateman C., and C.W. Mills (2007) *Contract and Domination*, Cambridge: Polity Press.

Peel Commission, *Palestine Royal Commission Report* (1937) Cmd. 5479, July, London: HMSO.

Peled, Y. (1992) 'Ethnic Democracy and the Legal Construction of Citizenship: Arab Citizens of the Jewish State', *American Political Science Review*, 86(2): 432–43.

————— (1998) 'Towards a Redefinition of Jewish Nationalism in Israel? The Enigma of Shas', *Ethnic and Racial Studies*, 21(4): 703–27.

————— (2006) '"No Arab Jews" There: Shas and the Palestinians', *Palestinian Studies in Society and History Review*, 1: 112–37 (in Arabic).

Peled, Y., and G. Shafir (1996) 'The Roots of Peacemaking: The Dynamic of Citizenship in Israel, 1948–93', *International Journal of Middle East Studies*, 28(2): 391–413.

————— (2002) *Being Israeli: The Dynamics of Multiple Citizenship*, Cambridge: Cambridge University Press.

Peteet, J.M. (1991) *Gender in Crisis: Women and the Palestinian Resistance Movement*, New York: Columbia University Press.

Putman, D.R. (2000) *Bowling Alone: The Collapse and Revival of American Community*, New York: Simon & Schuster.

Raday, F. (1991) 'The Concept of Gender Equality in a Jewish State', in B. Swirski and M. Safir (eds), *Calling the Equality Bluff: Women in Israel*, New York: Pergamon Press.

Raijman, R., and M. Semyonov (1997) 'Gender, Ethnicity, and Immigration: Double Disadvantage and Triple Disadvantage among Recent Immigrant Women in the Israeli Labour Market', *Gender and Society*, 11(1): 108–25.

————— (2004) 'Perceived Threat and Exclusionary Attitudes towards Foreign Workers in Israel', *Ethnic and Racial Studies*, 27(5): 780–99.

Ram, U. (1999) 'The State of the Nation: Contemporary Challenges to Zionism in Israel', *Constellations*, 6(3): 325–38.

————— (2003) 'From Nation-state to Nation: State: Nation, History and Identity Struggles in Jewish Israel', in N. Ephraim, *The Challenge of Post-Zionism: Alternatives to Israeli Fundamentalist Politics*, London: Zed Books.

Rayman, P. (1981) *The Kibbutz Community and Nation Building*, Princeton, NJ: Princeton University Press.

Raz-Krakotzkin, A. (2005) 'Broadcast Orientalism: Representations of Mizrahi Jewry in Israeli Radio, 1948–1967', in I.D. Kalmer and D.J. Penslar (eds), *Orientalism and the Jews*, Waltham, MA: Brandeis University Press.

Resnik, J. (2006) 'Alternative Identities in Multicultural Schools in Israel: Emancipatory Identity, Mixed Identity and Transnational Identity', *British Journal of Sociology of Education*, 27: 585–601.

Rodinson, M. (1979) *Israel: A Colonial Settler State?* New York: Pathfinder.

Rosenfeld, H. (1968) 'Change, Barriers to Change, and Contradictions in the Arab Village Family', *American Anthropologist*, 70(4): 732–52.

Rosenfeld, H., and M. Al-Haj (1987) *Social Change and Family Processes: Arab Communities in Israel*, Boulder, CO: Westview Press.

Rouhana, N. (1997) *Palestinian Citizens in an Ethnic Jewish State: Identities in Conflict*, New Haven CT and London: Yale University Press.

Rouhana, N., and A. Ghanem (1998) 'The Crisis of Minorities in Ethnic States: The Case of Palestinian Citizens in Israel', *International Journal of Middle East Studies*, 30(3): 321–46.

Rouhana, N., and N. Sultany (2003) 'Redrawing the Boundaries of Citizenship: Israel's New Hegemony', *Journal of Palestine Studies*, 33(1): 5–22.

Roy, S. (1995) *The Gaza Strip: The Political Economy of De-development*, Washington DC: Institute for Palestine Studies.

Sa'ar, A. (2007) 'Contradictory Locations: Assessing the Position of Palestinian Women Citizens of Israel', *Journal of Middle East Women's Studies*, 3(3): 46–74.

Sa'di, A.H., and N. Lewin-Epstein (2001) 'Minority Labour Force Participation in the Post-Fordist Era: The Case of the Arabs in Israel', *Work, Employment and Society*, 15(4): 781–802.

Safadiyyah, E., and O. Yiftahel (2003) 'Mizrahi Jews and Space: The Development of an Ethnic Class in Developed Countries', in A. Ghanem (ed.), *Identities and Politics in Israel*, Ramallah, Palestine: MADAR (Palestinian Centre for Israeli Studies) (in Arabic).

Said, E. (1994) *Representations of the Intellectuals*, New York: Pantheon.

Saporta, I., and Y. Yonah (2004) 'Pre-vocational Education: The Making of Israel's Ethno-working Class', *Race Ethnicity and Education*, 7: 251–75.

Sawt el-Amel/The Laborers' Voice (2010), www.laborers-voice.org/home-e.aspx.

Sayigh, R.M. (1979) *Palestinians: From Peasants to Revolutionaries*, London: Zed Books.

Schechla, J. (2001) 'The Invisible People Come to Light: Israel's "Internally Displaced" and the "Unrecognized Villages"', *Journal of Palestine Studies*, 31(1): 20–31.

Schwartz, M. (2005) 'Poverty: The Meeting Ground Between Arab and Jewish Women in Israel', *Mediterranean Women*, www.mediterraneas.org/print.php3?id_article=435.

——— (2006) 'The Role of Arab Women in Israeli Economy', *Mediterranean Women*, www.mediterraneas.org/article.php3?id_article=485.

Schwartz, M., and A. Agbarieh-Zahalka (2008) 'Arab Women in Israel: Obstacles to Emancipation', *Challenge*, 108, www.challenge-mag.com/en/article __203/arab_women_in_israel_obstacles_to_emancipation.

Segev, T. (1998) *1949: The First Israelis*, New York: Holt.

Semyonov, M. (1988) 'Bi-ethnic Labour Markets, Mono-ethnic Labour Markets, and Socioeconomic Inequality', *American Sociological Review*, 53(2): 256–66.

Semyonov, M., and Y. Cohen (1990) 'Ethnic Discrimination and the Income of Majority-group Workers', *American Sociological Review*, 55(1): 107–14.

Semyonov, M., and N. Lewin-Epstein (1994) 'Ethnic Labour Markets, Gender and Socioeconomic Inequality: A Study of Arabs in the Israeli Labour Force', *Sociological Review*, 35(1): 51–68.

———— (2009) *Israel and Palestine: Reappraisals, Revisions, Refutation*, London: Penguin.

Shadmi, E. (2003) 'Being Feminist Peace Activist-and Ashkenazi', *Nashim: A Journal of Jewish Women's Studies and Gender*, 6: 52–5.

———— (2004) 'The Israeli Woman and the Feminist Left in Israel', in Dan Leon (ed.), *Who's Left in Israel?: Radical Political Alternatives for the Future of Israel*, Brighton: Sussex Academic Press.

Shafir, G., and Y. Peled (1998a) 'Citizenship and Stratification in an Ethnic Democracy', *Ethnic and Racial Studies*, 21(3): 408–27.

———— (1998b) 'The Dynamics of Citizenship in Israel and the Israeli–Palestinian Peace Process', in G. Shafir (ed.), *The Citizenship Debates*, Minneapolis: University of Minnesota Press.

———— (2002) *Being Israeli: The Dynamics of Multiple Citizenship*, Cambridge: Cambridge University Press.

Shalhoub-Kevorkian, N. (1999) 'Law, Politics, and Violence against Women: The Case-study of Palestinian-Israelis', *Law and Policy*, 21(2): 189–211.

———— (2000) 'The Efficacy of Israeli Law in Preventing Violence within Palestinian Families Living in Israel', *International Review of Victimology*, 7: 47–66.

———— (2004) 'Militarization and Policing: Police Reactions to Violence against Palestinian Women in Israel', *Social Identities*, 10(2): 171–94.

Shalvi, A. (2002) 'Transformed by Joy', in N. Abdo and R. Lentin (eds), *Women and the Politics of Military Confrontation: Palestinian and Israeli Gendered Narratives of Dislocation*, London: Berghahn.

Shaw, M. (1997). 'Past Wars and Present Conflicts: From the Second World War to the Gulf', in M. Lunn and K. Evans (eds), *War and Memory in the Twentieth Century*, Leamington: Berg.

Shaw, J.V.W. (1945–46) *A Survey of Palestine* (prepared in December 1945 and January 1946 for the Information of the Anglo-American Committee of Inquiry).

Shenhav, Y. (2006) 'Arab Jews, Population Exchange, and the Palestinian Right of Return', *Palestinian Society and History Review*, 1 (Spring): 56–87 (Arabic).

Shepard, N. (2000) *Ploughing Sand: British Rule in Palestine, 1917–1948*, London: John Murray.

Shetrit, S.S. (2000) 'Mizrahi Politics in Israel: Between Integration and Alternative', *Journal of Palestinian Studies*, 29(4): 51–65.

Shilo, M. (1992) 'The Women's Farm at Kinneret, 1911–1917: A Solution to the Problem of the Working Women in the Second Aliyah', in D. Bernstein (ed.), *Pioneers and Homemakers: Jewish Women in Pre-State Israel*, Albany, NY: State University of New York Press.

Shiran, V. (2010) 'We Are Massouda from Sdarout', www.ha-keshet.org.il/articles/feminisim/anachnu_viki-shiran.htm (in Arabic).

Shlaim, A. (2001) *The Iron Wall: Israel and the Arab World*, London: Penguin.

Shohat, E. (1988) 'Sephardim in Israel: Zionism from the Standpoint of Its Jewish Victims', *Social Text*, 19–20 (Fall): 1–35.

——— (1997) 'The Narrative of the Nation and the Discourse of Modernization: The Case of the Mizrahim', *Critique: Critical Middle Eastern Studies*, 6: 3–18.

——— (1999) 'The Invention of the Mizrahim', *Journal of Palestine Studies*, 29(1): 5–20.

——— (2002) 'A Reluctant Eulogy: Fragments from the Memories of an Arab-Jew', in N. Abdo and R. Lentin (eds), *Women and the Politics of Military Confrontation: Palestinian and Israeli Gendered Narratives of Dislocation*, London and New York: Berghahn.

Sikkuy (2002) *The Sikkuy Report 2002: The Four Billion Shekel Plan*, www.sikkuy.org.il/english/reports.html.

——— (2003–2004) *The Sikkuy Report 2003–2004: Monitoring Civic Equality Between Arab and Jewish Citizens of Israel*, www.sikkuy.org.il/english/reports.html.

——— (2006) *Sikkuy Annual Activities and Financial Report*, www.sikkuy.org.il/english/papers/annual-2006.pdf.

Smith, D. (2005) *Institutional Ethnography: A Sociology for People*, London: Altamira.

Smooha, S. (1997) 'Ethnic Democracy: Israel as an Archetype', *Israel Studies*, 2: 198–241.

——— (1999) 'Transformations of Israeli Society – After Fifty Years', *Alpayim*, 17: 239–61 (in Hebrew).

Soysal, Y.N. (1994) *Limits of Citizenship: Migrants and Postnational Membership in Europe*, Chicago: University of Chicago Press.

——— (2001) 'Postnational Citizenship: Reconfiguring the Familiar Terrain', in K. Nash and A. Scott (eds), *Blackwell Companion to Political Sociology*, Oxford: Blackwell.

Stasiulis, D., and N. Yuval-Davis (eds) (1995) *Unsettling Settler Societies: Articulations of Gender, Race, Ethnicity and Class*, London: Sage.

Stein, K.W. (1984) *The Land Question in Palestine, 1917–1939*, Chapel Hill and London: University of North Carolina Press.

Stier, H. (2002) 'Does Women's Employment Reduce Poverty? Evidence from Israel', *Work, Employment and Society*, 16(2): 211–30.

Swirski, B. (2000) 'The Citizenship of Jewish and Palestinian Arab Women in Israel', in S. Joseph (ed.), *Gender and Citizenship in the Middle East*, Syracuse, NY: Syracuse University Press.

Swirski, B. (2006) 'A Gender Perspective on the Proposed 2006 Budget for the State of Israel', www.adva.org/uploaded/GenderPerspective2006Budget.pdf.

Swirski, B., and M.P. Safir (1991) *Calling the Equality Bluff: Women in Israel*, New York: Pergamon Press.

Swirski, S., and E. Konor-Attias (2004) *Israel: A Social Report*, www/adva.org/adva_israel_2004_english.pdf.

——— (2007) *Workers, Employers and the Distribution of Israel's National Income. Labor Report:* 2006, 30 May, www.adva.org/default.asp?pageid=1002&itmid=498.

Tabenkin, Y. (1985) *The Kibbutz: A Non-Utopian Commune*, Jerusalem: Yad Tabenkin.

Tekiner, R., S. Abed-Rabbo and N. Mezvinsky (eds) (1988) *Anti-Zionism: Analytical Reflections*, Brattleboro, VT: Amana.

Tibawi, A. (1956) *Arab Education in Mandatory Palestine: A Study of Three Decades of British Administration*, London: Luzac.

Tilley, V. (2005) *The One-State Solution: A Breakthrough for Peace in the Israeli–Palestinian Deadlock*, Ann Arbor, MI: University of Michigan Press.

Tirosh, R. (2004) 'Minutes of the Knesset Education and Culture Committee', 27 August, cited in *Sikkuy Report* 2004, www.sikkuy.org.il/english//2004/report_2003-4_health.pdf.

Toren, N., and V. Kraus (1987) 'The Effects of Minority Size on Women's Position in Academia', *Social Forces*, 65(4): 1090–100.

Tucker, J. (1988) 'Marriage and Family in Nablus, 1720–1856: Towards a History of Arab Marriage', *Journal of Family History* 13(2): 81–100.

——— (1993) 'The Arab Family in History: "Otherness" and the Study of the Family', in J. Tucker, *Arab Women: Old Boundaries, New Frontiers*, Bloomington: Indiana University Press.

——— (2000) *In the House of the Law: Gender and Islamic Law in Ottoman Syria and Palestine*, Berkeley and Los Angeles: University of California Press.

——— (2002) *Women in Nineteenth-century Egypt*, Cambridge: Cambridge University Press.

Tzfadia, E., and O. Yiftachel. (2001) 'Political Mobilisation in the Development Towns: The Mizrahi Struggle over Place', *Politika* [Israeli Journal of Political Science], 7: 79–96 (in Hebrew).

Tzfadia, E., and O. Yiftachel. (2004) 'Between Local and National: Mobilization in Israel's Peripheral Towns', *Cities*, 21(1): 41–55.

UNDP (2004) *Human Development Report 2004*, UNDP: New York, http://hdr.undp.org/en/media/hdr04_complete.pdf.

——— (2005) *Arab Human Development Report: Toward the Rise of Women in the Arab World*, UNDP: New York, http://rbas.undp.org/ahdr2005.shtml.

Walby, S. (1990) *Theorizing Patriarchy*, New York: Blackwell.

——— (1994) 'Is Citizenship Gendered?' *Sociology*, 28(2) (May): 379–95.

Warriner, D. (1936), *Land Tenure System in Palestine*. London.

Weiner-Levy, N. (2006) 'The Flag Bearers: Israeli Druze Women Challenge Traditional Gender Roles', *Anthropology and Education Quarterly*, 37: 217–35.

Ya'ar, E. (2005) 'Continuity and Change in Israeli Society: The Test of the Melting Pot', *Israel Studies*, 10(2): 91–128.

Yaffe, N., and D. Tal. (2002) 'The Arab Population in Israel', *Statistilite*, 27, Central Bureau of Statistics, State of Israel.

Yaish, M. (2001) 'Class Structure in a Deeply Divided Society: Class and Ethnic Inequality in Israel, 1974–91' *British Journal of Sociology*, 52(3): 409–37.

Yiftachel, O. (1999) '"Ethnocracy": The Politics of Judaizing Israel/Palestine', *Constellations: An International Journal of critical and Democratic Theory*, 6(3): 364–90.

———— (2006) *Ethnocracy: Land and Identity Politics in Israel/Palestine*, Philadelphia: University of Pennsylvania Press.

Yiftachel, O., and M. Segal (1998) 'Jews and Druze in Israel: State Control and Ethnic Resistance', *Ethnic and Racial Studies*, 21(3): 476–506.

Yonah, Y., and I. Saporta (2006) 'The Wavering Luck of Girls: Gender and Pre-vocational Education in Israel', *Journal of Middle East Women's Studies*, 2: 71–101.

Yuval-Davis, N. (1991) 'The Citizenship Debate: Women, the State, and Ethnic Processes', *Feminist Review*, 39: 58–68.

———— (1997) *Gender and Nation*, London: Sage.

———— (2003) 'Conclusion', in E. Nimni (ed.), *The Challenge of Post-Zionism: Alternatives to Israeli Fundamentalist Politics*, London: Zed Books.

———— (2006) 'Human/Women's Rights and Feminist Transversal Politics', in M.M. Ferree and A.M. Tripp (eds), *Global Feminism: Transnational Women's Activism, Organizing, and Human Rights*, New York: New York University Press.

Zahalka, J. (2009) 'Arab Female Educational Achievements at All Levels is Higher than that of Males', *Arabs*, 48 (July), www.arabs48.com/display.x?cid=1&sid=32&id=64651.

Zahalqa, J. (2008) 'Palestinian Women, Work, and Politics in Israel', paper presented to a conference held by Union of Palestinian Women, Nazareth, 9 February, www.rikaz.org/Summary.pdf.

Zeidani, S. (1995) 'Al-hizbel siyasi, wal-mujtama'a al-madani, wal-nizam al-dimocrati' [The Political Party, Civil Society and Democracy], in A. Bishara (ed.), *Azmat al-Hizb al-Siyasi Al-Falastini* [The Crisis of the Palestinian Political Party], Ramallah, Palestine: Muwatin (in Arabic).

Index

219